FINGAL COUNTY LIBRARIES

305. 30941

G000080025

Gender Roles

Gender Roles in Ireland: three decades ___ *titude change* documents changing attitudes toward the role of women ___ land from 1975 to 2005, a key period of social change in this society. ___ ook presents replicated measures from four separate surveys carried ___ over three decades. These cover a wide range of gender role attitude ___ as well as key social issues concerning the role of women in Ireland, inclu ling equal pay, equal employment opportunity, maternal employment, contraception, etc. Attitudes to abortion, divorce and moral issues are also presented and discussed in the context of people's voting behaviour in national referenda. Taken together, the data available in these studies paint a detailed and complex picture of the evolving role of women in Ireland during a period of rapid social change and key developments in social legislation. The book brings the results up to the present by including new data on current gender role issues from Margret Fine-Davis' latest research.

Margret Fine-Davis is Senior Research Fellow (Emeritus), Department of Sociology, School of Social Sciences & Philosophy, Trinity College Dublin and Director of the Social Attitude & Policy Research Group. Her research interests include social attitudes; changing gender role attitudes and behaviour and related social policy issues; attitudes to family formation and well-being. She is co-author of *Fathers and Mothers: dilemmas of the work–life balance – a comparative study in four European countries* (Kluwer, 2004; Italian version, Il Mulino, 2007).

Routledge Advances in Sociology

Gender Roles in Ireland

Three decades of attitude change

Margret Fine-Davis

Routledge
Taylor & Francis Group

LONDON AND NEW YORK

First published 2015
by Routledge
2 Park Square, Milton Park, Abingdon, Oxfordshire OX14 4RN

and by Routledge
711 Third Avenue, New York, NY 10017

First issued in paperback 2016

Routledge is an imprint of the Taylor & Francis Group, an informa business

© 2015 Margret Fine-Davis

The right of Margret Fine-Davis to be identified as author of this
work has been asserted by her in accordance with sections 77 and 78
of the Copyright, Designs and Patents Act 1988.

All rights reserved. No part of this book may be reprinted or
reproduced or utilised in any form or by any electronic, mechanical,
or other means, now known or hereafter invented, including
photocopying and recording, or in any information storage or
retrieval system, without permission in writing from the publishers.

Trademark notice: Product or corporate names may be trademarks or
registered trademarks, and are used only for identification and
explanation without intent to infringe.

British Library Cataloguing-in-Publication Data
A catalogue record for this book is available from the British Library

Library of Congress Cataloging-in-Publication Data
Fine-Davis, Margret.
Gender roles in Ireland: three decades of attitude change /
Margret Fine-Davis.
    pages cm. – (Routledge advances in sociology)
    1. Sex role–Ireland–Public opinion. 2. Women–Ireland–Public
opinion. 3. Women–Ireland–Social conditions. 4. Women–
Ireland–Economic conditions. 5. Feminism–Ireland–Public
opinion. 6. Public opinion–Ireland. I. Title.
HQ1075.5.I73F56 2014
305.309417–dc23   2014008917

ISBN 13: 978-1-138-21907-6 (pbk)
ISBN 13: 978-0-415-74308-2 (hbk)

Typeset in Baskerville
by Wearset Ltd, Boldon, Tyne and Wear

Contents

Figures

Tables

Foreword

During this decade of celebration, commemoration and remembrance of national and international events that changed Ireland and Europe so fundamentally, this volume of research by Dr Margret Fine-Davis is timely and important.

Present discussion and debate on the First World War, 1914–1918, the Easter Rising, 1916 and the Great Lockout of 1913 also include the suffragette/suffragist movement and the Irish Women Workers' Union. During that period, women activists diverted their energy into dealing with the terrible fall-out of the First World War and the turmoil of Easter week and afterwards. Then the history of that tumultuous period either ignored their participation and contribution, or airbrushed them out of sight.

That is why the research presented in this volume, comprising a synthesis of Fine-Davis' series of studies carried out over a period of 40 years, is so relevant now.

This book examines gender role attitudes in Ireland covering three decades from the mid 1970s to 2005, with more recent data included to bring the study up to the present day. Prior to her first study, carried out in 1975, essentially no research in this area had been conducted in Ireland.

In her introduction, Fine-Davis notes that changing gender roles constitute a major trend in our societies with vast social, political and economic implications and consequences. This published work, based on such solid and continuing updated research, demonstrates how far-reaching and life-changing these changes are. These changes came later in Ireland but the process has been very rapid.

A strong women's movement emerged after the publication of the Report of the Commission on the Status of Women in 1972 and Ireland becoming a member of the EEC in 1973. The level of legal and social discrimination against women identified in that report is breathtaking, particularly because of the political and social acceptance of the inferior status of women in Ireland at that time. The influence of the Catholic Church in Ireland powerfully upheld the traditional role of women and was reflected in the social and legal framework of the country. The political power of the Church was most evident in the debates and divisions during the referendum campaigns on divorce and abortion and its opposition to more liberal legislation on contraception.

Recent research carried out in 2010 on attitudes to religion and moral values suggests that most Irish people have adopted a relatively broad view of sex and sexual practices, in contrast with the Catholic Church teachings on the subject.

The greatest impetus to removing the discriminations against women came through legislation – much of it brought about by our membership of the then EEC – on equal pay, equal opportunity, positive action and the setting-up of the Employment Equality Agency, to monitor, influence and enforce this legislation.

Fine-Davis refers to the hostile reaction towards women working outside the home, citing the Commission of Inquiry into the Civil Service (1932–1935), which states:

> If a woman recruited to the post married after eight or ten years service the main purpose for which she has been employed entirely fails and she has moreover during that time been blocking the way of a man who could give the State good value for the service in question.

The "marriage bar", implemented in the 1930s continued until 1973, denying educated, trained women the opportunity to be promoted into decision-making areas where they could influence economic and social policy. The then Minister for Finance dismissed the women lobbying for equal pay and equal opportunity at that time as "a group of well-heeled articulate women".

Fine-Davis points out that the period of rapid social change, which occurred in Ireland from the mid 1970s to the mid 1980s coincided with the United Nations Decade for Women 1975–1985. International Women's Year, 1975, gave a huge boost to women's rights organisations. That first year revealed the discrimination against women worldwide and raised consciousness among UN member nations, which were required to give five-yearly reports on the progress of women's rights in their own country.

Whilst the overall picture is one of dramatic change, there is still a lingering residue of traditional attitudes concerning gender roles. Debate and discussion has moved on to work–life balance. There has been a disappointing lack of change in work-place structures. That brave new world of job-sharing, working from home, the sharing of domestic activities by both partners, has not been realised. The research shows that it is women with children who are most likely to perceive a male reluctance to do housework.

Women over the last 30–40 years have reached levels of attainment equal to those of men in education and lifelong employment. As Esping-Andersen

(2004) observed, it is the women who have done all the changing while the men still follow a model closely resembling that of their fathers and grandfathers.

The initiative by political parties to encourage women to run for election is to be welcomed. Policies are needed that will make it more attractive and possible for men to share family and home life. Women in parliament will add impetus to such change, not least in parliament itself!

Monica Barnes
Member of Dáil Éireann, 1982–1992, 1997–2002
Chair, Joint Oireachtas Committee on Women's Rights, 1987–1992

Acknowledgements

The research presented in this volume comprises a synthesis and integration of a series of studies, one building upon the other, carried out over a period of 40 years, beginning in 1973 with my doctoral research on attitudes toward the role and status of women in Ireland at Trinity College Dublin in the Department of Psychology (Professor D. W. Forrest, Head). I should like to thank Trinity College for providing a most supportive environment, as well as stimulating and congenial colleagues in the Department of Psychology, the Centre for Gender and Women's Studies and the Department of Sociology.

I should also like to acknowledge with thanks the organisations which supported the studies reported here. These include the Irish Department of Labour (1975 study), the Statistical Office of the European Communities, Luxembourg (1978 study), the Council for the Status of Women, Dublin (further analysis of the 1978 data set), the Second Joint Oireachtas Committee on Women's Rights (Joint Committee on Women's Rights of the 25th Dáil) (1986 study), the European Social Fund, EQUAL Initiative (2005 study) and the Family Support Agency (2010 study). I also wish to thank the Survey Unit of the Economic and Social Research Institute (ESRI) for its expertise in sampling, fieldwork and data analysis for the 1975, 1978, 1986, 2005 studies. Particular thanks are due to Professor Brendan Whelan and Professor James Williams. James Williams also contributed to the sampling design and other issues in the 2010 study. Aideen Mooney and Brian O'Byrne, Family Support Agency, and Dr Stephanie O'Keeffe also provided invaluable support and comments in relation to the 2010 study. Grateful appreciation is also due to Behaviour and Attitudes (Managing Director Ian McShane and Dean Howlin and Luke Reaper) for their expertise in sampling design and execution of the fieldwork and data analysis for the 2010 study. The views expressed in this book are solely those of the author and do not necessarily reflect those of any of the supporting agencies.

I would like to express particular thanks to Monica Barnes, former member of Dáil Éireann (Irish Parliament) and Chair of the Second Joint Oireachtas Committee on Women's Rights, for her encouragement, inspiration and support of the study of changing gender role attitudes carried out in 1986 and published in 1988. I am honoured and grateful to her for writing the Foreword.

My appreciation is also due to the late Michael O'Leary, Minister for Labour (1973–1977), whose Department supported the first study of attitudes toward the role and status of women in 1975. As Minister, he was instrumental in implementing much of the equality legislation during his tenure in office.

I wish to thank several scientific journals, including the *Journal of Personality*, *Psychology of Women Quarterly* and *Political Psychology* for permission to reproduce material from my articles previously published in these journals. I am also grateful to the Second Joint Committee on Women's Rights of the Irish Houses of the Oireachtas (Irish Parliament) for permission to reproduce material from two of my reports published by them. I also acknowledge with thanks permission from the Family Support Agency to reproduce selected material from my 2011 report.

Special thanks go to Amanda Holzworth for her contribution to the research in the 2010 study and for her excellent work in creating the majority of the tables and figures in this book and for formatting the final version of the manuscript.

I am indebted to Dr Gerald Morgan, Director, The Chaucer Hub, Trinity College Dublin, for his own example of scholarship and writing, as well as his incisive comments and encouragement throughout the writing of this book.

This book is dedicated to my late husband and colleague, Professor Earl E. Davis, formerly of the Economic and Social Research Institute, who opened up the world of social psychology and social research to me. He was my mentor and teacher in the early days of my career at the New School for Social Research, New York, and my collaborator and mentor through many exciting and productive years of research together in Dublin.

Margret Fine-Davis
Trinity College Dublin
March 2014

1 Introduction

1.1 Background

Changing gender roles constitute a major trend in our societies with vast social, political and economic implications and consequences. Inglehart and Norris (2003) have observed that "glacial shifts are taking place that move systematically away from traditional values and toward more egalitarian sex roles" (p. 9). These shifts in gender role roles have far-reaching implications. As Esping-Andersen asserts,

> women constitute the revolutionary force behind contemporary social and economic transformation. It is in large part the changing role of women that explains the new household structure, our altered demographic behaviour ... and, as a consequence, the new dilemmas that the advanced societies face
>
> (2004, p. v)

Ireland has been unique among developed Western societies in terms of the relative speed with which it has come to terms with these issues. While these changes came somewhat later in Ireland, the process of change has been very rapid.

The influence of various factors, including Ireland's economic development, the women's movement both internationally and in Ireland itself, and the impact of EU membership, served as catalytic forces to affect gender role attitudes as well as a spate of administrative and legislative reforms which enhanced the role and status of women. These included the removal of the marriage bar – which had required women to give up their jobs upon marriage – legislation for equal pay, equal opportunity, contraception and taxation of married women. All of these changes profoundly affected the role and status of women in Ireland and facilitated their increasing participation in the labour market. As a result of this, new issues have come to the fore, including the need for flexible working, work–life balance and childcare. Other issues which have also been the focus of public debate in Ireland over more than three decades include divorce, abortion and the role of women in the Church. Of these, the issue of divorce was resolved with a national Referendum in 1995 and legalised in 1996; yet the issues of abortion and, to a lesser extent, women's role in the Church are still sources of controversy. As of this writing, the issue of abortion was being debated in the houses of the Oireachtas (the Irish Parliament) as the Government tried to legislate to introduce a limited form of abortion; this legislation was finally passed in December 2013. The book examines attitudes to all of these issues, many of them over a period of three decades.

1.2 Changing gender role attitudes – the international context

The decade from the late 1960s to the late 1970s witnessed a heightened international awareness of the role and status of women in society. This awareness led to a marked increase in research devoted to studying changes in gender role attitudes and behaviour. Gender role attitudes have been shifting in Western societies since the late 1960s. Social scientists have attempted to capture these shifts, along with related shifts in values, through longitudinal studies of attitudes. One of the earliest studies of attitude change was carried out in Finland (Haavio-Mannila, 1972), yet the vast majority of the research in the early period was carried out in the US. These earlier studies captured the initial effects of the women's movement (e.g. Mason, Czajka and Arber, 1976; Thornton and Freedman, 1979). This train of research continued in the US through the 1980s and beyond and has continued to the present day (e.g. Thornton, Alwin and Camburn, 1983; Mason and Lu, 1988; Thornton and Young-DeMarco, 2001; Cotter, Hermsen and Vanneman, 2011). This train of research has also taken place in several European countries, including the Netherlands (e.g. van der Wal and Oudijk, 1985), the UK (e.g. Hinds and Jarvis, 2000; Scott, 2006, 2008), and Ireland (Fine-Davis, 1983a, 1988a; Fine-Davis, McCarthy, Edge and O'Dwyer, 2005) as well as in Australia (van Egmond, Baxter, Buchler and Western, 2010). Measures of gender role attitudes have been included in cross-national surveys, including the Eurobarometre, European Values and World Values surveys and International Social Survey Programme (ISSP) and trends in Ireland have been discussed by several authors (Wilcox, 1991; Banaszak and Plutzer, 1993; Whelan and Fahey, 1994; Hayes, McAllister and Studlar, 2000; Treas and Widmer, 2000; Inglehart and Norris, 2003; and O'Sullivan, 2007, 2012).

The vast majority of the research cited above has found gender role attitudes have become significantly less traditional over time. Most of these studies have found that attitudes to maternal employment have become more accepting (e.g. Mason and Lu, 1988; Fine-Davis, 1988a; Thornton and Young-DeMarco, 2001; O'Sullivan, 2007, 2012). Yet, several of the studies have shown that men continue to hold more traditional attitudes than women (e.g. Fine-Davis, 1988a; Fine-Davis *et al.*, 2005; Treas and Widmer, 2000) and opposition to maternal employment tends to be expressed through concern about its effects on children (e.g. Mason and Lu, 1988; Treas and Widmer, 2000; Fine-Davis, 2011). Mason and Lu (1988) concluded that "for many men, support for equal family roles is highly qualified" (p. 46).

Thornton and Young-DeMarco (2001) and Cotter *et al.* (2011) both conclude that attitudes to gender roles in the US may have plateaued up to the mid 1990s. Van Egmond *et al.* (2010) also found that gender role attitudes in Australia became more egalitarian up to the 1990s, but then flattened and in some cases reversed after that period. These authors asked if it was "a stalled revolution?" (Ibid) explored reasons for the slowing down of change in gender role attitudes in the US, including the possibility of a "backlash effect", a concept introduced earlier by Faludi, (1991). Braun and Scott (2009), writing from the UK and looking at cross-cultural data, also explored if the trend reversal was real, pointing to possible measurement issues in comparative research, and concluded that observed changes in gender role attitudes over time did not support "a story of revolutionary change and backlash", though they did find some evidence of "egalitarianism reaching a peak and retreat" (pp. 365–366).

This book examines gender role attitudes in Ireland over a comparable period of time, covering three decades from the mid 1970s to 2005, with more recent data also included to bring the study up to the present day. While many of the issues examined here share common ground with the numerous international studies cited above, the present volume, reporting a series of studies, also includes measures of attitudes to social policy issues relevant to the status of women in Ireland and documents attitude change in the context of legislative and policy changes which took place during a period of rapid social change beginning in the early 1970s.

1.3 Socio-cultural and historical background to study

Prior to the first study presented here, which was carried out in 1975, essentially no research in this area had been conducted in Ireland. This was due in large part to the relatively recent emergence of pressure for change in the status of women. Such pressure for change was facilitated by Ireland's relatively more recent economic and industrial development, together with its entrance in 1973 into the European Economic Community (EEC), now referred to as the European Union (EU). Because Ireland was just beginning to undergo transition in the area of gender role attitudes and behaviour at the time of the first data collection (1975), it offered an opportunity to collect baseline data at a unique period in its history.

While many other countries also experienced significant changes in gender role attitudes and behaviour during this period – coinciding with the Women's Movement (Inglehart and Norris, 2003) – for a number of unique reasons, Ireland's transformation began somewhat later and in many ways Ireland had much farther to go in order to catch up with developments in the status of women in most other developed Western societies. Part of the lag in Ireland's transition in the gender role sphere may have been due to its island status and consequent geographic isolation from the rest of Europe. Ireland had also been primarily an agrarian society, and its economic and industrial development did not gain momentum until the early 1960s. The agrarian nature of the culture had a historical impact on the nature of gender roles in the society by virtue of economic considerations, as discussed by Lee (1978). A further important factor influencing the role and status of women in this country has been the strong influence of the Roman Catholic Church, to which 95% of the population belonged in the 1970s; this figure has slightly reduced over the past three decades.

1.3.1 The social context and influence of the Church

Ireland is unique among developed Western societies in relation to the constraints on women's roles which continued well into the 1970s and 1980s (Commission on the Status of Women, 1972; Beale, 1986; Galligan, 1998; O'Connor, 1998; Kennedy, 2001) and which still remain concerning the issue of abortion (Smyth, 1992; Kingston, Whelan and Bacik, 1997). This was due in large part to the strong influence of the Catholic Church in promulgating and supporting a traditional role for women and in shaping attitudes to gender roles (Flanagan, 1975; Robinson, 1978; Inglis, 1998; Ferriter, 2009), as well as in contributing to the social conditions and legal framework in the country. While the influence of religion on the development of gender role attitudes and behaviour has been well documented (e.g. Reuther, 1974; Daly, 1975; Farley, 1976), the influence of the Catholic Church in Ireland was particularly strong (Garvin, 2004), surpassing that in other Catholic countries (Chubb, 1971) particularly concerning women's roles (Flanagan, 1975; Robinson, 1978) and issues related to sexuality and relationships, such as contraception, divorce and abortion. The influence of Church teachings on the norms and values of the society have been complemented by laws of the State, and underpinned by passages in the Irish Constitution concerning the role of women (Constitution of Ireland, 1937, Article 41.2):

> 2.1 In particular, the State recognises that by her life within the home, woman gives to the State a support without which the common good cannot be achieved.

> 2.2 The State shall, therefore, endeavour to ensure that mothers should not be obliged by economic necessity to engage in labour to neglect of their duties in the home.
>
> (Article 41.2, Constitution of Ireland, 1937)

Attitudes toward the role of women in Ireland are part of a larger belief system in which religiosity is a central component (Fine-Davis, 1979a, 1989) and which also has elements reminiscent of the authoritarian personality syndrome (ibid.; Adorno, Frenkel-Brunswik, Levinson and Sanford, 1950), a feature noted earlier by both Chubb (1971) and Whyte (1971).

1.3.2 Social change in Ireland

In spite of the fact that Ireland was a more traditional society relative to many other Western countries, the process of change from the mid 1970s was very rapid. The influence of various factors, including Ireland's economic development, the women's movement – both internationally and in Ireland itself – and the impact of Ireland's membership of the European Community from 1973 onwards, served as catalytic forces to affect gender role attitudes. These were reinforced by a series of administrative and legislative changes which had implications for the role and status of women. These included the removal of the marriage bar (1973) – which had prevented married women from being employed in the public service – followed in rapid succession by legislation for equal pay (passed in 1974, implemented in 1975), employment equality (1977), contraception (1979) and taxation of married women (1980). Legislation concerning equal pay and equal employment were direct results of EU membership, as they followed EU directives. There was extensive public debate on contraception in the early 1970s and the 1973 McGee case – in which the Supreme Court ruled that contraceptives could be imported for personal use – helped to precipitate legislation in 1979 in this area. Further significant changes followed, including the legalisation of divorce (1995), following two national referenda in 1986 and 1995, the latter successful by a very small margin (O'Connor, 1998).

Many of these developments profoundly affected the role of women in Ireland and in many cases removed impediments to their freedom and labour force participation. Increasing numbers of married women entered the labour force from the 1970s onwards (Callan and Farrell, 1991) and this trend has continued to the present day. Married women's labour force participation was almost negligible in 1971 at 7.5%. By 1977 this figure had doubled and in the 20 years from 1989 to 2009, a period of economic growth, the figure increased from 23.7% to 54%, with employment among married women in the childbearing age group much higher at 72.6% (CSO, 2009a).

Thus, for a number of reasons, progress toward the attainment of equal status for women has not been as rapid in Ireland as it has been in most other European countries or in the United States. However, while these factors may help to explain the reasons for Ireland's relative traditionalism and lag in progress vis-à-vis other European countries and the US, they do not explain the *context* from which the attitudes toward women arose. In order to more fully understand attitudes toward the role and status of women today, it is important to try and understand where they came from historically. Thus, it may be useful to step back into Irish history – if however briefly and sketchily – in order to identify some of the socio-cultural and historical roots of more current attitudes toward the role of women in Ireland. In the following section we shall review some of the key facts and events which have been relevant to women's status in Ireland over the centuries up to the present time. While many sources have been consulted, we have relied extensively on the excellent collection of articles edited by MacCurtain and Ó Corráin (1978). For a more comprehensive discussion of each topic touched on below, the reader is referred to the work of the individual Irish historians cited here.

1.3.3 The historical context – the role of women in Ireland through the ages

The earliest information about the role and status of women in early Irish society comes from mythology and folklore. Irish mythology began to be written down in the sixth century; however, there is little agreement as to the dating of the culture being written about and, in fact, a potential span from 1000 BC to AD 1000 is possible, although there is general agreement that Irish mythology involves much pre-Christian information (Wood, 1985).

It is clear that in Ireland goddesses were worshipped, as well as gods. These goddesses were primarily associated with fertility, protection of flocks and herds and with the security of land and people. The principal goddess referred to in Irish myths was the goddess of sovereignty, who symbolised the land of Ireland. In these stories the prospective king was required to perform the "banfheis rigi, or marriage of sovereignty, with the goddess of the land to ensure the acceptance of his kingship by its people" (ibid., p. 16, citing MacCana, 1980). MacCana (1980) points out that "in Irish tradition it would be hard to exaggerate the importance of this idea of the land and its sovereignty conceived in the form of a woman" (p. 7).

However, not all of the goddesses were gentle and protective. There is a rich history of Irish war goddesses. One "triple" goddess who is well-documented in Irish history was the triad of Morrigan, Badb and Macha. Their role in war was, however, not a combative one but rather involved tactics of "psychological warfare". They apparently instilled terror and panic in the opponent through magical powers and by their very presence (Wood, 1985). This tactic would appear to have been mirrored in the Sheela-na-gigs of the fifteenth and sixteenth centuries. These blatant images of female sex-uality were put high up over doors and windows in churches and castles in the probable hope that they would give protection against destructive forces (ibid.). While some of the warrior goddesses did not fight, others did. The most famous of these was Queen Medb (Maeve), who is generally accepted as a goddess in human form. She was commander of her army, expert in the use of weapons and an active participant in battle. Another famous legendary figure in this tradition, though from a somewhat later period, was Grace O'Malley, better known as Grainne Mhaol, who was a "pirate queen" and power-broker. Like the mythical Macha, who had to race against horses – and won – she too was roused from childbirth to fight (O hOgain, 1987). The historical evidence for women engaging in battle in Celtic societies occurs not only for Ireland, but also for Britain and Gaul and apparently in Ireland this behaviour is documented until well into the Christian era (Wood, op. cit.).

Historical evidence further reveals that from the tenth century on queens emerged in their own right. Whereas prior to that time the terminology used was "the queen of the king of Tara", after that point the usage was simply "the queen of Tara". Ó Corráin (1978) sees this as reflecting a major rise in the status of women. The queens of this time exercised considerable political and social influence (ibid.).

It is clear from this that female images – whether they were goddesses or actual living people who took on a legendary character – were seen as powerful. Indeed women were believed to have special powers that men did not have (O hOgain, op. cit.). This power can also be seen in the mythical figure of the banshee – "a solitary, crying, female supernatural being" who has the power to "proclaim deaths which are imminent or have just occurred" (Lysaght, 1985). However, while many legendary female figures were portrayed as powerful, Irish folklore also provides evidence that the average woman's primary responsibilities were indoors and those of men outdoors. In describing women's lives in the fairy legends, Bourke (1987) observes that women's power is "emotional and moral", whereas men's is "economic and political". Women are the "interpreters"; they "know what is going on" (ibid.).

Ó Corráin notes that "early Irish society was patriarchal: the legal and political life was governed by men" (1978, p. 1). This state of affairs apparently held for the earliest period for which there are written records – the sixth and early seventh centuries. However, from the late seventh and early eighth century the situation changed fairly rapidly. The reasons for this are a matter of debate among scholars (ibid.). Women were granted extensive rights during this period, particularly with regard to marriage, divorce and property rights. It is to be emphasised that we are referring here to *secular* law. Under early Irish *Church* law, while separation or divorce was possible in the case of adultery, one could not take another spouse during the lifetime of the first. Ó Corráin observes that

> the balance of the evidence, secular and ecclesiastical alike, would tend to indicate that at least among the aristocracy the older customs remained the norm. And despite the intense activity of the 12th

century reformers, secular marriage, with its tolerant attitude to divorce continued in Ireland until the close of the middle ages.

(Ibid., p. 7)

The wide-ranging and flexible grounds for divorce available to women under the Brehon Laws "served as a guarantee of extensive women's rights and protected women in a way which was remarkably different from the customs of other European countries" (ibid., p. 8). Quoting the German scholar Knoch (in Binchy, 1936, p. 262), Ó Corráin goes on to state:

> The possibility of more or less easy dissolution of marriage will be evaluated differently according to one's outlook, but the care which is evident for the individual personality of the woman in Irish marriage law is a widely shining landmark in this early period of western history as compared with the unrespected position of women in earlier times and other societies.
>
> (Ó Corráin, 1978, p. 8)

Ó Corráin believes that historical developments which followed, beginning with the Norman invasion in 1169 and followed by the imposition of English law in the early seventeenth century had the effect of curtailing the natural development of these Gaelic customs: "As a result, in its attitude to women and their place in society – as in its attitude to many other matters – modern Ireland enjoys no continuity with its Gaelic past" (Ó Corráin, 1978, p. 11).

Following the Norman invasion, Ireland was partly conquered and colonised. For approximately four hundred years two different communities – the Gaels and the Anglo-Normans – lived side by side, each with their own legal system. The Gaels continued to live under the Brehon Laws, although these were modified to some extent in the later period, and the Anglo-Normans lived under the system of English Common Law. The latter, which reflected standard practice in most of Western Europe, was less egalitarian than the Brehon Laws in the rights it accorded to women (Simms, 1978).

Thus the position of Irish women did not deteriorate until the conquest and plantations of the sixteenth and seventeenth centuries by the English. From then until the Famine, women were totally without formal political rights:

> ... their property and inheritance rights both within and outside of marriage were now governed by English common law, and ... theirs was a subject and subsidiary role to the male, and it was performed, for the most part, within a domestic context.
>
> (Ó'Tuathaigh, 1978, p. 26)

The Great Famine of 1846 further weakened the position of women in Irish society. Prior to the Famine women had had an important role both in the agricultural and non-agricultural sectors. The Famine affected this situation in various ways. One major effect was to essentially wipe out domestic spinning, which had been the major source of women's independent income. Women's role in agriculture also diminished as it became more focused on livestock and less on tillage, and thus became less labour intensive (Lee, 1978). The deterioration in the economic status of women affected their marriage prospects and made them vulnerable to male dominance – hence the growing importance of the dowry after the Famine. As the woman made what was perceived as a lesser contribution to the farm, her "capital" became more important. Thus, daughters became more dependent on their fathers and had less independence in choosing a mate (ibid.). In discussing the position of women in Irish society following the Famine, Lee (1978) explains that:

> Farmers would not normally dower two daughters. That would dissipate their savings, and drag the family down in the social scale. Marriage might be a sacrament, but for the farmer the marriage contract was essentially a commercial transaction, and it devalued the family currency to put two daughters on the marriage market. A society dominated by strong farmers, and providing little female employment, inevitably denied most of its children the chance of rearing a family in the country. It was therefore crucial to maintain the economic dominance of the new order that all thoughts of marriage in Ireland should be banished from the minds of the majority of Irish youth. Temptation must not be placed in their way. Sex, therefore, must be denounced as a satanic snare, in even what had been its most innocent pre-Famine manifestations. Sex posed a far more subversive threat than the landlord to the security and status of the family. Boys and girls must be kept apart at all costs. Economic circumstances therefore conspired to make Ireland an increasingly male dominated society after the Famine.
>
> (p. 38)

Echoes of this are seen in the widespread practice of keeping the sexes separate through single sex schools. Lee notes that the rise of the strong farmer coincided with the growth in clerical power and a new public obsession with sex. Whereas in 1840 there was only one Catholic priest for every 3,000 lay people, by 1960 this had risen to one priest for every 600 people. Similarly the ratio of nuns to lay persons increased from one to 7,000 in 1841 to one to 400 a century later (ibid.). Lee observed that

> the doctrines inculcated in Maynooth and other seminaries, in the convents, and in Trinity College, Dublin, where the Church of Ireland clergymen were educated, reinforced the assumptions the young

aspirants brought with them. In Maynooth sex was equated, for all practical purposes, with sin. Trinity College Divinity School ... produced clergy who suspected sex and Catholicism with equal fervor. It is therefore hardly surprising that the post-Famine clergies displayed a much greater preoccupation with sex than earlier clerical generations.... It is one of the ironies of the intellectual history of modern Ireland that at a period when Catholic propagandists ... were prone to denounce England as decadent, they imbibed unconsciously ... the prudish values of Victorian middle class morality, which simultaneously idealised and repressed women.

(Ibid., p. 40)

Echoing the sentiments of Ó Corráin (1978) concerning Ireland's lack of continuity with its Gaelic past regarding its attitude to women, Lee (1978) points out

there was nothing natural or normal or even inherently Irish about the "traditional" values. The wheel is coming full circle, as women begin once more to enjoy something of the economic independence many of them knew before the Famine. Men are adapting, however reluctantly, to the implications of this change, and the clerical image of women, like the male image of woman in general, is being refurbished accordingly. The past century may soon come to be seen as no more than a sharp but temporary deviation from the main course of the history of women in Ireland.

(pp. 44–45)

The increase in the number of women pursuing religious vocations increased dramatically after the Famine, probably in part as a result of the decreased marriage prospects for women. This coincided with the expansion of the educational system and the greater involvement of the churches in education. Lee points out that "it is ironic that at a moment when educational opportunities increased for Irish women, the educational system began to be more systematically used to indoctrinate them into adopting as self-images the prevailing male image of woman" (ibid., p. 41). These traits included "obedience, docility and resignation to the role assigned to them" (ibid., p. 42).

Political scientists have also written about religion and related values and attitudes in Ireland. Chubb (1971) compared Irish Catholicism with continental Catholicism and found it to be more anti-intellectual in character than that in other Catholic countries. He also pointed to the Augustinian tradition in Ireland, which puts a priority on abstemiousness. Chubb (ibid.) and Whyte (1971) also discuss the presence of authoritarianism in Irish culture. Mary Robinson (1978), who wrote as a feminist lawyer and academic, prior to becoming the first woman President of Ireland in 1990, commented on Chubb's identification of authoritarianism, loyalty and anti-intellectualism in Irish political culture, saying she found it surprising that his analysis

> does not dwell at all on the position of women in this whole structure. The analysis is a completely male orientated one.... Yet it is clear that the characteristics of authoritarianism, loyalty and anti-intellectualism reinforced prevailing attitudes about the different roles of the sexes in society...
>
> (p. 60)

A different, yet analogous critique was made by the theologian Flanagan (1975) of the Report of the Commission on the Status of Women (1972):

> It is a fascinating thing that in all its length the Report on the Status of Women never once mentions the word "religion" or "religious", not even under the heading "education" in the Index. This is a notable and significant omission in an Irish context where "traditional values" are so carried and formed by religion and where the system of education is so dominated by conservative and traditionalist religious values. Religion in Ireland may be, in fact, the ultimate source and sanction of many of those traditional discriminatory thought-patterns which exist undetected in the Irish mind.
>
> (p. 235)

Thus, it would appear that analyses of the position of women have not always been integrated into analyses of other key aspects of Irish life, notably politics and religion, and vice versa. The position of women is clearly the result of multiple forces – historical, economic, political, social and religious. To understand it, one needs to be aware of and examine the interconnections among all of these influences. This is the challenge of interdisciplinary research. The present volume, while primarily presenting social-psychological data, attempts to place this data in its socio-cultural context. While it is never possible to be completely thorough in carrying out interdisciplinary work, it is our view that attempting to bring in other relevant contextual material will help to elucidate the attitudinal data which are the main focus of this book.

Clearly religion has been a key shaper of attitudes towards women in general and in Ireland in particular. Flanagan (1975) points out that discriminatory attitudes toward women are in part rooted in a belief that women are inferior to men. Many of these attitudes have a scriptural basis: e.g.

> women were created for the sake of men (1 Cor. 11:10) and are a reflection of man's glory. (1 Cor. 11:8). Man did not come from

woman but woman from man (1 Cor. 11:8; cf. Gen. 2:21f). Adam was formed first and Eve afterwards (1 Tim. 2:14)

(Ibid., p. 237)

Flanagan suggests that the inegalitarian approach to women in the Church was influenced in part by a basic fear of women as evil. He notes that in the patristic record women are described as "volatile, shallow minded, morally weak" (ibid., p. 238). He asserts that this misogyny has deep roots in the Christian ascetic tradition and touches not only males, but females as well who have come to see themselves as second-class citizens. Another theologian, Margaret Farley (1976), elaborates upon some of these ideas noting that

> Eve had not only been an agent in Adam's sin, she was by nature derivative from Adam and hence by nature subordinate to him. The identity of every woman could easily be seen as derivative, then, in some way from a man.
>
> (p. 167)

This implication, of female inferiority was, of course, reinforced by the "refusal by Christian theology to attribute the fullness of the *imago Dei* (the image of God) to women" (ibid., p. 166). Farley also emphasises that the sources of Christian misogynism are very much related to "ancient myths identifying women with chaos, darkness, mystery, matter and sin" (ibid., p. 164). These notions became echoed in Christian interpretation "of the body as defiled, of sexuality as contaminating, and thence of woman as temptress, as a symbol of sin" (ibid.). Other sources of misogynism can be found in ancient blood taboos and Hebrew connections between nakedness and shame (ibid., p. 165). Paradoxically, Farley points out,

> Christian theology exalted woman and her role at the same time that it made her inferior. She was at once the symbol of sin and the symbol of all virtue.... When woman was placed on a pedestal what was perceived too easily as sacred was also perceived too easily as profaned.
>
> (Ibid., p. 166)

Because of the increasing influence of the Church since the Famine and its control of the educational system in Ireland, it was inevitable that many of these underlying ideas would find their way into the psyches of Irish people, men and women alike, and thereby have a profound effect on shaping attitudes toward the role of women and indeed on shaping the role itself.

To return to our historical journey, in traditional Irish life there was no rigid distinction between domestic duties and other types of work and women performed a wide variety of duties (Daly, 1978; Ó Corráin, 1978). However, with the Industrial Revolution, beginning in the late 1800s, many jobs which had once been performed in the home were now performed in factories. In 1841 there had been half a million female textile workers, mainly outworkers, in Ireland. By 1881 this dropped to just 100,000. The only growth area for women's employment was domestic service. In 1911 one out of three working women was a servant. The other large group of women workers was in agriculture. During the 1930s the number of women employed in factories grew steadily, however they tended to be concentrated in lower paid jobs (ibid.).

At a time when women began to become involved in the trade union movement, Daly points out that it is ironic that restrictions against women in employment began to appear (ibid.). In 1932 the Government proposed to ban the employment of married women as national teachers. While this move was strongly opposed by the Irish National Teachers Organisation (INTO), they eventually acquiesced on the condition that existing teachers be exempted (ibid., pp. 75–76). A ban on married women in the civil service was also under active discussion in the 1930s and later implemented. In the Report of the Commission of Inquiry into the Civil Service, 1932–1935 (the Brennan Commission) it states:

> If a woman recruited to the post married after eight or ten years service the main purpose for which she has been employed entirely fails and she has moreover during that time been blocking the way of a man who could give the State good value for the service in question.
>
> (para. 180)

Thus, Daly (1978) points out, the marriage bar in the civil service also proved detrimental to single women, as it destroyed their promotion prospects, since they were treated as if they were going to marry and leave at any time. Attitudes in the civil service toward equal pay for women were also hard-line, reflecting, according to Daly, public opinion on this issue. Citing the Brennan Commission again, she quotes:

> In those cases in the Civil Service where men and women may be employed indifferently we find special reason for supposing that on the whole when all relevant aspects are taken into account the woman does not give as good a return of work as a man.
>
> (Commission of Inquiry into the Civil Service, 1932–1935, Para. 180)

Daly observes that

> they also argued that differential rates of pay between men and women were accepted by Irish society and that it was not the role of the Civil Service to alter this practice: "if the Government were to grant equal pay the result would be a disproportionate influx (of women) into State employment".
>
> (Daly, 1978, p. 76)

Daly concludes that:

> Attitudes towards women working were extremely hostile – the
> Brennan Commission could actually raise the suggestion of barring
> women from Executive Grades in the Civil Service. In a climate of job
> shortages, many male trade unionists were equally hostile towards
> women working and their attitudes reflected the conventional opin-
> ions of contemporary society.
>
> (Ibid., p. 77)

The job shortages during this period, which influenced the attitudes
toward women working would seem to have been caused by the rapid
changeover from an agricultural to a non-agricultural society and the
failure of economic policies at that time. The period from Independence
to the mid 1950s was characterised by policies of "self-sufficiency, protec-
tionism, home-market orientation, in short economic nationalism"
(Redlich, 1978, p. 84).

Other retrograde measures which affected women emerged during this
period. Prior to 1937, while there was no divorce law, it was theoretically
possible to obtain a divorce by means of a private bill in the Irish Parliament, but this recourse was effectively blocked by an amendment to standing orders introduced in 1925 by the Taoiseach of the time, W. T.
Cosgrave (Whyte, 1971). However, in the 1937 Constitution (Article
41.3.2), a prohibition on divorce was officially enacted. Indeed attitudes
concerning appropriate gender roles were enshrined in the 1937 Constitution (Article 41.2.1 and 41.2.2), as cited above.

In spite of the introduction of the "marriage bar" and the prohibition
on divorce, many important gains for women were made in the late nineteenth and early twentieth centuries, including obtaining the vote, the
right to hold political office and to become cabinet ministers (MacCurtain, 1978).

Following the 1950s, which were characterised by economic depression,
gloom and high emigration, the 1960s ushered in a period of economic
development, expansion and optimism, as well as a greater openness to
the rest of the world; and the early 1970s marked the beginning of the
women's movement in Ireland (see Beale, 1986). With Ireland's entrance
into the European Community in 1973, together with an increasing awareness on the part of the population, as a result of such factors as exposure
to British and American television and greater opportunities for foreign
travel, etc., a period of rapid social change began to occur in the early
1970s and has continued to the present day.

1972 was a significant year for women's equality in Ireland, as it marked
the publication of the *Report of the Commission on the Status of Women*. This
Report, to the then Minister for Finance, Charles J. Haughey, TD, who was
later to become Taoiseach (Prime Minister), documented areas of

discrimination in all areas of Irish life and made wide-ranging recommendations for policy changes. However, in addition to such concrete recommendations, the Report also acknowledged the important role played by attitudes in perpetuating discrimination:

> the removal of ... actual discriminations leaves untouched a larger and more subtle area of discrimination consisting of those factors which limit women's participation even in the absence of formal discrimination, that is, the stereotyped role that is assigned to women, the inculcation of attitudes in both boys and girls in their formative years that there are definite and separate roles for the sexes.... It is from this type of cultural mould that formal discrimination arises...
>
> (p. 12)

Subsequent to the publication of this Report, there followed a series of significant administrative and legislative changes as well as political developments which would have far-reaching consequences for gender role behaviour in Ireland and would also have been likely to have affected attitudes, particularly during the 1970s and 1980s. These included:

1 The removal of the marriage bar in 1973 which had required that women resign from their jobs upon marriage;
2 Ireland's entrance to the European Community in 1973;
3 Passage of the Anti-Discrimination (Pay) Act of 1974 (implemented in 1975);
4 Passage of the Employment Equality Act of 1977;
5 The establishment in 1977 of the Employment Equality Agency, whose role it was to enforce the Anti-Discrimination legislation and to promote equality in the workplace;
6 Legislation in 1979 which legalised the sale of contraceptives;
7 The Supreme Court Decision of 1980 removing the discriminatory tax laws against married women.

Parallel with, and probably to a great extent a result of, the many administrative and legal reforms referred to above, the labour force participation rate of married women increased significantly, rising from 7.5% in 1971 to 19.5% in 1984. The increase among young married women of childbearing age (25–34) was particularly striking – going from 8.8% in 1971 to 26.9% in 1984 (Blackwell, 1986, Table 3.5, p. 22). This trend was also evident in other European countries (Eurostat, 1981) as well as in the US (Nye, 1974; Klein, 1975). However, Ireland was unique in that, as late as 1961, the base was unusually low – with just 5.2% of married women working (Blackwell, op. cit.) – and the rate of increase was particularly rapid, quadrupling in just over two decades. However, whereas in the US, the boom in married female labour force participation occurred during the period 1940–1960 and involved an increase from 17% to 37%, the Irish increase from 5% to 20% occurred some 20 years later, i.e. from 1961 to the early 1980s. While the participation rate was still quite low during the 1970s and 1980s compared with the US and most other European countries, it was expected that the Irish level would continue to increase and approximate European norms (Sexton, 1981; Working Party on Child Care Facilities for Working Parents, 1983). This in fact came to pass, as illustrated in Table 1.1. By 2004 the labour force participation of married women stood at 49.4%. It is notable that the participation rate of those in the childbearing age group (25–34) was lower than that of all married women in 1961 (4.8% vs 5.2%), reflecting social norms that women with young children should not work outside the home. Yet this ratio began to gradually change. By 1989, while 23.7% of married women of all ages were working outside the home, 39% of married women of childbearing age were. This trend gained momentum and by 2004 65.5% of married women of childbearing age were employed, compared with 49.4% of married women of all ages. By 2009 72.6% of married women in the childbearing age group were employed, compared with 54% of married women overall (CSO, 2009a).

In the early period the increase in married female labour force participation was due to the spate of administrative and legal changes in the area of gender equality and the removal of deterrents to married women working. In the later period women's participation was associated with economic growth and indeed was seen to contribute to the Celtic Tiger (Fahey and FitzGerald, 1997). At all points in time, from the 1970s onwards, the participation of women in the prime childbearing age group of 25–34 increased at an even more rapid rate than that of other groups of married women.

Concomitant with the increasing labour force participation of married women came a decrease in the fertility rate (Sexton and Dillon, 1984), which was particularly notable in the Irish context, since this country has traditionally had the highest fertility rate in Europe. Irish fertility rates continued to decline over the following decades from the 1980s, as shown in Table 1.2. While Ireland still has one of the highest total fertility rates in Europe, where we are now seeing fertility rates well below replacement level in many countries, this still reflects a decrease of roughly 50% over

Table 1.1 Married women's labour force participation in Ireland, 1961–2009 (%)

	1961	1971	1977	1981	1989	1994	1997	2001	2004	2009
All ages	5.2	7.5	14.4	16.7	23.7	32.4	37.3	46.4	49.4	54.0
Age 25–34	4.8	8.8	16.7	21.6	39.0	54.5	58.2	64.7	65.5	72.6

Sources: CSO: Labour Force Surveys (1971–97); Callan and Farrell (1991); CSO: Quarterly National Household Surveys (1999–2009).

Table 1.2 Total fertility rate, 1960–2007 for selected high and low fertility EU countries

	1960	1970	1980	1990	2000	2004	2006	2007
HIGH								
Ireland	3.76	3.93	3.25	2.11	1.90	1.99	1.90	2.03
France	2.73	2.47	1.95	1.78	1.88	1.90	2.01	1.98
Denmark	2.57	1.95	1.55	1.67	1.77	1.78	1.85	1.85
LOW								
Poland	2.98	2.20	2.28	2.04	1.34	1.23	1.27	1.31
Hungary	2.02	1.98	1.92	1.87	1.32	1.28	1.35	1.32
Italy	2.41	2.42	1.64	1.33	1.24	1.33	1.35	1.34
Germany	2.37	2.03	1.56	1.45	1.38	1.36	1.34	1.39
EU-15	2.59	2.38	1.82	1.57	1.50	1.54	–	–
EU-25	2.59	2.34	1.88	1.64	1.48	1.49	–	–
EU-27	–	–	–	–	–	–	1.53	1.56

Sources: Eurostat (2006), from Table D-4, p. 76; Eurostat (2008), Table 4, p. 6; CSO. (2009b), Table 7.9, p. 58.

the last three decades. The average number of children per woman was just under four in 1970 whereas from 1990 onwards it has hovered at around two. It has been predicted by the Central Statistics Office that this will further decrease (CSO, 1999, 2007) and that Ireland's birth rate is likely to continue to fall in line with European norms (approximately 1.5) unless policies intervene to change this trend.

1.4 Overview of studies

Against this background, the author carried out a series of studies on attitudes to the role of women at five points in time over a 35-year period – from 1975 to 2010.

1.4.1 1975 study

Shortly after the publication of the Report of the Commission on the Status of Women (1972), the first detailed and comprehensive study of attitudes toward the role and status of women in Ireland was carried out during the period 1973–1975, with main test data collection taking place in 1975 (Fine-Davis, 1976, 1977). This study examined the nature and dimensions of such attitudes (Fine-Davis, 1983a), their demographic determinants (ibid.) and personality and other social-psychological correlates (Fine-Davis, 1979a) – as well as the social-psychological predictors of labour force participation of married women (Fine-Davis, 1979b). The study provided baseline data at the approximate beginning of a period of rapid social change concerning gender roles in Ireland.

1.4.2 *1978 study*

Several key items measuring attitudes toward gender roles from the original 1975 study were replicated in a larger nationwide representative study (N=1,862) which was carried out in 1978 (Fine-Davis, Davis and Bolger, 1981; Fine-Davis, 1983a) as part of a harmonised cross-cultural study of subjective social indicators of the quality of working life sponsored by the Statistical Office of the European Communities. Additional items concerning attitudes to social issues in Ireland were added to the questionnaire fielded in Ireland.

1.4.3 *1986 study*

A third major study was conducted in 1986 – 11 years after the first 1975 study (Fine-Davis, 1988a, 1988b, 1988c). Because of the major legislative and administrative changes which occurred in Ireland from the early 1970s until the early 1980s, as well as changing gender role behaviour, as exemplified by the increased labour force participation of married women and a decreasing fertility rate, it would be expected that attitudes concerning gender roles would also have changed. Tentative evidence from two Irish surveys carried out in 1978 (Fine-Davis, 1983b) and in 1981 (Fine-Davis, 1983c) which replicated several sets of items contained in the 1975 study, indicated that attitudes seemed to be moving in a more egalitarian direction (Fine-Davis, 1983b), at least on the part of women. However, the persistent and increasing high rates of unemployment in Ireland might well have created a backlash effect and a counterforce on attitudes. The earlier research indicated that negative attitudes toward married female labour force participation were linked to a fear of job loss for men. The belief seemed to be that men were more entitled to jobs than women (ibid.).

Further evidence pointing to a possible reversion to earlier attitudes was manifested by two national referenda – the first on abortion (1983) and the second on divorce (1986). In both cases, the conservative option was chosen: a Constitutional amendment, recognising the equal right to life of the unborn child, was passed in 1983, thereby strengthening the already illegal status of abortion. The referendum on divorce similarly yielded a result in which two-thirds rejected introducing divorce – leaving Ireland among the handful of countries in the world which did not allow divorce.

In view of the countervailing trends cited above, it would not have been possible to state with any degree of certainty how people felt in 1986, nor would it have been possible to assess the attitudinal effects of the major legislative and other social changes which had occurred in the interim period, unless the attitudes involved were actually measured.

In addition to measuring change in attitudes from 1975 to 1986 in the area of gender roles and equal opportunity, the 1986 study also examined attitudes to other current issues. These included divorce and abortion as well as information on how people had voted in the two recent referenda on these issues. This made it possible to examine the relationships between attitudes and voting behaviour on these two issues which were highly germane to the status of women. It was hoped that these analyses would shed light on the attitudes underlying the 1983 and 1986 referenda results.

The 1986 study also addressed such emerging issues as barriers to women's career advancement, attitudes to parental leave, flexible working hours, childcare arrangements, men's participation in household activities and childcare.

Comparative results from these two surveys conducted in 1975 and 1986, as well as those from the 1978 nationwide representative survey replicating some of the key items, were published as a series of reports by the Joint Oireachtas Committee on Women's Rights – an inter-party committee of the Irish Parliament, the body which sponsored the 1986 study (Fine-Davis, 1988a, 1988b, 1988c).

1.4.4 2005 study

The most recent survey in this series was conducted in 2005 (Fine-Davis *et al.*, 2005), 30 years following the first study in 1975, and 19 years following the 1986 survey. This latter period included the time period from the 1990s to 2005, a period of economic boom – referred to as the 'Celtic Tiger', a period much more prosperous than that which preceded, and indeed, followed it.

1.4.5 2010 study

The results from the four studies referred to above, covering the period 1975– 2005, will be augmented by selected results from a study of "Changing Gender Role Attitudes and Behaviour: Implications for Family Formation in Ireland" (Fine-Davis, 2011). This study examined current gender role attitudes and attitudes to family formation of Irish men and women. The measures from this study are new and reflect how gender roles and gender relations are evolving in Ireland. The results from this study provide a timely counterpoint to the previous four studies by showing how these issues are perceived today and which new issues are perceived as important.

In this volume we shall present the time series data and discuss it in light of social changes which occurred alongside the attitudinal change. This series of four studies (1975, 1978, 1986 and 2005) has produced a wealth of data relating not only to gender role attitudes but also to attitudes to key social policy issues of the last three decades.

The current volume thus provides a synthesis of the key results from the earlier studies together with more recent data from 2010. The bringing together of the results of these five studies carried out over a 35-year period provides a unique picture of how attitudes toward the role and status of women in Ireland have evolved in the context of a period of rapid social and legislative change. This longer time period enables us to chart attitudes from a base of a very traditional, economically poorly developed country to one which has gone through a social and economic transformation.

We shall document attitudinal change in light of social, economic and legislative change during the period 1973–2013, with key empirical data from 1975–2005 and more current data from 2010 (Fine-Davis, 2011) and discuss how attitudes have been a key factor, together with other elements of social change, in the development of public policy and social legislation during this period. Through this approach we will examine the sequential relationships between social attitudes and the development of public policy and vice versa and attempt to interpret their reciprocal effects on each other.

We shall also draw upon the historical, sociological, legal and policy work which has been written about gender issues and social change in Ireland in order to place the time series attitudinal data in an interdisciplinary context. In addition we will draw upon relevant news reporting of the period, particularly from *The Irish Times*, considered the newspaper of record, in order to locate the attitudinal findings in the socio-economic, legislative and political context of the day.

The purpose of the series of studies reported here was to examine changing gender role attitudes during a period of rapid social change in Ireland, initially the mid 1970s to the mid 1980s, coinciding approximately with the United Nations Decade for Women (1975–1985). The data for the first study were collected in 1975 – International Women's Year – and the data collection for the first follow-up study were collected in 1986. The timing of these key international events underlines the importance accorded to women's issues throughout the world at this time.

2   Method

Balbriggan
Library
Ph: 8704401

2.1 Overview of studies: 1975–2010

In this book we present findings from five studies carried out over the period 1975–2010. The initial four studies carried out in 1975, 1978, 1986 and 2005, containing replicated measures of attitudes to gender roles and related social issues, comprise the major body of the data to be presented here, whilst the most recent study (2010) contains primarily newer measures of attitudes to gender roles, together with a few of the original gender role items.

The variables in the first four studies include measures of gender role attitudes and stereotypes as well as attitudes to several of the major social policy issues of the day: maternal employment, equal pay, equal opportunity, taxation of married women, and contraception. These issues resulted in developments in public policy over this period, including in many cases to legislation. The availability of comparable attitudinal data at several points in time over this key period of social change enables us see to what extent attitudes may have stimulated legislation and public policy and to what extent changes in legislation and public policy may have in turn facilitated further attitude change. The passage of legislation concerning equal pay (implemented in 1975), employment equality (1977), contraception (1979) and taxation of married women (1980) after collection of baseline data in 1975 offers a unique natural experiment which makes it possible to examine attitudes towards these issues both before the legislation and at two points afterwards. While we cannot definitively attribute causation here, we can assume that public attitudes contributed to a readiness to enact legislation and changes in legislation and related public policies were likely in turn to have facilitated further attitude change.

The first four datasets have several methodological advantages over much of the previous empirical research in this area. First, the measures were based, in part, on earlier, more comprehensive measures developed in the US (Kirkpatrick, 1936; Levinson and Huffman, 1955; Spence and Helmreich, 1972) as well as on issues specifically relevant to the Irish context. These new measures were developed using factor analysis (Fine-Davis, 1983a), yielding composite scores which are more robust and reliable than individual items. Finally, the set of measures tap a wider range of attitudes and issues than many previous studies in the area of gender role attitudes do. Thus, the series of studies which form the basis of this volume is unique in that it includes an extensive range of measures all of which have been developed in Ireland, yielding results which are robust and reliable over a significant time period. The advantage of having a differentiated set of items from the early period is that it provides a baseline against which to measure the effects of key legislation relating to gender equality which was passed in the period 1975–1980 in the immediate aftermath and also allows for the measurement of change over time.

However, because the main set of items replicates the original items from 1975, it only includes policy issues which were salient in 1975, as well as global attitudes to women and gender roles. However, the study carried out in 1986 includes measures of attitudes to the emerging issues of divorce and abortion, the studies carried out in 2005 and 2010 contain extensive data on attitudes to work–life balance and related social policies, and the study from 2010 includes newer measures of gender role attitudes, including those eliciting a "response" to changes in men and women's roles. Thus, the combined datasets offer a unique opportunity to measure attitude change over a considerable period of time, whilst also examining attitudes to newer issues as they have emerged.

The methodology of each of the studies is described below.

2.2 1975 study

2.2.1 Pilot and pre-test

The 1975 study was the first of its kind to be carried out in Ireland. Thus, careful preliminary work was necessary, including review of literature of related work in other countries and well as an in-depth pilot study. The pilot study was carried out in April 1975 with 27 subjects varying in sex, age, socio-economic status and marital status. Face-to-face interviews were conducted using a semi-structured questionnaire to try out the questions as well as to gain new insights and perspectives on attitudes towards gender roles. Interviews lasted approximately one hour. For a fuller description of this phase of the research see Fine-Davis (1976).

The pilot study was followed by an instrument pre-test using a stratified sample of 122 male and female Dublin adults. The instrument consisted of 60 attitude statements presented in Likert format concerning the role and status of women in Ireland. Many of the items were selected from instruments developed in the US (i.e. Kirkpatrick, 1936; Levinson and Huffman, 1955; Spence and Helmreich, 1972). Spence and Helmreich's (1972) Attitude toward Women Scale was the most widely used instrument at that time. When they carried out their study, Spence and Helmreich reported a dearth in the literature of scales measuring attitudes toward the status of women. Although they drew in part upon the work of Kirkpatrick (1936), they found that his items were in general quite outdated and that male-female relationships and sex role behaviour in the United States had changed considerably from 1936 to 1972. However, in the context of the present study – Ireland in the mid 1970s – many of Kirkpatrick's much earlier items were still relevant and indeed many of Spence and Helmreich's that were relevant in the United States in 1972 were not yet appropriate for Ireland. Therefore, a careful selection of items was necessary. Some of these were modified and others newly developed – in part on the basis of the pilot interviews – in an attempt to elicit attitudes particularly relevant to the Irish context.

The pre-test data were factor analysed to examine the dimensionality of the attitudes as well as for purposes of data reduction (Fine-Davis, 1976). On the basis of this analysis, 33 items were selected for inclusion in the main test instrument. In general, items were selected on the basis of having high loadings on the resulting factors; however, in some cases an item was retained because of the interest and importance of its content even if it was not among the highest loading items. Factor analysis was also carried out in the main 1975 study (ibid.) and the results of this are presented in Chapter 3.

2.2.2 Sample

The main 1975 study was based on a sample of 420 Dublin adults, aged 18–65, who were selected using stratified quota sampling procedures. Names and addresses from high and low SES neighbourhoods, randomly selected from the Dublin Electoral Register, were used as starting points, in order to optimise randomness. The sample was stratified on the basis of sex, age, socio-economic status and marital status. In order to examine the effect of employment status of married women on their attitudes, the sample included an oversampling of married women ($n=240$) who were stratified both by employment status and presence or absence of dependent children (see Fine-Davis, 1979b).

The research design of the main study consisted of two overlapping or "nested" factorial designs that would permit the use of analysis of variance. Given the nature of the research design which necessitated obtaining respondents with very specific combinations of characteristics (e.g. an employed married woman over 35 of lower socio-economic status with dependent children), it would have been quite inefficient, if not impossible, to utilise strictly random sampling procedures. Stratified quota sampling thus seemed the most appropriate procedure to use; however, within this framework, attempts were made to optimise randomness in subject selection.

Each of 13 interviewers was given six starting points (names and addresses randomly selected from the Dublin Electoral Register). Three of the six were in high SES neighbourhoods and three in low SES neighbourhoods. Interviewers were instructed to start with the initial name and address and then if that person did not satisfy the characteristics required by their quota, to go from one house to the next on the same side of the street to locate respondents to fill their quotas. Once a completed interview was obtained, the interviewer was instructed to skip five houses. This was to reduce the likelihood of respondents knowing one another as well as to spread the sample out geographically. Once five interviews were obtained in one area, the interviewer was instructed to move to a new starting address. Interviewing was conducted in the evening as well as during the day to facilitate contact with males and employed females.

Each of the stratification categories was defined as follows:

1   *Socio-economic status* was based on own or, in the case of married women, husband's occupational status in terms of the Hall-Jones (1950) Scale of Occupational Prestige, as adapted to the Irish context by Hutchinson (1969). Categories 6, 7 and 8 (skilled manual, semi-skilled manual and unskilled manual routine) were classified as "low SES" and categories 1–5 (professionally qualified/high administrative, lower professional/managerial and executive, supervisory – higher and lower grades, and routine grades – non-manual) were classified as "high SES". This dichotomy was essentially based on a blue collar/ white collar distinction.

2   *Age:* The age range of respondents was 18–65; as 65 is the usual retirement age, it was used as the upper age limit, since employment status was part of the factorial design. Respondents were dichotomised at age 35, since it was felt that any higher age, such as 40, would probably not adequately reflect age-related attitudinal differences. Thus, those aged 18–34 constituted the "young" group and those 35–65 constituted the "old" group.

3   *Employment status:* The factorial design required that all males and single females be employed. However, married women were stratified by this characteristic, with half being employed and half non-employed. Employment was defined as "paid employment outside the home". No lower limit of hours worked was placed. This flexible definition of employment was based on (1) the realisation that it would be difficult to obtain the necessary number of married females in all of the appropriate categories if the definition were too stringent, (2) the fact that part-time work is quite a common form of employment for married women and therefore should not be excluded from study, and (3) the belief that a job that may take a woman outside the home for even a few hours may be just as psychologically meaningful for her as a job that involves a greater number of hours outside the home.

4 *Presence or absence of dependent children:* This stratification characteristic was also applied only to married women. "Dependent children" were defined as children in primary school or younger. The rationale for this was based on the assumption that children of post-primary school age are usually more self-sufficient and their care would not likely be as significant a factor for the mother as in the case of younger children. The women "without dependent children" included both women without any children and women with one child or more of post-primary school age, but with no children of primary school age or younger.

A breakdown of the sample by demographic characteristics may be thus summarised as follows: The total sample of 420 consisted of 300 females and 120 males. The 300 females consisted of 240 married women and 60 single women, all of whom were stratified by age and socio-economic status. The 240 married women were further stratified by employment status and presence or absence of dependent children. The 120 males, of whom 60 were married and 60 were single, were further stratified by age and socio-economic status.

2.2.3 Instrument and data collection procedures

The main test questionnaire included the following sets of variables:

a *Attitudes toward the role and status women.* A set of 33 items measuring attitudes toward the role and status of women, which constituted the main focus of the study. These were presented in modified Likert format, i.e. a six-point scale ranging from "strongly disagree" to "strongly agree", with three levels of agreement (strong, moderate and slight) and three levels of disagreement. The scale was constructed in such a way as to encourage an "agree" or "disagree" response and to discourage a "don't know" response. The scale was however coded as if it were a seven-point scale with a code of "4" being the theoretical midpoint. This code accommodated those respondents who insisted on making a mark in between the two sides of the continuum, indicating a "Don't Know" response.
b *Social-psychological and personality characteristics.* A set of 33 items measuring social-psychological and personality constructs was also presented in a similar Likert format ranging from strongly disagree to strongly agree.

The questionnaire was administered to the respondents in their own homes by trained interviewers of the Survey Unit of the Economic and Social Research Institute (ESRI), Dublin. The Likert items were self-administering and the remaining sections were administered by the interviewer. All of the questionnaires were completed in September and October 1975.

2.3 1978 study

2.3.1 Sample

Several key items measuring attitudes toward gender roles from the original 1975 study were replicated in a larger nationwide representative study (N = 1,862) of the quality of working life and attitudes to social issues in Ireland carried out in 1978 (Fine-Davis *et al.*, 1981; Fine-Davis, 1983b) as part of a harmonised cross-national survey of social indicators of working life sponsored by the Statistical Office of the European Communities. The sample was of the adult population of the Republic of Ireland living at non-institutional addresses. The availability of this data enabled nationwide comparisons to be made between 1978 and 1986 and specifically enabled rural–urban comparisons to be examined with regard to attitude change during this period.

The sample was selected using a computer-based system (RANSAM) which employs the Electoral Register as the sampling frame; the procedure also relies on supplementary information about the population in order to improve the efficiency of the estimates derived from the sample (Whelan, 1977, 1979). The refusal rate was 5% which is quite low by international standards, but quite typical for Irish surveys at that time. The sex ratio and other demographic characteristics of the sample were found to correspond fairly closely to official statistics. The questionnaires were administered to respondents in their own homes by trained interviewers. The data from Likert items reported here were self-administered by the respondents. All interviews were carried out in September–October 1978.

2.3.2 Instrument

The measures contained in the 1978 questionnaire included 40 Likert items presented on six-point scales ranging from "strongly disagree" to "strongly agree". Twelve of these items replicated key gender role items developed in the original 1975 study (Fine-Davis, 1976, 1983a). These were high loading items from four of the main factors which emerged in factor analysis in the 1975 study. The other 28 items measured social-psychological and personality constructs, as developed in prior factor analytic work described above (Davis, Fine-Davis, Breathnach and Moran, 1977).

2.4 1986 study

2.4.1 Sample

The 1986 study was a replication and extension of the original 1975 Dublin study. The replication was to enable attitude change to be measured over the intervening years and the extension was to provide policy makers with a picture of attitudes in the country at large and in particular to include rural respondents to allow for rural/urban comparisons. This was an express wish of the Joint Oireachtas Committee on Women's Rights, a committee of the Irish Parliament (Dáil), which supported the study. The sampling and data collection procedures were identical to those used in the original study except for the addition of 300 rural subjects and a consequent slight diminution of the number of urban respondents, from 420 to 300, resulting in a total of 600 respondents – 300 urban and 300 rural. "Rural" was defined as a village or open country or a town of between 1,000 and 3,000 inhabitants. All 26 counties in Ireland were included except for Longford and Laois. Cities and towns with populations over 3,000 were left out of the sample, apart from Dublin. Thus, this sample provided a clear comparison between rural and urban, with urban being defined as Dublin. The sample was limited to adults between the ages of 18 and 65.

The sample was based on stratified quotas, so as to meet the requirements of a factorial design. For this reason, it does not constitute a national representative sample; however, every attempt was made to maximise randomness in subject selection within the context of the stratification design. There were a total of 83 sampling points (starting points) – 30 in rural areas and 53 in Dublin. Starting addresses were generated from the Electoral Register by means of the Economic and Social Research Institute's (ESRI) sampling system, RANSAM (Whelan, 1977, 1979). In addition, when percentage results for the total sample are presented they have been re-weighted so as to reflect the exact proportions of the groups as they actually exist in the population. Thus, any re-weighted results presented are representative of the groups which were studied in the survey, i.e. men and women aged 18–65 from Dublin and rural Ireland. The survey includes employed and non-employed married women, employed single women and employed married and single men. It does not include other groups such as the retired, the unemployed or non-employed single women. Thus, the results may be generalised to the groups studied, but not to the country as a whole. Differences measured between groups are quite reliable indicators since the sampling techniques used to obtain respondents within categories were essentially random, using strict quota sampling procedures. The sampling, fieldwork and data processing for the study were carried out by the Survey Unit of the Economic and Social Research Institute. The 1986 survey was carried out in September–December 1986.

2.4.2 Instrument

The content of the 1986 questionnaire was identical to that used in the 1975 study with regard to the key sets of items, and additional items concerning more current issues were added. The replicated items included:

a   27 of the original 33 Likert items from the 1975 study measuring attitudes toward the role and status of women.
b   27 of the original 33 Likert items from the 1975 study measuring social-psychological and personality characteristics.

The new items in the 1986 questionnaire included:

a   Attitudes to social issues: 42 Likert items measuring attitudes to a range of social issues, including ten items measuring attitudes to divorce; these were balanced with five framed in pro-divorce and five in an anti-divorce direction; and 11 new items measuring attitudes to gender roles.
b   The Divorce Referendum: A set of questions regarding voting behaviour in the Divorce Referendum of 1986 was included. These included, *inter alia*, questions concerning the perceived extent to which various sources of information (e.g. television, church sermons, national and provincial newspapers) were perceived as important in influencing the respondent prior to the referendum.
c   The Abortion Referendum: A set of questions was included concerning voting behaviour in the 1983 Abortion Referendum, as well as current attitudes to abortion. These included whether or not respondents thought abortion should be prohibited "under any and all circumstances" or whether they thought there may be "certain circumstances" under which it might be permissible. Those indicating the latter were then presented with a list of seven possible circumstances and asked to indicate on Likert scales the extent to which they agreed or disagreed that abortion should be permissible under each of them. Respondents were asked if they had voted in the 1983 abortion referendum and, if so, how they had voted.

A further set of questions was included which tapped attitudes toward treatment for a pregnant woman with a serious illness. Respondents were also asked how much "say" they thought various individuals (the woman herself, the woman's husband, the doctor, a priest or a clergyman) should have in making such a decision.

2.5   2005 study

2.5.1   Sample and sample selection

The sample used in the 2005 study was a random, nationally representative sample of the adult population living in private households. As in the case of the 1978 sample, the institutional population was excluded from the sampling frame.

The sample for the 2005 study was also selected by the Survey Unit of the ESRI using its computer-based, random sampling procedure, RANSAM

(Whelan, 1977, 1979) which uses the Electoral Register as the sampling frame. Sample selection was on a two-staged clustered basis. At the initial stage of selection a set of Primary Sampling Units (or sampling points) were selected based on District Electoral Divisions or parts thereof. The primary sampling units were formed on the basis of a minimum population criterion, in this case 1,000 persons. When the primary sampling units were selected a random systematic sample of respondents was selected from within each for contact by the interviewer.

The specific respondent within a household selected for interview was identified on the basis of the "next birthday" rule. This was used as a simple but highly effective selection of respondent from all adults in the household. The target respondent was identified as the household member who had the next birthday – regardless of their age on the birthday. This provides a random sample of respondents within households.

A total of 2,200 names were issued to interviewers. Questionnaires were successfully completed with 1,218 respondents (a total of six of these were not included for analysis due to missing information in important areas of the questionnaire), resulting in a final sample of 1,212. The gross response rate for successfully completed questionnaires was 55%. If one includes only the households successfully contacted in the course of fieldwork the figure rises to a response rate of 67%.

2.5.2 Re-weighting the data

The purpose of sample weighting is to compensate for any biases in the distributional characteristics in the completed sample as compared to the population of interest, in this case the population of all adult persons who are resident in private households in the Republic of Ireland. The weighting adjustment is used to account for biases that occur because of sampling error, due to the nature of the sampling frame or as a result of differential response rates within different groups of the population.

Regardless of the source of the discrepancy between the sample and population distributions we used the statistical adjustment or re-weighting procedure to adjust the distributional characteristics of the sample in terms of characteristics such as age, sex, economic status and so on in order to match the corresponding structures in the population. This is achieved by comparing sample characteristics to external population figures. These latter were principally derived from the *Census of Population 2002* supplemented with figures from the most recent record of the *Quarterly National Household Survey* (QNHS) – both conducted by the Central Statistics Office.

The variables used in the weighting scheme in the current project were:

- number of adults in the household (five categories);
- gender by age cohort (ten categories);
- gender by marital status by age (12 categories);

- gender by age by highest level of educational attainment (12 categories);
- gender by age by region (18 categories);
- gender by age by principal economic status (21 categories).

The weighting procedure involved constructing weights so that the marginal distributions of each of the characteristics of responding individuals were equal to the distribution of characteristics for the population. To achieve this we used a so-called minimum information loss (minimum distance) algorithm to adjust an initial weight so that the distribution of characteristics in the sample matched those of the set of control totals.

2.5.3 Data collection procedures

The data were collected on a face-to-face basis by experienced interviewers from the ESRI's standing panel of field staff. Approximately 60 interviewers – both male and female, distributed throughout the country – were used in the Survey. Interviewers working on the project attended a dedicated training session at which the survey, its design, protocols and implementation were explained by the Survey Unit staff and the research team from Trinity College.

Interviewers were allocated 20 names in each work assignment or cluster. The interviewer approached the household, presented his/her photo ID card along with a brochure, explaining the survey. The "next birthday rule" was explained and the target respondent identified for interviewers. The interview may have taken place on the first call or a visit arranged for a time convenient for the respondent.

A total of four calls were made to each household – the initial call plus three call-backs. The timing and day of the week of call-backs was changed on each attempt to visit the household. All questionnaires were completed on a paper and pencil basis with subsequent entry onto the ESRI's computer system by their data-entry staff. When interviewers completed their first two questionnaires these were returned to the ESRI for checking – with comments (as appropriate) being sent back to the interviewer. All questionnaires were extensively checked before data entry. Standard computer checking at point-of-entry (cross-variable consistency, range checks, etc.) were also implemented. Questionnaires took approximately 45 minutes to complete. All interviews took place in the respondent's home during the period September 2004–January 2005.

2.5.4 Instrument

The questionnaire included 14 of the original items measuring attitudes to gender roles. These were collected in the context of a larger survey concerning work–life balance and social inclusion (Fine-Davis *et al.*, 2005).

2.6 2010 study

2.6.1 The qualitative study

An in-depth qualitative study was carried out in late 2008–early 2009 as a precursor to the quantitative study. The purpose of the qualitative study was to obtain in-depth qualitative information and insights into current attitudes to gender roles and gender relations and attitudes to family formation and childbearing. The results of the qualitative study played an essential role in identifying key issues for inclusion in the questionnaire to be administered in the quantitative study (Fine-Davis, 2011, 2014).

The sample used in the qualitative study consisted of 48 adults selected to mirror the types of respondents which were to be included in the main quantitative phase. The sample was stratified by gender, age (20–34/35–55 years), family status (single/cohabiting/married and living with spouse), socio-economic status and geographic location (Dublin/other towns and cities/rural areas).

Most of the questions were open-ended and designed specifically for this study. Interviews were carried out on a one-to-one basis in a variety of locations. They were conducted primarily in the respondent's home, the interviewer's home or in Trinity College Dublin. All interviews were tape recorded. Interviews lasted from 39 minutes to one hour and 58 minutes, with the average interview length being one hour. The full results of the qualitative study are contained in Fine-Davis (2009).

2.6.2 Pilot study

Following the development of an extensive questionnaire, a pilot study was carried out in the summer of 2010 on a stratified sample of 150 respondents throughout the country. The results of the pilot were used in developing the questionnaire to be used in the main study. Factor analyses were carried out to identify underlying dimensions of attitudinal items and to provide an empirical basis for retaining the best items for inclusion in the main questionnaire.

2.6.3 Main study

2.6.3.1 Research design and sample

The population under investigation was adults of childbearing age (20–49 years) in the Republic of Ireland. A stratified sampling design was employed. This was based on gender, family status (single, cohabiting, married), age (20–34 and 35–49 years), having one or more children or not, and rural vs urban location. "Single" was defined as not living with a partner; it did not refer to marital status per se and "married" was defined as married and living with one's spouse. Presence of a child was defined as the respondent having given birth, fathered or adopted one or more children; it did not require that the child be resident with the respondent. This design was employed so that the sample would include people in all possible combinations of these characteristics, including married with children, married without children, single with and without children, etc. as this would allow for the use of analysis of variance – one of the primary multivariate statistical techniques used in the study. A major goal in creating this design was to allow for comparisons between single, cohabiting and married people, while controlling for the effects of gender, age and other key demographic variables.

A multi-staged quota controlled sampling design with randomly selected starting addresses from the Geo Directory was used. This was based on a total of 200 randomly selected sampling points throughout the country with six interviews conducted per point. A "random walk" from the random starting point was adopted within each sampling point. A total of 1,254 interviews were conducted during the main fieldwork phase, with the additional 150 pilot survey questionnaires boosting the final sample to 1,404. Because of the comparability of the questionnaires and the quality of responses elicited at the pilot stage, the pilot data were thus incorporated into the final data set prior to analysis.

In order to obtain the final sample of 1,404 a total of 10,596 contacts were made. Of these, 38% were ineligible, 32% were not at home and 1% was derelict properties. Twenty-eight per cent of the total contacts were eligible, i.e. they fulfilled the characteristics of the quota sample design. Of these eligible respondents, there was a 51% response rate in urban areas and a 42% rate in rural areas, for an overall response rate of 47%.

2.6.3.2 *Data collection procedures*

All interviewing was conducted on a face-to-face basis in respondents' homes by experienced and pre-briefed interviewers from Behaviour and Attitudes. Computer Aided Personal Interviewing (CAPI) was utilised. Some of the sections of the questionnaire were self-completed by respondents on the laptops – Computer Aided Self-Completion Interviewing (CASI). This protected the privacy of the respondent in providing answers to more sensitive questions and, accordingly, enhanced data quality. Fieldwork for the main survey took place from mid August to early November, 2010. The average interview time was 45 minutes.

2.6.3.3 *Instrument of main study*

The questionnaire used in the main study included, *inter alia*, the following sections: (1) demographics, (2) attitudes to relationships; (3) relationships and relationship history; (4) attitudes to having children; (5) attitudes to gender roles; and (6) attitudes to work–life balance and related social policies.

Most of the items were developed on the basis of the qualitative study, while others were replications of items used in previous research by the author and others. Some of the items concerning gender role attitudes were replicated from Fine-Davis (1983a, 1988a) while some items concerning work–life balance were replicated from Fine-Davis, Fagnani, Giovannini, Højgaard and Clarke (2004) and Fine-Davis *et al.* (2005). Selected items measuring attitudes to childcare and other family policies were replicated from Fine-Davis (1983b, 1983c) and Fine-Davis *et al.* (2004, 2005). Likert items were used extensively. These were presented on seven-point scales ranging from "strongly disagree" to "strongly agree". Within each set, items were presented in a randomised order for each respondent, so that there would be no ordering effects.

2.6.3.4 Weighting of the sample and comparison with population estimates

In line with best practice in all sample surveys, the completed sample was statistically adjusted or re-weighted to ensure that it reflected the socio-demographic structure of the relevant sub-group of the population under investigation. Table 2.1 presents details on the structures of (a) the unweighted sample, (b) the weighted sample and (c) the relevant sub-group of the population. Forty-eight individual weighting variables were set which reflected the population breakdown of 20–49 year olds in terms of gender, age, family status, presence of children and area. Additional educational and SES (occupational status) weights were applied. All population figures were derived from the 2006 Census of Population.

A comparison of Sections A and C of Table 2.1 illustrates that the completed sample, notwithstanding the quota controls, was slightly under-represented in terms of family composition by single and married respondents and over-represented in terms of cohabitees. This is due to the fact that certain groups, including cohabitees, were oversampled in order to have sufficient respondents in each cell of the design to make it possible to carry out analyses of variance. Other groups in the completed sample are largely in line with the population figures.[1] Comparison of Columns B (the re-weighted sample) and C (the Census figures) shows that the structure of the re-weighted sample is very close to the population figures. Thus, we may be confident that the re-weighted data is representative of the population in the childbearing age group.

In the final weighted sample there are 50% males and 50% females. There are 54% in the age group 20–34 and 46% in the age group 35–49. The final weighted sample consists of 45% single people, 44% married people and 11% cohabiting people.

The breakdown by occupational status shows that 8% of the re-weighted sample consists of professional workers, 29% managerial and technical workers, 22% non-manual workers, 22% skilled workers, 15% semi-skilled workers and 5% unskilled workers.

Table 2.1 Comparison of unweighted sample, weighted sample and CSO population estimates for key demographic characteristics

	A. UNWEIGHTED SAMPLE		B. WEIGHTED SAMPLE		C. CSO POPULATION ESTIMATES (Census 2006)		
	%	Sample (N)	%	Weighted sample (N)	%	Population estimate (N)	% Excluding "All others"
OCCUPATIONAL STATUS							
Total	100	1,404	100	1,404	100	1,916,814	
Professional workers	8	107	8	111	7	128,878	8
Managerial and technical	24	338	29	412	25	479,715	29
Non-manual	29	403	22	303	18	352,530	22
Skilled manual	19	267	22	305	18	354,492	22
Semi-skilled	16	225	15	205	12	238,308	15
Unskilled	5	64	5	68	4	78,944	5
All others	0	0			15	283,947	
GENDER							
Total	100	1,404	100	1,404	100	1,916,814	
Male	49	691	50	706	50	964,396	
Female	51	713	50	698	50	952,418	
AGE							
Total	100	1,404	100	1,404	100	1,916,814	
20–34	56	780	54	759	54	1,035,825	
35–49	44	624	46	645	46	880,989	

FAMILY STATUS

Total	100	1,404	100	1,404	100	1,916,814
Single	42	590	45	625	45	853,319
Married	36	510	44	619	44	845,442
Cohabiting	22	304	11	160	11	218,053

PRESENCE OF CHILDREN

Total	100	1,404	100	1,404	100	1,916,814
Without child	52	735	54	753	54	1,027,689
With child	48	669	46	651	46	889,125

LOCATION

Total	100	1,404	100	1,404	100	1,916,814
Urban	43	609	40	556	40	759,251
Rural	57	795	60	848	60	1,157,563

The proportion of rural and urban respondents is 40% urban and 60% rural in the final re-weighted sample. Again, this was adjusted somewhat by the weighting to conform to the proportions of these groups in the population. The final re-weighted sample includes 46% with children and 54% people without children, reflecting a minor readjustment from the original sample.

2.7 Data analysis techniques

Factor analysis was used in the 1975 study and again in the 1978 study to confirm the factor structure of the earlier study. It was also used in the 1986 survey to explore the dimensionality of new sets of items, including items measuring new gender role attitudes, attitudes to divorce, etc. It was used in the 2005 and 2010 studies to develop new measures of gender role attitudes, attitudes to family formation and attitudes to social policies. Analysis of variance was the second major multivariate method used, with attitudinal measures, derived through factor analysis, as the dependent measures and demographic characteristics as the independent measures. Multiple regression was used selectively as appropriate when a larger number of independent variables were examined as predictors of a single key dependent variable.

In order to measure change in attitudes over time, the mean composite scores representing the attitudinal dimensions, identified through factor analysis in the 1975 study, were compared using t-tests and analysis of variance with the comparable 1986 data for Dublin respondents. Comparable data for the 1978 and 1986 surveys were compared for Dublin and rural Ireland. Analysis of variance was also employed to make comparisons between comparable composite scores from three time periods: 1978, 1986 and 2005, in addition to comparisons of percentage responses.

2.8 Comparisons of datasets

The nature of the research presented here is that it measures phenomena in a natural social setting. As such it is not amenable to a strict experimental design, with control groups, etc. However, the research designs employed in all of the studies were of a quasi-experimental design. Their major strengths involve the randomness of subject selection, the availability of data in a time series and the use of identical measuring instruments over time (Campbell and Stanley, 1963).

Chapter 6 shows how attitudes changed over the period 1975–2010. We summarise below how the various samples described above will be compared.

2.8.1 Dublin samples – 1975–1986

The first set of comparisons is for Dublin only. It includes the 1975 data for Dublin (N=420) and the 1986 data for Dublin only (N=300). These samples are comparable and while they are based on stratified sampling, they include the most complete sets of variables, covering the full gamut of social policy issues relevant to gender equality at the time, as well as measures of traditional vs non-traditional gender roles, perception of females as inferior and perceptions of limitations in the housewife role. They provide a comparison over an 11-year period at the first stage of social change.

2.8.2 Nationwide samples – 1978, 1986 and 2005

The second set of comparisons is for the country as a whole. It includes the datasets from 1978, 1986 and 2005. The 1978 (N=1,862) and 2005 (N=1,212) datasets are based on representative nationwide samples selected using probability sampling. The 1986 data for Dublin and rural Ireland (N=600) are re-weighted to reflect the proportions of the groups studied in the country as a whole. While the 1986 sample is not strictly comparable to the 1978 and 2005 datasets, it is a national sample which provides a third comparison point between 1978 and 2005. The advantage of the comparisons between these three datasets is that they are of the country as a whole, and in the case of the 1978 and 2005 surveys, the comparison is of representative nationwide samples. However, the sets of variables are more limited in the case of the 1978 and 2005 datasets. Data from these three points in time allow for an examination of attitude change over a 27-year period in two phases – the earlier phase (1978–1986) and the later phase (1986–2005).

2.8.3 2010 data set

The 2010 data set is primarily new and consequently not directly comparable in most cases to the earlier datasets. We include it here because it shows us where attitudes are today in relation to gender roles and gender relations. It is an interesting counterpoint to the data from the earlier periods. Furthermore, the sample consists of people in the childbearing age group (20–49) and hence it is not comparable to the other datasets which included respondents aged 18–65. However, there are four comparable gender role items which are interesting to compare with the earlier data, as well as measures concerning social policies, including work–life balance and childcare.

Note

1 Note that the Census figures on Social Class contain an undefined "Other" category which was not in the survey data.

3 Dimensions of attitudes toward the role and status of women

As discussed in Chapter 1, the late 1960s and early 1970s witnessed a heightened international awareness of the role and status of women in society. This awareness not only manifested itself in an international social movement, but it also led to a marked increase in research devoted to studying sex role attitudes and behaviour. While the vast majority of the studies in this area were carried out in the US, important contributions in these early days came from Britain (Bailyn, 1970; Fogarty, Rapoport and Rapoport, 1971); Finland (Haavio-Mannila, 1971, 1972); Greece (Safilios-Rothschild, 1971); Austria (Haller and Rosenmayr, 1971) and elsewhere. However, prior to the 1975 study reported here, essentially no research in this area had been conducted in Ireland. This was due in large part to the relatively recent emergence of pressure for change in the status of women. Such pressure for change was facilitated by Ireland's comparatively recent economic and industrial development, which gained momentum in the early 1960s, together with its entrance in 1973 into the European Economic Community (EEC), as well as the emerging women's movement in Ireland (Beale, 1986; O'Connor, 1998). Because Ireland was just beginning to undergo transition in the area of sex role attitudes and behaviour at the time of data collection (1975), it offered an opportunity to collect baseline data at a unique period in its history.

As outlined in Chapter 1, the mid 1970s to the early 1980s were a period of rapid social change in areas central to women's status. Several key issues were a focus of public debate at this time, as people became aware of how women were treated unequally under the law in several key areas. This included a lack of equal pay, equal employment opportunity and lack of access to contraception. It also included unfair treatment by the tax code, which discriminated against married women employed outside the home. In relation to pay, women earned 37.6p per hour, compared with 65.5p per hour earned by men, which amounted to just 57% of the average hourly earnings of men in 1972 (Purcell, 1980). Prior to 1980 a wife's earnings were treated as part of her husband's. The tax system involved aggregating the husband's and wife's income, so that the wife's *total* income was taxed at her husband's highest marginal rate, which in the late 1970s reached 60–77% in the higher income brackets. As Hederman (1980) points out, under the Income Tax Act of 1967 a married woman's income was deemed for income tax purposes to be the income of her husband. This resulted in her paying a substantially higher rate of tax than either married men or single people. Because her income was added to that of her husband she was not able to benefit from the lower rates of tax available to every other tax payer on the lower bands of his income. Hederman concludes that this "effectively precluded most women from achieving through their own efforts financial independence of their husbands, ignored the fact that the women's earnings were generated by their labour and denied them fair remuneration for effort" (ibid., p. 58).

The fight to legalise contraception began in the early 1970s. Senator Mary Robinson, who later became the first woman President of Ireland, tried in 1971 to introduce the first bill to liberalise the law on contraception in the Seanad, but it was not allowed a reading. It was not until 1973 that the first success towards its legalisation came with the McGee case, which provided for the importation of contraceptives for personal use. In terms of legislation in the Dáil (the Irish Parliament), the first bill to legalise contraception was introduced by Charles Haughey, Minister for Health, in 1978 with the Health (Family Planning) Bill. This bill limited the provision of contraceptives to *bona fide* "family planning or for adequate medical reasons". Contraceptives could only be sold by a pharmacist on the presentation of a prescription from a doctor. The 1979 Act came into effect in 1980. It was described by Haughey as "an Irish solution to an Irish problem". This law clearly had restrictions and was unpopular. The law was further liberalised in 1985, with the Health (Family Planning) (Amendment) Act, which allowed condoms and spermicides to be sold to people over 18 without a prescription. This was further modified in 1992 to make these available to people over 17 (Health (Family Planning) (Amendment) Act, 1992).

Apart from specific and concrete ways that women were discriminated against, there were also the widespread attitudes which underpinned them. As the Commission on the Status of Women pointed out in 1972:

> the removal of ... actual discriminations leaves untouched a larger and more subtle area of discrimination consisting of those factors which limit women's participation even in the absence of formal discrimination, that is, the stereotyped role that is assigned to women, the inculcation of attitudes in both boys and girls in their formative years that there are definite and separate roles for the sexes.... It is from this type of cultural mould that formal discrimination arises...
>
> (p. 12)

Thus, while legislative and administrative reforms were and are of critical importance, there was also a great need to examine the role played by social attitudes in perpetuating inequality and rigid sex role behaviour. It was the investigation of these traditional attitudes toward sex roles and related issues that constituted the focus of the present series of studies. One of the main aims of the first study carried out in 1975 was to examine the nature and factor structure of attitudes toward the role and status of women in Ireland, the interrelationships among these attitudes, and their demographic determinants (Fine-Davis, 1983a).

3.1 Factor structure of attitudes toward the role and status of women

As described in Chapter 2, 33 Likert items measuring attitudes toward the role and status of women were included in the original 1975 study. Factor analysis was performed on the responses to these items in order to identify the underlying attitudinal dimensions in the items. Principal Axis factors were extracted using the Principal Components technique. These Principal Axis factors were then orthogonally rotated to simple structure using the Varimax criterion (Kaiser, 1958). After an inspection of several solutions, an eight factor solution was found to provide optimal psychological interpretability. Because of the meaningfulness of the factors, this solution was chosen in spite of the fact that a few of the factors had fewer items than would be ideally desirable. Accordingly, greater confidence may be placed in the more robust factors containing a greater number of items. This solution fairly closely mirrored the solution obtained in the pre-test (Fine-Davis, 1976). Thus the relatively fewer items used in the main test were in fact representative of a larger pool of 60 items. The names given to the factors together with the items that loaded on them are presented in Table 3.1.

Factor I, entitled *Traditional Sex Role Orientation,* explained the greatest percentage of variance of all of the factors (9.8%). It is the most global measure of attitudes towards sex roles. The term "sex roles" was commonly used when this first study was carried out in the mid 1970s. Now the term "gender roles" is more commonly used. We shall use the term "sex roles" when referring to this factor but will use the terms interchangeably throughout the course of the book. Factor I was found to embody several threads: these included a belief in women's role being home-centred and a man's work-centred, with a simultaneous belief in male superiority in the home, as expressed in the item, "Some equality in marriage is a good thing, but by and large the husband ought to have the main say in family matters." The factor also embodies the belief that women are most gratified and fulfilled by the wife and mother role, as reflected in the item, "Being a wife and mother are the most fulfilling roles any woman could want." Respondents high on this factor tended to believe that "most women need and want the kind of protection and support that men have traditionally given them", suggesting that an implicit rationale for traditional sex roles is the belief – or the wish to believe – that women are "delicate" and dependent. A further implicit rationale for maintaining the status quo, suggested by the factor, was the fear that "if equal job opportunities are opened to women, this will just take away jobs from men who need them more". Such a fear was logically inconsistent with other attitudes comprising the factor; for example, if women were in fact so fulfilled and gratified by the wife and mother roles, there would be no reason to fear that they would compete with men for jobs. Thus, mixed with traditional sex role attitudes were some anxieties as well as rationalisations to help allay these anxieties.

Factor II, *Positive Attitude to Contraception,* concerned the controversial issue of contraception, which had not yet been legalised at the time of the first study (1975) and was a subject of heated public debate at the time. The highest loading item was, "The sale of contraceptives should be legalised in Ireland." The second and third highest loading items expressed the view that "It is a basic human right to be able to control whether or not one has a child through the use of contraceptives," and "It is perfectly healthy and natural for couples to have sexual intercourse, even if they don't want to conceive a child." It is of interest to note that, somewhat unexpectedly, an item concerning co-education also loaded on this factor ("There would probably be more communication and understanding later on if boys and girls got to know each other earlier by going to the same schools"). The directionality of the loadings of the various items indicated that those who opposed legalisation of contraception also tended to oppose co-education. Conversely, those who favoured legalisation of contraception also tended to favour co-education. The loading of these items on the same factor suggests that co-education may have been linked in respondents' minds with sexuality, suggesting that resistance to co-education may in part have been related to a fear that it might lead to greater permissiveness.

Factor III, *Belief in Equal Opportunity,* contained two items, one concerning equality in the workplace and the other equality in the home ("People should be employed and promoted strictly on the basis of ability regardless of sex" and "The daughters in a family should have the same privileges and opportunities as the sons"). Equal opportunity was not yet enshrined in legislation and the first item gave expression to the reality that women were not treated equally in the workplace at that time. With regard to the second item, sons were often given preference in terms of opportunity for third level education and it was also the custom for sons to inherit the family farm in rural areas.

Factor IV, *Positive Attitude to Maternal Employment,* was one of the most robust of the factors, explaining 6.9% of the variance. It consisted of several attitudes related to employment of married women and, in particular, mothers. Those high on the factor believed that "A woman who has a job she enjoys is likely to be a better wife and mother, because she has an interest and some fulfillment outside the home." Those "low" on the factor believed that "Women with children should not work outside the home if they don't need the money" and that "It is bad for young children if their mothers go out and work, even if they are well taken care of by another adult." It is of interest to note that those low on the factor expressed – in addition to an apparent concern for the welfare of children – a belief that married women were less entitled to jobs than men during times of high unemployment.

Factors I and IV provided evidence to suggest that traditional attitudes toward sex roles and resistance to social change in gender roles were linked to a fear of job loss for men, as expressed in the items "If equal job opportunities are opened to women, this will just take away jobs from men who need them more" and "When there is high unemployment married women should be discouraged from working." This indicated that the road to equality for women would be considerably more difficult in an economic climate characterised by high unemployment – a situation which characterised the 1970s and 1980s.

Factor V, *Belief in Equal Pay*, included three items, two of which loaded negatively and reflected the status quo, e.g. "It is only fair that male workers should receive more pay than women even for identical work." The data were collected at a time when the issue of equal pay was a controversial one. Equal pay legislation had just been passed by the Oireachtas (Irish Parliament), following a directive from the European Community, and was due to come into effect within a few months; however, there was discussion in the media of the negative effect that implementation of equal pay would have on certain companies. Factor V contains items reflecting the divergent opinions on the issue (e.g. "Even if it means financial difficulties for some companies, equal pay for equal work should be given immediately").

Factor VI, *Belief in Higher Tax for Married Women*, contained two items on the tax issue (e.g. "It is only fair that a married couple [both working] pay more tax than two single people"). While this factor was not as robust as some of the others, it was retained because of the importance of this issue at the time.

Factor VII, *Perception of Females as Inferior*, contained four items (e.g. "Generally speaking, women think less clearly than men" and "Women are, by nature, too highly strung to hold certain jobs") and explained the second greatest amount of variance (7%) after Factor I. The factor contains a mixture of stereotypes that some might argue have nothing to do with perceiving women as inferior to men, but rather as different from men (e.g. "highly strung"). However, it appears that such beliefs, no matter how benignly held, are likely to inhibit access to equal opportunities for women. This is evident from the "highly strung" item which explicitly connects this perceived trait with access to jobs. It is further reinforced by an item concerning training ("It's a bad idea for employers to spend money training women, since they will more than likely get married, have children and leave the job"). This attitude was in fact the one which underpinned the introduction of the marriage bar in the 1930s, as expressed in the Brennan Commission (1932–1935) (see Chapter 1).

Factor VIII, *Perception of Limitations in Housewife Role*, contained two items (e.g. "Housework is basically dull and boring" and "Being at home with children all day can very often be boring for a woman"). This factor was also less robust than many of the other factors, but was retained because of the interest and uniqueness of its content.

Composite scores were computed for each factor. These scores were then used in subsequent analyses. Items that were composited are noted in Table 3.1 with an asterisk.

3.2 Relationships among attitudes toward the role and status of women

Once the dimensions of attitudes toward the role and status of women had been identified the next step undertaken was an examination of the inter-relationships among these various dimensions. While factor analysis with orthogonal rotations – the procedure used here – identifies factors which are the most unrelated, or orthogonal, to each other, it does not wipe out all relationships between the factors. Hence it is of interest to explore the correlations between the factors to gain a greater understanding of the relationships among the various factors. Inter-correlations among the composite scores, based on the preceding factor analysis, are presented for the whole sample (N = 420) in Table 3.2.

Traditional Sex Role Orientation – which is the most basic and global measure of the eight – was found to be significantly related to attitudes toward a number of issues relevant to women's rights and equality. Those with more traditional sex role attitudes were significantly less likely to support social change in areas that would lead to greater equality for women (e.g. equal pay ($r=-0.43$; $p<0.001$), contraception ($r=-0.24$; $p<0.001$), maternal employment ($r=-0.43$; $p<0.001$) and taxation of married women ($r=0.26$; $p<0.001$). Those holding traditional sex role attitudes were also significantly more likely to perceive women as inferior ($r=0.41$; $p<0.001$). On the other hand, those who tended to perceive women as inferior were less likely to favour maternal employment ($r=-0.30$; $p<0.001$) or to support equal pay ($r=-0.31$; $p<0.001$) or the legalisation of contraception ($r=-0.14$; $p<0.001$) and they further tended to believe that employed married women should pay higher taxes than others ($r=0.24$; $p<0.001$).

Attitudes toward the various social policies relevant to the status of women were significantly interrelated. Those favouring change in one area were likely to favour it in another. For example, those favouring maternal employment were also more likely to have positive attitudes to contraception ($r=0.31$; $p<0.001$) and to favour equal pay ($r=0.31$; $p<0.001$).

Table 3.1 Factor analysis of 33 Likert items measuring attitudes toward the role and status of women – selected items from eight Varimax rotated factors (N=420)

Item no.		Varimax rotated loading
Factor I: Traditional Sex Role Orientation		
*3.	Some equality in marriage is a good thing, but by and large the husband ought to have the main say in family matters.	−0.73
*18.	A husband has the right to expect that his wife will be obliging and dutiful at all times.	−0.64
*2.	Being a wife and mother are the most fulfilling roles any woman could want.	−0.63
*20.	If equal job opportunities are opened to women, this will just take away jobs from men who need them more.	−0.50
*25.	The political and business leadership of a community should be largely in the hands of men.	−0.46
*1.	Most women need and want the kind of protection and support that men have traditionally given them.	−0.44
% Variance: 9.8 Cumulative % Variance: 9.8		
Factor II: Positive Attitude to Contraception		
*32.	The sale of contraceptives should be legalised in Ireland.	−0.76
*12.	It is a basic human right to be able to control whether or not one has a child through the use of contraceptives.	−0.74
*21.	It is perfectly healthy and natural for couples to have sexual intercourse, even if they don't want to conceive a child.	−0.70
4.	There would probably be more communication and understanding later on if boys and girls got to know each other earlier by going to the same schools.	−0.41
% Variance: 6.4 Cumulative % Variance: 16.2		
Factor III: Belief In Equal Opportunity		
*16.	People should be employed and promoted strictly on the basis of ability, regardless of sex.	0.66
*17.	The daughters in a family should have the same privileges and opportunities as the sons.	0.64
% Variance: 4.7 Cumulative % Variance: 20.9		
Factor IV: Positive Attitude to Maternal Employment		
*28.	A woman who has a job she enjoys is likely to be a better wife and mother, because she has fulfillment outside the home.	0.70
*26.	Women with children should not work outside the home if they don't need the money.	−0.59

*8. It is bad for young children if their mothers go out and work, even if they are well taken care of by another adult.	−0.58
*33. Women should be more concerned with bringing up their children than with desires for careers.	−0.45
27. When there is high unemployment married women should be discouraged from working.	−0.40

% Variance 6.9   Cumulative % Variance: 27.8

Factor V: Belief in Equal Pay

*13. Even if it means financial difficulties for some companies, equal pay for equal work should be given immediately.	0.72
*6. A married man should be paid more than a woman for performing the same job.	−0.64
**5. It is only fair that male workers should receive more pay than women even for identical work.	−0.47

% Variance: 5.6   Cumulative % Variance: 33.4

Factor VI: Belief in Higher Tax for Married Women

*9. It is only fair that a married couple (both working) pay more tax than two single people.	0.73
*23. Married women should be taxed more than single women.	0.73

% Variance: 5.5   Cumulative % Variance: 38.9

Factor VII: Perception of Females as Inferior

*29. Generally speaking women think less clearly than men.	0.76
*15. Women are, by nature, too highly strung to hold certain jobs.	0.68
*10. Female workers, even if qualified and experienced, are in some ways less reliable, less committed and less serious than men.	0.57
30. It's a bad idea for employers to spend money training women, since they will more than likely get married, have children and leave the job.	0.44

% Variance: 7.0   Cumulative % Variance: 45.9

Factor VIII: Perception of Limitations in Housewife Role

*7. Housework is basically dull and boring.	−0.79
*24. Being at home with children all day can very often be boring for a woman.	−0.66

% Variance: 4.7   Cumulative % Variance: 50.7

* Items which were composited for further analyses.
** Also loaded at 0.50 on Factor 1, but interpretation more consistent with this factor.

Table 3.2 Intercorrelations among composite scores based on factors measuring attitudes toward the role and status of women: total sample (N=420)

Factor	I	II	III	IV	V	VI	VII	VIII
I. Traditional Sex Role Orientation	–	–0.24**	–0.03	–0.43**	–0.43**	0.26**	0.41**	–0.07
II. Positive Attitude to Contraception		–	0.01	0.31**	0.22**	–0.18**	–0.14*	0.13*
III. Belief In Equal Opportunity			–	0.05	0.14*	–0.13*	–0.11*	0.02
IV. Positive Attitude to Maternal Employment				–	0.31**	–0.31**	–0.30**	0.21**
V. Belief in Equal Pay					–	–0.28**	–0.31**	0.07
VI. Belief in Higher Tax for Married Women						–	0.24**	–0.06
VII. Perception of Females as Inferior							–	0.09
VIII. Perception of Limitations in Housewife Role								–

* $p < 0.01$
** $p < 0.001$

3.3 Determinants of attitudes toward the role and status of women: analyses of variance

The next logical question that one would want to answer is how are these attitudes distributed in the population? Who holds more egalitarian attitudes and who holds more traditional attitudes? An examination of the demographic determinants of these attitudes was undertaken in order to understand the ways in which groups in the society differed with regard to their perceptions of the role and status of women, to obtain insight concerning which attitudes were more potent or salient, which were less so, and for whom, and, finally, to obtain a picture of where in the society change was occurring and where there was resistance to such change.

3.3.1 Demographic determinants of gender role attitudes in the total 1975 sample

As noted in the Method section (Chapter 2), the research design involved a series of overlapping or nested factorial designs. In the first factorial design, analysis of variance was carried out to determine the effects of four independent or exogenous demographic variables on variance in the dependent measures, which consisted of summary scores on the eight factors presented above. The analyses of variance were based on a $2 \times 2 \times 2 \times 2$ factorial design of respondent characteristics, varying two levels each of sex (male/female), marital status (married/single), age (18–34/35–65), and socio-economic status (low/high).

The results of this analysis are summarised in Table 3.3. It may be seen that the independent variable that controlled a significant amount of variance in the greatest number of factors was the respondent's sex. This variable was responsible for main effects in six of the eight factors. The overwhelming tendency was for males to express significantly more traditional attitudes toward the role and status of women than females. In addition to having a significantly more traditional overall sex role orientation ($F=10.32$, $p<0.01$), they were also more likely to perceive females as inferior ($F=19.66$, $p<0.001$) and less likely to support equal pay ($F=10.46$, $p<0.01$) or equal opportunity ($F=6.75$, $p<0.01$) than were females. They believed women's proper role was in the home and they were significantly more likely than women to perceive limitations in the housewife role ($F=32.41$, $p<0.001$). The only exception to this overall trend of greater conservatism among males was a tendency for them to be somewhat more favourable toward contraception ($F=7.23$, $p<0.01$). This is not terribly surprising since liberalisation of the contraception laws in Ireland would have had an obvious relevance for males as well as for females. This finding was consistent with previous findings which showed that Irish males were significantly less religious than Irish females (MacGréil, 1974; Fine-Davis, 1976) and religiosity was significantly correlated with attitudes regarding

Table 3.3 Summary of four-way analysis of variance: mean scores and significance of F-ratios for main effects of four independent variables on eight factors measuring attitudes toward the role and status of women (N=420)

Factor	Sex		Marital status		Age		Socio-economic status (SES)	
	Male	Female	Married	Single	18–34	35–65	Low	High
1. Traditional Sex Role Orientation	$F=10.32$** 4.59	4.09	4.37	4.32	$F=14.08$*** 4.05	4.64	$F=26.47$*** 4.74	3.94
2. Positive Attitude to Contraception	$F=7.23$** 5.67	5.18	5.61	5.25	$F=23.42$*** 5.87	4.98	5.34	5.51
3. Belief in Equal Opportunity	6.26	6.56	6.34	6.47	$F=6.75$** 6.43	6.38	6.40	6.41
4. Positive Attitude to Maternal Employment	$F=6.36$* 3.65	3.96	4.03	3.58	$F=14.85$*** 4.15	3.46	$F=13.06$*** 3.49	4.13
5. Belief in Equal Pay	$F=10.46$** 4.67	5.31	5.03	4.95	$F=17.11$*** 5.40	4.58	4.87	5.10
6. Belief in Higher Tax for Married Women	3.00	3.08	$F=11.42$*** 2.68	3.40	$F=20.76$*** 2.55	3.53	3.24	2.84
7. Perception of Females as Inferior	$F=19.66$*** 3.44	2.64	2.94	3.13	2.93	3.15	$F=11.97$*** 3.35	2.72
8. Perception of Limitations in Housewife Role	$F=32.41$*** 5.41	4.27	$F=6.23$* 5.09	4.59	4.83	4.85	4.72	4.96

Mean scores ranged from 1 (strongly disagree) to 7 (strongly agree); F-ratios and asterisks indicate significant differences between the means.

* $p<0.05$
** $p<0.01$
*** $p<0.001$

contraception (Fine-Davis, 1979a). The overall results obtained concerning sex differences are consistent with findings obtained in the United States at approximately the same time (e.g. Spence and Helmreich, 1972; Tomeh, 1978; Yorburg and Arafat, 1975) and in Finland (Haavio-Mannila, 1972).

The next most important determinant of attitudes toward the role and status of women was age. There was a very strong tendency for older people to express more traditional attitudes and younger people more egalitarian attitudes. Older people were significantly less likely to favour contraception ($F=23.42$, $p<0.001$), maternal employment ($F=14.85$, $p<0.001$) and equal pay ($F=17.11$, $p<0.001$) and were more likely than younger people to support a policy of higher taxation of married women ($F=20.76$, $p<0.001$). All of these attitudes toward policy issues were underpinned by a significantly more traditional sex role orientation ($F=14.08$, $p<0.001$). Older people were not, however, more likely than younger people to perceive women as inferior ($F=1.45$, N.S.), suggesting that this particular factor may be less a component of "traditional" norms than it is of sexist norms. The importance of age as a determinant of attitudes toward women's rights and sex role ideology had been noted in previous research in the United States (Spence and Helmreich, 1972; Welch, 1975; Yorburg and Arafat, 1975). The results concerning greater conservatism among older people on the issue of contraception corroborate previous results obtained in Ireland just prior to the present study (Hibernia Review/Irish Marketing Surveys Ltd, 1974; Wilson-Davis, 1974).

After sex and age, the third most important determinant of attitudes toward the role and status of women was socio-economic status (SES). This characteristic was highly significant for three of the eight attitude factors. The direction of the effect was consistent in all cases and indicated a clear tendency for respondents from lower socio-economic backgrounds to hold more traditional attitudes than those from higher SES backgrounds. This effect was particularly strong on the factor *Traditional Sex Role Orientation* ($F=26.47$, $p<0.001$). Lower SES respondents were also more likely to perceive women as inferior to men ($F=11.97$, $p<0.001$). However, they manifested more conservative views on only one specific issue: maternal employment ($F=13.06$, $p<0.001$). And even on this issue, a significant interaction effect showed that there was no significant SES effect among married people ($F=11.50$, $p<0.001$), suggesting that lower SES individuals may change their views about maternal employment upon marriage, perhaps out of economic necessity. It is of further interest to note that there were no SES differences on any of the other issues, namely equal pay, contraception, taxation of married women and equal opportunity. This would suggest that, in spite of a generally more traditional sex role orientation, people from lower SES backgrounds were as supportive of change as people from higher SES backgrounds. This seeming discrepancy may indicate a "lag effect" between traditional social norms, on the one hand, and a desire for social change on the other. While traditional gender role attitudes may have been prevalent in lower socio-economic groups, this may have been an idealised set of norms which was becoming more and more inconsistent with the economic realities which included the increased participation of women in the labour force. This, in turn, may have contributed to the more egalitarian views on related social issues such as equal pay, contraception, maternal employment and taxation.

Marital status was not as significant a determinant of attitudes as the other three characteristics of sex, age and socio-economic status. It did, however, determine significant amounts of variance in three of the eight dependent measures. Interestingly, all three were particularly relevant to married people. Married respondents were significantly more likely than single people to perceive limitations in the housewife role ($F=6.23$, $p<0.05$). They were also more likely to favour maternal employment ($F=6.36$, $p<0.05$) and to oppose the prevailing policy of higher taxation of married women ($F=11.42$, $p<0.001$). The differences between married and single people were the greatest on this last factor concerning higher taxes for married women, a factor which directly impinged on the economic well-being of married people.

A significant two-way interaction effect indicated that single respondents from lower SES backgrounds expressed significantly less favourable attitudes to maternal employment than did lower SES married respondents or indeed higher SES respondents of either marital status ($F=11.50$; $p<0.001$). A similar interaction effect was obtained concerning support for higher taxes for married women ($F=4.68$, $p<0.05$). It appears that once lower SES people get married they modify their views on these issues, perhaps, as suggested above, for economic reasons. It will be noted in this context that *older* low SES single people were the least favourable toward maternal employment ($F=6.21$, $p<0.05$). This can be interpreted in terms of the fact that young single people are more likely to anticipate marriage themselves and the possibility of either themselves or their spouse working after marriage, whereas older people are less likely to marry and therefore may tend to have less empathy for the working married woman and some may even feel resentful of her presence in a competitive job market.

3.3.2 Demographic determinants of gender role attitudes of married women

Since employment on the part of married women was an unusual phenomenon in the mid 1970s (only 7.5% of married women were employed according to the 1971 Census) it was of interest to examine how employed and non-employed married women differed in their gender role attitudes. Were they distinctly different? While the previous analysis could tell us about the sample as a whole, it could not tell us about more specific characteristics of married women. Thus a second set analyses were carried out focusing solely on married women (N = 240) in order to tease out the effects of employment status, while controlling for the relevant variables of age, socio-economic status and presence or absence of dependent children.

Table 3.4 presents these results. As one might have expected, employment status on the part of married women was a very significant determinant of sex role attitudes in several areas. It was most significant in relation to attitudes toward maternal employment ($F = 35.17$, $p < 0.001$). It was also – not surprisingly – a significant predictor of attitudes toward taxation of married women ($F = 9.62$, $p < 0.01$) and equal pay ($F = 4.61$, $p < 0.05$). Employed married women were also significantly more likely to perceive limitations in the housewife role ($F = 5.08$, $p < 0.05$) and less likely to perceive females as inferior ($F = 4.22$, $p < 0.05$). Their overall sex role orientation was also less traditional than that of non-employed married women ($F = 6.30$; $p < 0.05$). While one might have expected differences between the two groups on attitudes to contraception, there were none ($F = 1.83$; N.S.). Nor were there differences in attitudes to equal opportunity ($F = 0.03$; N.S.). Thus, the main area in which employed and non-employed women differed strongly in the mid 1970s concerned attitudes to maternal employment and the related issue of taxation of married women. Regarding contraception, while attitudes of the two groups did not differ significantly, their actual contraceptive use did. Employed married women were significantly more likely to use contraceptives than their non-employed counterparts ($F = 5.20$; $p < 0.05$). However, an interaction effect indicated that this mainly applied to women of higher socio-economic status ($F = 3.90$; $p < 0.05$) (Fine-Davis, 1979b). This corresponded to a smaller expected family size on the part of employed married women ($F = 7.84$: $p < 0.01$) (ibid.). In spite of this difference, there was no difference in ideal family size; both groups saw four children as the ideal (ibid.). The preference for relatively large families in Ireland was in contrast to British attitudes of the time, which tended to favour two to four children, with two being more commonly favoured than three or four (Data from Office of Population and Censuses and Surveys, Central Statistics Office, London, as reported in "Fewer Births Trend Shown," *Irish Times,* 5 May 1976, p. 7).

Whether or not married women had dependent children (children under age 12) had virtually no effect on their attitudes toward the role and status of women, with one exception. Those with dependent children were somewhat *more* likely to be positive toward maternal employment ($F = 5.10$, $p < 0.05$). This is particularly interesting since age was controlled for and the effect could not be attributed to attitudes of younger women only. This finding is consistent with Census data which showed that the increasing labour force participation of married women was particularly pronounced among those of childbearing age (see Table 1.1, Chapter 1).

Table 3.4 Summary of four-way analysis of variance: mean scores and significance of F-ratios for main effects of four independent variables on eight factors measuring attitudes toward the role and status of women ($N=240$ married women)

Factor	Dependent children		Age		Socio-economic status (SES)		Employment status	
	Yes	No	18–34	35–65	Low	High	Employed	Non-employed
1. Traditional Sex Role Orientation	4.23	4.25	$F=17.58^{***}$ 3.86	4.60	4.25	4.21	$F=6.30^{*}$ 4.01	4.45
2. Positive Attitude to Contraception	5.63	5.33	$F=27.75^{***}$ 5.98	4.98	5.38	5.58	5.61	5.35
3. Belief in Equal Opportunity	6.60	6.46	6.55	6.50	6.42	6.63	6.52	6.54
4. Positive Attitude to Maternal Employment	$F=5.10^{*}$ 4.33	3.88	$F=13.48^{***}$ 4.47	3.74	4.01	4.20	$F=35.17^{***}$ 4.69	3.52
5. Belief in Equal Pay	5.04	5.30	$F=7.96^{**}$ 5.48	4.86	5.18	5.16	$F=4.61^{*}$ 5.41	4.93
6. Belief in Higher Tax for Married Women	2.50	2.53	$F=6.63^{**}$ 2.23	2.80	2.54	2.50	$F=9.62^{**}$ 2.17	2.86
7. Perception of Females as Inferior	2.64	2.63	$F=10.99^{***}$ 2.32	2.95	2.76	2.52	$F=4.22^{*}$ 2.44	2.83
8. Perception of Limitations in Housewife Role	4.47	4.69	4.55	4.60	4.40	4.76	$F=5.08^{*}$ 4.83	4.33

Mean scores range from 1 (strongly disagree) to 7 (strongly agree); F-ratios and asterisks indicate significant differences between the means.

* $p<0.05$
** $p<0.01$
*** $p<0.001$

However while increasing labour force participation was particularly pronounced among married women in the childbearing age group, our attitudinal data showed that women of all ages who had dependent children were more positive towards maternal employment than women without dependent children. This suggests that women who have children – whether working or not – are more likely to be supportive of mothers working since they can identify with them.

3.4 Discussion

It has been shown that traditional sex role attitudes were associated with a belief in a sharp differentiation of tasks and roles of men and women as well as a belief in male superiority and female inferiority, the latter of which was often couched in terms of socially acceptable stereotypes, but was in fact directly linked to discriminatory attitudes and practices. Such an orientation was also found to be related to opposition to social change in issues directly relevant to the status of women – equal pay, contraception, and employment and taxation of married women.

Sex was found to be the overriding determinant of traditional sex role attitudes. Males were markedly more traditional than women in sex role orientation, as well as consistently resistant to social policy changes related to improving the status of women.

The significant differences found between age groups suggests that attitudes were already changing in a more egalitarian direction, although this can only really be tested in longitudinal studies, since age differences at one point in time could potentially merely be a cohort effect. Our subsequent studies over time will shed some light on this question. Similarly, differences observed between socio-economic groups suggested that as people continue to become better educated and more affluent, their attitudes are likely to change in an egalitarian direction. Socio-economic status was found to be largely related to the more global attitudes and less related to specific policy issues, suggesting attitudes toward policy issues that have an immediate relevance for individuals (e.g. equal pay, contraception, taxation, etc.) may be more amenable to change than more deepseated, culturally reinforced, global attitudes.

The results concerning differences between employed and nonemployed married women also have implications for social change in Ireland. While it is not clear whether employment on the part of married women contributes to the development of egalitarian sex role attitudes or whether such attitudes contribute to a woman's decision to become employed, obviously the two are related. Because of reforms in legislation and taxation, married women in Ireland increasingly entered the labour force, as had been the trend in other developed countries. This phenomenon was to have reverberations in many spheres – the home, the workplace, etc. – and inevitably on basic sex role attitudes.

The position of women in Ireland changed dramatically in the period from 1970 onwards. Ireland had recently passed anti-discrimination legislation in the area of employment. The Anti-Discrimination (Pay) Act had been passed in 1974, introducing equal pay, with effect from December 1975. The Employment Equality Act had come into effect in July 1977. This act made it unlawful to discriminate on the grounds of sex or marital status in recruitment, conditions of employment, access to training, or in the provision of opportunities for promotion. Both of these acts fulfilled recommendations made by the Commission on the Status of Women (1972), in addition to conforming to EEC guidelines and directives. Further progress was made with the establishment of the Employment Equality Agency, an independent permanent body whose role it was to promote and encourage equality of opportunity between men and women in employment. Moreover, it had power to enforce the anti-discrimination legislation.

At the time this first study was conducted in 1975 many further reforms were yet to be achieved. Among the more important of these were legalisation of the sale of contraceptives and repeal of the punitive taxation laws that acted as a strong deterrent to married women's working (Fine-Davis, 1976, 1977; Walsh, 1973). In 1979 legislation allowing for the sale of contraceptives was passed and came into effect in November 1980. However, this legislation was considered to be far from ideal in that it only provided for the sale of contraceptives to married people with a doctor's prescription. This was later liberalised.

Another important advance occurred in 1980 with a High Court ruling that declared the current system of taxation, in which a wife's earnings were treated as part of her husband's, to be unconstitutional (Scannell, 2000). Because the system involved aggregating the husband's and wife's income, the wife's *total* income was taxed at her husband's highest marginal rate, which in recent years has been as high as 60–77% in the higher income brackets. This ruling, which was appealed by the Government but upheld by the Supreme Court, now means that married women may be taxed as single individuals and are no longer penalised financially by the taxation system.

The legislative machinery was thus largely there. However, the importance of law is not only that it prohibits or eliminates prejudiced behaviour but that it *changes* the situations and practices that breed prejudiced behaviour and attitudes. Since these situations and practices create a framework and a context in which prejudices develop, law can be seen as an educational agent in restructuring these situations and practices (Raab and Lipset, 1959). The existence of the employment equality legislation meant that men would increasingly see women in the workplace as equals. The effect of the change in the tax law meant that many married women who had formerly stayed at home would be returning to the workforce and single women would no longer be leaving the workforce in as great numbers upon marriage as they did previously. As a result of all of these changes, adult males as well as children of both sexes would be faced with a new picture of women that would ultimately help reshape their attitudes. Women themselves would also have more options, which would lead to new behaviours, which in turn would have an effect upon their own attitudes.

The process of social change began in the 1970s and intensified in the subsequent decades. Such change involved a two-way causal process: as people's behaviour changed – as a result of a variety of factors, including legislation and other policy changes – this began to influence attitudes; similarly, as people's attitudes changed, further behavioural changes were likely to follow. This process would inevitably have far-reaching implications in many spheres, affecting not only social norms and lifestyles, but the role of the Church in Irish society, as well as future Government policies.

4 Social-psychological and personality correlates of attitudes toward the role and status of women

4.1 Background and literature review

One of the main goals of the initial 1975 study was to examine the relationships between personality and related social-psychological characteristics, on the one hand, and attitudes toward sex roles and issues relevant to the status of women, on the other. One of the main constructs of interest was that of religiosity, since the Church had been so influential in encouraging a traditional role for women in Ireland and had explicitly expressed attitudes towards women and gender roles in its teachings and scriptures, as has been referred to above. However, other social-psychological and quasi personality characteristics were also of interest. The underlying objective was to see if attitudes toward the role and status of women varied depending on the personality and other social-psychological characteristics of the respondents. We have already seen that demographic characteristics, such as sex, age, socio-economic status and rural–urban location were systematically and significantly related to attitudes to gender roles. Could personality and related psychological variables also be systematically related? Other research suggested that they could be.

In this phase of the research factor analytically derived measures of personality and related social-psychological characteristics were developed in parallel with the development of measures of attitudes toward the role and status of women, as described above (Davis *et al.*, 1977). The purpose of this preliminary factor analytic work was to develop a set of measures of quasi personality and social-psychological constructs which were relevant to the Irish context.

While the legal and administrative reforms of the 1970s and into the 1980s were of critical importance in redressing inequality, it was also important to understand the attitudinal underpinnings of these inegalitarian attitudes and practices, since it was clear that attitudes also played a key role in perpetuating inequality and rigid sex role behaviour (Commission on the Status of Women, 1972; Flanagan, 1975). Thus, while law and social policy had and have a key role to play in combating inequality, social psychology can contribute to our fuller understanding by examining the possible causes of the development of attitudes which are inconsistent with equality and with modern concepts of mental health, including self-actualisation and fulfillment on the part of women.

This issue was of interest to psychologists in the 1970s as the women's movement was beginning to have an influence on scholarly research and the new interdisciplinary field of women's studies was beginning to be born (e.g. Safir, Mednick, Israeli, and Bernard, 1985). Several studies in this train of research showed that demographic characteristics such as sex and age explained a great deal of variance in sex role attitude differences (e.g. Spence and Helmreich, 1972; Yorburg and Arafat, 1975; Fine-Davis, 1983a); however, other studies indicated that polarisation of support occurred within each group and was associated with a variety of person-ality variables (e.g. Worell and Worell, 1977). These studies suggested that opposition to equal status for women in political, economic, social and legal areas existed among both sexes and reflected a complex matrix of motivational and belief systems that militated against sexual equality (Worell and Worell, 1977).

The majority of these studies were carried out in the United States and largely utilised college samples. Most also tended to examine atti-tudes of women, dichotomising them in terms of whether or not they supported the goals of what was broadly described as the "Women's Lib-eration Movement". Worell and Worell (1977), using a variety of meas-ures, found that the "one compelling characteristic" that set the female supporter off from other American college women was her "very strong desire for autonomy". In comparison both to women who were opposed to the movement and to college girls in general, she was found to want to be independent, self-sufficient and free from external control. In fact, several investigators of the time found that autonomy was a significant variable differentiating these two groups (Tangri, 1970; Cherniss, 1972; Fowler and van de Reit, 1972; O'Keefe, 1972; Stoloff, 1973) and hence seemed to be a critical personality variable determining attitudes to the role of women.

Other characteristics, closely associated with autonomy, were also found to characterise women who supported women's liberation: Ryckman, Martens, Rodda and Sherman (1972) found these women to be more internal in locus of control; Pawlicki and Almquist (1973) found that they manifested greater feelings of control over their environment; and Cher-niss (1972) found them to be more assertive. Other qualities characteris-ing supporters included greater achievement orientation and less abasement (O'Keefe, 1972); increased personal risk-taking, creativity and originality (Joesting, 1971); greater self-actualisation, self-confidence and aggression (Fowler and van de Reit, 1972); greater humanitarianism (Stoloff, 1973); less authoritarianism (Pawlicki and Almquist, 1973; Worell and Worell, 1977); and greater tolerance of ambiguity (Pawlicki and Almquist, 1973). In contrast, women opposed to liberation were found to be more self-protective, fearful of danger, risk-avoiding, resistant to change and low in curiosity and flexibility (Worell and Worell, 1977).

Several researchers (Broverman, Vogel, Broverman, Clarkson and Rosenkrantz, 1972; Gump, 1972; Nielson and Doyle, 1975) also found pro-liberation women to have healthier self-concepts than traditional women and to have a higher regard for women in general. Gump (1972) found that differences in ego strength were associated with plans for marriage and career: high ego strength subjects were actively pursuing both object-ives, leading Gump to conclude that ego strength may be negatively related to adoption of the traditional female sex role. Along these same lines, Broverman *et al.* (1972) reported that, among Catholic women college students in the US, those who perceived themselves as more com-petent planned to combine employment with children, whereas women who perceived themselves as less competent indicated that they planned to stop working when they became mothers. Those with high competency self-concepts also had a smaller ideal family size than those with lower competency self-concepts. Plans to have fewer children, on the part of women favouring the women's liberation movement, were also found by O'Keefe (1972).

In light of the research findings concerning the personality characteris-tics of women favouring women's liberation versus those of traditional women, Lott (1973) expressed concern that it was the more traditional women who expressed a greater desire to have children. The ones whom she felt would make the better mothers in terms of their personality char-acteristics (independence, flexibility, democratic orientation, creativity) were the least interested; they were opting for careers, for smaller families and more frequently for childlessness or "childfreeness".

In addition to the more classical "personality" characteristics, other social-psychological variables have also been examined in relation to atti-tudes toward sex roles. One of the main constructs which has attracted attention in this connection is religiosity. In a study of women in a mid-western US city, Welch (1975) found that religious practice was negatively related to support for women's rights; those who attended church regu-larly, whether Protestant or Catholic, were less likely to be supportive of women's rights than those who did not attend regularly. Religious practice was also found to be correlated with perceptions of women as incompe-tent. Similar findings concerning the relationship between support for the women's movement and church attendance were obtained in Ireland by Philbin Bowman (1976, 1977).

It was against this background that this phase of our research was carried out. The goal was to develop measures of more general personality and related social-psychological characteristics which were relevant to the Irish context in parallel with the development of measures of attitudes toward the role and status of women in order to examine possible relation-ships between these two sets of measures in an Irish sample.

4.2 Method

4.2.1 Pretest

The development of measures of attitudes toward the role and status of women has been described in Chapter 3. A second pretest was also conducted in order to develop measures of personality and related social-psychological constructs with an Irish sample. A large number of items were selected from widely used measures and scales mostly developed in the US (Robinson and Shaver, 1973). These tapped a range of constructs including trust in people, life satisfaction, self-esteem, anomia, alienation, authoritarianism, intolerance of ambiguity, etc. Many of these items and scales had not been subjected to factor analysis before and it was not always certain that they were uni-dimensional constructs to begin with. Moreover, since they had been developed on American samples, it could not be assumed that they were necessarily relevant for Irish respondents. At least it seemed an empirical question which should be subjected to empirical research.

A stratified sample of 412 male and female Dublin adults responded to a pretest instrument in March 1975. Responses to the items were factor analysed and items from several of the resulting factors were selected for inclusion in the main-test instrument of the present study. The results of this pretest as well as subsequent research along these lines are described more fully by Davis *et al.* (1977).

4.2.2 Sample

The sample employed in this phase of the research was the 1975 Dublin sample, consisting of 420 male and female adults, aged 18–65, as described in more detail in Chapter 2. A stratified quota sampling procedure was used, with randomised starting points, based on names and addresses randomly selected from the Dublin Electoral Register. The sample was stratified by sex, age, socio-economic status and marital status, and on the part of married women by employment status and presence of dependent children.

4.2.3 Factor analysis of measures of personality and related social-psychological constructs

The pretest carried out prior to the main study resulted in a number of measures of personality and related social-psychological characteristics, many of which represent well-known constructs in the psychological literature (Davis *et al.*, 1977). Thirty-three high loading items from several of the factors which emerged in this pretest were included in our main-test and then re-factor analysed. A six-factor solution provided optimal psychological interpretability. The names given to these factors with an example of high loading item from each are as follows: Factor I: *Religiosity* (e.g. "Prayer is something which is very important in my life"); Factor II: *Self-Deprecation with Powerlessness* (e.g. "I certainly feel useless at times"); Factor III: *Life Satisfaction* (e.g. "All things considered, I would say that I am very happy with my life these days"); Factor IV: *Need for Order and Predictability* (e.g. "I always see to it that my work is carefully planned and organised"); Factor V: *Trust in People* (e.g. "If you don't watch yourself, people will take advantage of you" – loaded negatively); Factor VI: *Self-Esteem* (e.g. "I feel that I am a person of worth, at least on an equal basis with others"). The full factor analytic results are presented in Table 4.1.

Summary scores for each respondent on each of the factors were computed and these were intercorrelated with summary scores based on the eight factors measuring attitudes toward the role and status of women. Several patterns emerged from this analysis of this data as may be seen in Table 4.2. Tables 4.3 and 4.4 present the results of correlational analysis for females and males separately.

The factor most strongly related to attitudes toward the role and status of women was Religiosity. The more religious a person was, the more likely he/she was to have a traditional sex role orientation. The more religious were also significantly less favourable in their attitudes to the legalisation of contraception and related questions. Several other significant relationships were consistent with this pattern. The more religious respondents were, the more likely they were to be opposed to maternal employment, the more likely they were to oppose equal pay, and the more likely they were to favour higher taxes for married women. More religious people were also less likely to perceive limitations in the housewife role than were the less religious. Among women, greater religiosity was also found to be associated with a tendency to perceive women as inferior (Table 4.3).

Subjects manifesting a high *Need for Order and Predictability* (sometimes referred to in the literature as rigidity or compulsivity) were also found to manifest more traditional attitudes toward the role of women and to be more opposed to social change in the status of women. Similar findings were obtained in the US by Worell and Worell (1977), who found women opposed to liberation to be resistant to change and low in flexibility.

Several other findings emerged from this analysis. There was a consistent pattern of significant correlations between *Self-Deprecation and Powerlessness* on the one hand and attitudes toward the status of women on the other. People who were self-deprecating and felt powerless tended to express traditional sex role ideology and to be opposed to social change which would lead to greater equality in the status of women; such individuals were also more likely to perceive females as inferior. Similar relationships have been obtained by other researchers. For example, Pawlicki and Almquist (1973) found women's liberation supporters to manifest greater feelings of control over their environment. Nielson and Doyle (1975) found pro-liberation women to have a higher regard for women in general.

Relationships were also observed between the variable *Trust in People* and several measures of attitudes toward the role and status of women. Greater trust in people was associated with perceiving women as equal and not as inferior to men. Aside from this relationship, *Trust in People* was unassociated with attitudes toward the status of women among females; however, it was quite salient for males. Men with high trust in people were more likely to support equal pay and more likely espouse egalitarian sex roles.

The variables *Life Satisfaction and Self-Esteem* were not significantly related to any of the attitudes to social issues; however, they were moderately correlated with *Traditional Sex Role Orientation,* suggesting that those holding traditional sex role attitudes are not particularly disturbed by them. They have somewhat higher life satisfaction and higher self-esteem than those with less traditional views; such attitudes may well be so culturally acceptable that those holding them are relatively comfortable and satisfied. However, these relationships were not as strong and did not present as coherent a pattern as did relationships with the other personality variables. Moreover, as has been shown in other studies (cf. Robinson and Shaver, 1973), these measures are subject to social desirability response set.

4.3 Path analysis

Separate analyses of variance had indicated that age was a significant predictor of a number of attitudes toward the role and status of women. It was also found to be a significant predictor of *Religiosity* in the direction of older people being more religious (Fine-Davis, 1979a). Thus, in order to determine whether or not there was a direct effect of *Religiosity* on attitudes toward the role and status of women, a path analysis, which took age and other demographic variables into account, was performed using two of the attitude factors as endogenous variables in the path model. This path model may be seen in Figure 4.1. By examining direct and indirect effects, the path analysis clarified the extent of the role of age as a predictor variable. It became clear that age was particularly important in determining *Religiosity,* but was a less significant direct predictor of *Traditional Sex Role Orientation* (the first key factor) and, in fact, had no direct effect on *Attitudes to Maternal Employment* (the second key factor). Thus, the apparent effects of age on *Traditional Sex Role Orientation* and *Positive Attitude to Maternal Employment* were found to be largely *indirect,* mediated by *Religiosity.* Only one criterion variable – *Attitude to Maternal Employment* – was used; however, it was hoped that the path analysis for this variable would be illustrative of the kinds of patterns that would be likely to occur with other similar variables (such as other issues relevant to the role and status of women) which had been found in other analyses to be similarly related to age and to *Religiosity* (Fine-Davis, 1979a).

Table 4.1 Factor analysis of 33 Likert items measuring general social-psychological and personality constructs – selected items from six Varimax rotated factors (N=420)

Item no.	Varimax rotated loading
Factor I: Religiosity	
*15. Prayer is something which is very important in my life.	−0.81
*3. One's religious commitment gives life a certain purpose which it could not otherwise have.	−0.77
*29. How often do you attend Mass or other worship services? (7 = daily; 1 = rarely or never).	−0.76
*10. I believe the miracles happened just as the Bible says.	−0.72
*30. I know God really exists and I have no doubts about it.	−0.71
% Variance: 10.8 Cumulative % Variance: 10.8	
Factor II: Self-Deprecation with Powerlessness	
*7. Most people are better liked than I am.	0.64
*17. I certainly feel useless at times.	0.60
*31. In spite of what some people say, the life of the average man is getting worse, not better.	0.57
*6. Most of the things I do now are boring or monotonous.	0.55
*9. It is useless to plan for tomorrow, all we can do is live for the present.	0.53
*16. There are only two kinds of people in the world: the weak and the strong.	0.52
*24. I often wish I were very different than I am.	0.46
*26. I would prefer to be told what to do than tell others.	0.45
% Variance: 7.8 Cumulative % Variance: 18.7	
Factor III: Life Satisfaction	
*23. All things considered, I would say that I am very happy with my life these days.	0.75
*19. In almost every way, I'm very glad to be the person I am.	0.72
*18. I am just as happy or happier now than when I was younger.	0.68
% Variance: 7.4 Cumulative % Variance: 26.0	

Factor IV: Need for Order and Predictability

*22. I always see to it that my work is carefully planned and organised.	-0.75
*32. I always like to keep my things neat and tidy and in good order.	-0.71
*12. It bothers me when something unexpected interrupts my daily routine.	-0.45
*21. Every person should live by a few good and unchanging rules of conduct, that way he can never go wrong.	-0.43

% Variance: 6.2   Cumulative % Variance: 32.2

Factor V: Trust in People

*13. If you don't watch yourself, people will take advantage of you.	-0.72
*2. It is safest to assume that all people have a vicious streak and it will come out when they are given the chance.	-0.62
*8. Most people are inclined to look out for themselves than to help others.	-0.51
4. I don't like things to be uncertain and unpredictable.	-0.47
*25. You can trust most people.	0.46
27. There is only one right way to do anything.	-0.45
5. A good job is one where what is to be done and how it is to be done are always clear.	-0.41

% Variance: 7.8   Cumulative % Variance: 40.1

Factor VI: Self-Esteem

*33. I usually rely on my own opinions rather than on other people's.	-0.72
*14. I feel that I am a person of worth, at least on an equal basis with others.	-0.54
*28. I'm popular with people my own age.	-0.45
**20. I think that I am an average type of person.	-0.42

% Variance: 5.6   Cumulative % Variance: 45.6

* Items which were composited for further analyses.
** Also loaded at 0.46 on Factor III, but interpretation somewhat more consistent with this Factor (item not composited).

Table 4.2 Correlations between attitudes toward the role and status of women and other social-psychological and personality characteristics: total sample (N=420)

Attitudes toward the role and status of women	Other social-psychological and personality characteristics					
	Factor I: Religiosity	Factor II: Self-deprecation with powerlessness	Factor III: Life satisfaction	Factor IV: Need for order and predictability	Factor V: Trust in people	Factor VI: Self-esteem
I. Traditional Sex Role Orientation	0.34**	0.31**	0.12*	0.29**	-0.16**	0.16**
II. Positive Attitude to Contraception	-0.40**	-0.06	-0.08	-0.18**	-0.04	0.01
III. Belief in Equal Opportunity	0.04	-0.01	0.09	0.01	0.05	0.02
IV. Positive Attitude to Maternal Employment	-0.28**	-0.21**	0.01	-0.17**	0.13*	-0.04
V. Belief in Equal Pay	-0.17**	-0.15**	0.00	-0.10	0.09	0.00
VI. Belief in Higher Tax for Married Women	0.12*	0.22**	-0.06	0.14*	-0.13*	0.00
VII. Perception of Females as Inferior	0.10	0.29**	-0.04	0.19**	-0.24**	0.09
VIII. Perception of Limitations in Housewife Role	-0.18**	0.09	-0.10	-0.06	-0.10	0.01

* $p<0.01$

** $p<0.001$

Table 4.3 Correlations between attitudes toward the role and status of women and other social-psychological and personality characteristics: all females (N=300)

Attitudes toward the role and status of women	Other social-psychological and personality characteristics					
	Factor I: Religiosity	Factor II: Self-deprecation with powerlessness	Factor III: Life satisfaction	Factor IV: Need for order and predictability	Factor V: Trust in people	Factor VI: Self-esteem
I. Traditional Sex Role Orientation	0.40**	0.34**	0.16*	0.29**	-0.08	0.16*
II. Positive Attitude to Contraception	-0.38**	-0.09	-0.04	-0.18**	-0.02	0.00
III. Belief in Equal Opportunity	0.05	0.02	0.06	-0.03	0.07	0.03
IV. Positive Attitude to Maternal Employment	-0.36**	-0.23**	-0.01	-0.15*	0.11	-0.04
V. Belief in Equal Pay	-0.23**	-0.16*	-0.09	-0.11	0.02	-0.01
VI. Belief in Higher Tax for Married Women	0.17**	0.23**	-0.03	0.11	-0.12	-0.02
VII. Perception of Females as Inferior	0.20**	0.32**	0.07	0.24**	-0.20**	0.05
VIII. Perception of Limitations in Housewife Role	-0.16*	0.16*	-0.13*	-0.04	-0.06	0.05

* $p<0.01$
** $p<0.001$

Table 4.4 Correlations between attitudes toward the role and status of women and other social-psychological and personality characteristics: all males (N=120)

Attitudes toward the role and status of women	Other social-psychological and personality characteristics					
	Factor I: Religiosity	*Factor II:* Self-deprecation with powerlessness	*Factor III:* Life satisfaction	*Factor IV:* Need for order and predictability	*Factor V:* Trust in people	*Factor VI:* Self-esteem
I. Traditional Sex Role Orientation	0.36**	0.27**	0.11	0.30**	-0.31**	0.16
II. Positive Attitude to Contraception	-0.42**	0.07	-0.13	-0.17	-0.06	0.03
III. Belief in Equal Opportunity	-0.04	-0.13	0.09	0.09	-0.03	0.03
IV. Positive Attitude to Maternal Employment	-0.25*	-0.21*	0.00	-0.24*	0.14	-0.04
V. Belief in Equal Pay	-0.18	-0.21**	0.11	-0.10	0.20*	0.02
VI. Belief in Higher Tax for Married Women	0.07	0.22*	-0.11	0.21*	-0.14	0.04
VII. Perception of Females as Inferior	0.08	0.31**	-0.15	0.13	-0.25*	0.18
VIII. Perception of Limitations in Housewife Role	-0.08	-0.04	0.07	-0.08	-0.08	-0.09

* p < 0.01
** p < 0.001

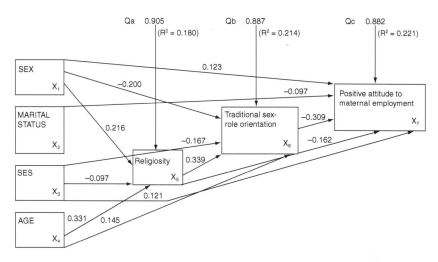

Figure 4.1 A path analysis model of predictors of attitudes toward maternal employment (N = 420).

The implications of this analysis are considerable. It has demonstrated that *Religiosity* is directly related to *Traditional Sex Role Orientation* as well as to a specific issue highly relevant to the status of women, namely *Attitude to Maternal Employment.* This direct effect exists even when age and other key demographic variables are controlled. While path analysis cannot establish causality, these results support the hypothesis that the formation of traditional sex role attitudes and attitudes toward social policy in the area of equal rights for women are, directly or indirectly, influenced by the norms and teachings of the Church.

4.4 Discussion

It has been suggested both from outside as well as from within the religious community (e.g. Reuther, 1974; Daly, 1975; Flanagan, 1975; Farley, 1976) that sex role stereotypes and the perpetuation of traditional sex role attitudes and behaviour have been influenced historically to a great extent by the Judaeo-Christian tradition and through its institutions. Flanagan (1975) points to the androcentric structure of the Church itself, as well as to scriptural bases which have provided a justification for women's submissive role, such as that

> women were created for the sake of men (1 Cor. 11:10) and are a reflection of man's glory (1 Cor. 11:8). Man did not come from woman but woman from man (1 Cor. 11:8; cf. Gen. 2:21 f). Adam was formed first and Eve afterwards (1 Tim. 2:14).
>
> (Flanagan, 1975, p. 237)

Flanagan suggests that the inegalitarian approach to women in the Church was influenced in part by a basic fear of women as evil. He notes that in the patristic record women were described as "volatile, shallow minded, morally weak" (ibid., p. 238). Flanagan asserts that this misogynism has deep roots in the Christian ascetic tradition and touches not only males, but females as well who have come to see themselves as second-class citizens.

The few studies that have examined these variables tend to support these assertions. They are further supported by the results of the present study which has shown that religiosity on the part of women is significantly correlated with perceptions of females as inferior as well as the more general findings that religiosity on the part of both men and women is associated with an overall traditional sex role orientation as well as opposition to social change in policies that would lead to greater equality.

In addition to the clear findings concerning religiosity, some of the other relationships are also worth commenting upon briefly. It will be recalled that men with greater trust in people were more likely to support equal pay and generally more likely to espouse egalitarian sex roles. Men with low trust in people are possibly too insecure to contemplate giving women more freedom and are more comfortable with the *status quo,* whereas men who have greater trust in people are not as threatened by increased flexibility in sex role behaviour. Since they basically trust people – including women – perhaps they do not fear that they will be "taken advantage of" if women are given greater opportunities.

In spite of the significance of these relationships, it should be pointed out that other analyses not presented here indicated that socio-economic status was a significant determinant of several measures of attitudes toward the role and status of women, including perceptions of females as inferior, as well as of some of the personality characteristics, notably *Self-Deprecation with Powerlessness, Need for Order and Predictability* and *Trust in People* (Fine-Davis, 1979a).

The mediating role of socio-economic status is worth reflecting upon briefly. There was a very strong relationship between being from a lower socio-economic background and having feelings of self-deprecation and powerlessness. Such a relationship is not altogether surprising since, compared to other groups, this group is, in fact, relatively powerless. Perhaps in this social context, women become in part a scapegoat on whom men project their own feelings of frustration and inadequacy. Frustrated groups have long been known to project their own frustrations on a visible, weaker group, rather than on the real source of their frustration (Allport, 1958). As for women of lower socio-economic status, perhaps they pick up male attitudes regarding women (from their fathers and husbands) and incorporate these into their own self-image.

Subjects of lower socio-economic status were also found to have less trust in people and a higher need for order and predictability. It is not surprising that they should manifest less trust in people since society has given them a difficult time – economically, in terms of educational opportunities, and in many other ways. With regard to their greater need for order and predictability, such a personality syndrome has been interpreted by Adorno *et al.* (1950) as a defence mechanism against anxiety. In the context of the life of adults of lower socio-economic status, the anxiety against which they are defending is likely to be in large part due to economic deprivation. That this group is less supportive of social change in the area of women's rights is not surprising, since such change would upset the sense of order and predictability that for them may be a necessary psychological defence. Furthermore, it may be hard to bring oneself to grant greater rights and opportunities to another disadvantaged group – women – in the light of one's own hardships.

However, while the mediating role of socio-economic status is certainly a factor to be aware of, it by no means completely explains the obtained relationships. The data demonstrate a very consistent pattern that those who are resistant to social change in the area of sex role behaviour are more rigid, express greater religiosity, are less trusting of people, more self-deprecating and more likely to manifest feelings of powerlessness. Worell and Worell (1977) point out that according to research on authoritarianism and dogmatism, resistance to change appears to be motivated by fear or anxiety. In the case of sex role attitudes and behaviour, the source of the fear may stem from a rigid conceptual system in which "the new patterns of social behaviour suggested by the women's movement present a degree of risk-taking and uncertainty to which the individual cannot easily accommodate" (p. 12). This interpretation would seem to be supported by the relationships obtained in the present study. The manifestation of rigid thinking is apparent from the high scores on *Need for Order and Predictability*, the uncertainty and fear expressed through a low trust in people, and the high levels of religiosity suggest an adherence to familiar and accepted forms of social behaviour.

In view of data presented by Davis *et al.* (1984) on a nationwide Irish sample concerning the low levels of trust in people, high levels of religiosity, rigidity and anomia in the country, the outlook for attitude change in the area of gender equality looked rather bleak at this time. Certainly social change in this area would depend upon leadership from men and women who were characterised by somewhat different personal qualities. However, on the more positive side, the results clearly demonstrated that attitudes favouring gender equality were associated with generally healthier personality structures.

5 Attitudes toward the role of women as part of a larger belief system

5.1 Introduction

It is clear from the findings in Chapter 4, based on a Dublin sample, that personality and related social-psychological characteristics, including religiosity, were systematically related to attitudes to the role of women. Because of the strong and systematic relationships found in the Dublin sample, we decided to extend our analyses to a larger and more representative sample of the Irish population to see if these relationships held up. We replicated a number of the key variables from the 1975 study reported above in a nationwide representative sample survey carried out three years later in 1978. This offered the opportunity to see not only to what extent the relationships obtained in the 1975 data on a Dublin sample held in a more representative nationwide sample, but also to explore to what extent attitudes toward the role of women were part of a larger set of social attitudes and beliefs.

5.2 Method

The Method for the 1978 survey has already been described in Chapter 2. As noted there, the survey was carried out on a nationwide representative sample of 1,862 Irish adults aged 18 and over. The questionnaire contained 40 Likert items, attitude statements presented on seven-point scales ranging from strongly disagree to strongly agree. These included 28 items measuring a wide range of social-psychological attitudes and beliefs. These were developed in prior factor analytic work to develop measures of major social-psychological constructs in an Irish sample (Davis *et al.*, 1977). The set of 40 Likert items also included 12 which measured attitudes toward the role and status of women in Ireland. These 12 were selected from the earlier factor analytic work in the 1975 study (Fine-Davis, 1976, 1983a) to develop measures of attitudes toward the role and status of women in Ireland (Fine-Davis, 1976, 1983a), as described in Chapter 3. The 12 items selected were high loading items from four of the most robust and timely of the original eight factors.

The questionnaires were administered to respondents in their own homes by trained interviewers. The Likert items shown here were self-administered by the respondents to help eliminate any interviewer bias. All interviews were carried out in September–October 1978.

5.3 Results: the societal context

The following tables present data concerning attitudes of the nationwide sample regarding the woman's role and specifically her potential role in the workplace. Table 5.1 presents factor analytic results, followed by percentage responses of the nationwide sample to items which loaded on three factors measuring attitudes related to the role of women, grouped by factor in Table 5.2. The factor analysis was based on a Principal Components analysis; the Principal Axis factors which were extracted were rotated orthogonally to simple structure using the Varimax criterion (Kaiser, 1958).

Factor I, *Traditional Sex Role Orientation with Perception of Female Inferiority*, represents a convergence of two separate factors which were identified in the original 1975 study, which had a larger number of items in this domain (Fine-Davis, 1983a). These two separate factors were *Traditional Sex Role Orientation* (represented by items 1 and 2) and *Perception of Females as Inferior* (represented by items 3, 4 and 5). The convergence of these previously separate factors indicates the close link in people's minds between these two constructs, i.e. female inferiority is seen as a basic component of and inextricably linked with traditional sex role attitudes.

Attitudes in the general population concerning the role of women appear to be at least somewhat ambivalent (Table 5.2). While a slim majority gives lip service to equal participation (i.e. 61% disagree that "the political business leadership of the community should be largely in the hands of men"), a large majority (78%) feels that "being a wife and mother are the most fulfilling roles any women could want". Thus, while the home would appear to be the place where most people would prefer that Irish women fulfil themselves, a majority of the population nevertheless believes that it is the male's prerogative to have the "main say" even in family matters. While a majority does not perceive females as inferior, disturbingly high minorities (ranging from 26% to 42%) do. Furthermore, such beliefs are positively correlated with support for male superiority and may be used as conscious or unconscious rationales for avoiding equality.

Factor III, *Positive Attitude to Maternal Employment*, further illustrates the existence of ambivalent attitudes, in this case concerning employment of married women, particularly those with children. Sixty-four per cent acknowledge that "a woman who has a job she enjoys is likely to be a better wife and mother, because she has an interest and some fulfillment outside the home". Yet, at the same time, close to 70% believe that "it is bad for young children if their mothers go out and work, even if they are well taken care of by another adult". The "bottom line" is perhaps best

Table 5.1 Factor analysis of 12 Likert items measuring attitudes toward the role of women (N = 1,862)

Items	Varimax rotated loading
Factor I: Traditional sex role orientation with perception of female inferiority	
1. The political and business leadership of a community should be largely in the hands of men.	0.67
2. Some equality in marriage is a good thing, but by and large, the husband ought to have the main say in family matters.	0.60
3. Generally speaking, women think less clearly than men.	0.74
4. Women are, by nature, too highly strung to hold certain jobs.	0.63
5. Female workers, even if qualified and experienced, are in some ways, less reliable, less committed and less serious than men.	0.69
% Variance: 26.9 Cumulative % Variance: 26.9	
Factor II: Support for higher taxation of married women	
1. It is unfair to make a women pay more tax just because she is married.	−0.70
2. Married women should be taxed more than single women.	0.77
3. It is only fair that a married couple (both working) pay more tax than two single people.	0.72
% Variance: 13.1 Cumulative % Variance: 40.0	
Factor III: Positive attitude to maternal employment	
1. It is bad for young children if their mothers go out and work, even if they are well taken care of by another adult.	0.74
2. Being a wife and mother are the most fulfilling roles any woman could want.	0.62
3. A woman who has a job she enjoys is likely to be a better wife and mother, because she has an interest and some fulfillment outside the home.	−0.45
4. When there is high unemployment, married women should be discouraged from working.	0.60
% Variance: 9.6 Cumulative % Variance: 49.6	

reflected in the responses to Item 4, "When there is high unemployment, married women should be discouraged from working", to which 71% responded in the affirmative.

Thus, the apparent concern for the welfare of children was not the only justification for opposition to maternal employment. There was also a strong belief that married women were less *entitled* to jobs than men and young people newly entering the job market. This clearly indicated that the road to equality would be considerably more difficult in an economic climate characterised by high unemployment, a climate which prevailed and even worsened in the years following the study, through the 1980s. However, as illustrated by the items on Factor II, *Support for Higher Taxation of Married Women*, there was some evidence of a liberalisation of attitudes. Quite a large majority (71%) felt that it was unfair to make a woman pay more tax just because she was married. This feeling led in 1980 to the revision of the tax code with respect to married women (Scannell, 2000), thereby removing a strong deterrent to their employment.

Further evidence of potential change was suggested by the data in Table 5.3, which show differences between groups in the society on these measures. It is clear that the most conservative attitudes were held by males, older people, those of lower socio-economic background and those living in rural areas. While the sex difference was overwhelming concerning the most global measure (*Traditional Sex Role Orientation with Perception of Female Inferiority*), it was less strong concerning the more specific social issues. Thus, with progressive change resulting from liberalisation of social policies affecting women, some of the global attitudes – which were shown in previous research to be correlated with attitudes to these social policies (Fine-Davis,1983a) – were likely to shift in a more liberal direction. Also, legislation inducing *behavioural* change (e.g. the Employment Equality Act 1977)[1] was also likely to lead to attitude shifts, since – as cognitive dissonance theory (Festinger, 1957) would predict – attitudes change to become congruent with behaviour.

Regarding the age effect, American research, which has studied attitude shifts over time using the National Opinion Research Center's General Social Survey, has noted that both "conversions" (i.e. even the oldest groups tend to shift in a liberal direction when the rest of society changes) and "cohort replacement" effects occur. Since the younger generation is better educated and education is associated with liberalism, as the older cohorts die and younger, better educated cohorts enter the population, attitude shifts can be quite pronounced (Davis and Smith, 1982).

5.4 Results: attitudes toward the role of women as part of a larger belief system

In order to examine the relationship between attitudes toward the role of women and other attitudes and beliefs, the three composite scores

Table 5.2 Percentage distributions of responses to Likert items measuring attitudes toward the role of women, grouped by factor (N = 1,862)

Items	Disagree			DK etc.	Agree		
	Strong	Moderate	Slight		Slight	Moderate	Strong
Factor I: Traditional sex role orientation with perception of female inferiority							
1. The political & business leadership of a community should be largely in the hands of men.	26.6	20.1 **(60.6%)**	14.0	0.5%	12.4	13.1 **(38.9%)**	13.4
2. Some equality in marriage is a good thing but, by and large, the husband ought to have the main say in family matters.	19.3	13.2 **(43.1%)**	10.6	0.6	16.5	19.6 **(56.3%)**	20.2
3. Generally speaking, women think less clearly than men.	36.6	22.0 **(73.6%)**	14.9	0.8	12.9	7.8 **(25.7%)**	5.0
4. Women are, by nature, too highly strung to hold certain jobs.	24.8	19.2 **(56.8%)**	12.9	0.8	19.8	13.8 **(42.4%)**	8.8
5. Female workers, even if qualified and experienced, are in some ways less reliable, less committed and less serious than men.	34.4	22.1 **(70.8%)**	14.3	0.8	12.6	10.3 **(28.4%)**	5.5
Factor II: Support for higher taxation of married women							
1. It is unfair to make a woman pay more tax just because she is married.	12.3	9.1 **(28.0%)**	6.6	0.8%	11.9	19.2 **(71.2%)**	40.1
2. Married women should be taxed more than single women.	40.6	20.6 **(72.4%)**	11.2	1.0	10.4	8.1 **(26.5%)**	8.1
3. It is only fair that a married couple (both working) pay more tax than two single people.	31.4	18.0 **(61.0%)**	11.6	1.4	13.0	11.3 **(37.6%)**	13.4

Factor III: Positive attitude to maternal employment

1. It is bad for young children if their mothers go out and work, even if they are well taken care of by another adult.	10.3	11.4	8.1	0.6	13.3	20.7	35.7
	–	**(29.7%)**	–		–	**(69.7%)**	–
2. Being a wife and mother are the most fulfilling roles any woman could want.	4.9	7.1	8.8	1.0	15.6	23.3	39.2
	–	**(20.8%)**	–		–	**(78.2%)**	–
3. A woman who has a job she enjoys is likely to be a better wife and mother, because she has an interest and some fulfillment outside the home.	9.0	12.3	13.0	1.6	21.6	21.0	21.4
	–	**(34.3%)**	–		–	**(64.0%)**	–
4. When there is high unemployment married women should be discouraged from working.	10.7	9.6	8.7	0.4	18.7	20.8	31.1
	–	**(29.0%)**	–		–	**(70.6%)**	–

Note:
The percentages in bold indicate summary agree and disagree responses.

Table 5.3 Summary of analysis of variance results: source level means and significant F-ratios for main effects of five independent variables on attitudes related to the role and status of women (N = 1,803)

Attitudes toward the status of women	Sex		Age				Socio-economic status			Marital status		Rural vs urban location	
	Male (n=886)	Female (n=917)	18–24 (n=238)	25–39 (n=557)	40–54 (n=433)	55+ (n=575)	Low (n=839)	Med. (n=668)	High (n=296)	Married (n=1,169)	Other (n=634)	Rural (n=1,152)	Urban (n=651)
1. Traditional sex role orientation with perception of female inferiority	($F=201.42$)***		($F=19.27$)***				($F=12.72$)***			($F=4.54$)*		($F=15.70$)***	
	3.80	2.92	2.93	3.18	3.44	3.62	3.43	3.41	3.00	3.30	3.45	3.44	3.18
2. Support for higher taxation of married women	($F=5.67$)*		($F=5.27$)***				($F=6.04$)**			($F=21.21$)***		($F=15.11$)***	
	3.08	2.90	2.76	2.85	3.11	3.13	3.01	3.09	2.70	2.85	3.25	3.10	2.79
3. Positive attitude to maternal employment	($F=10.18$)***		($F=34.54$)***				($F=11.76$)***			($F=0.99$)		($F=7.58$)**	
	3.22	3.41	3.82	3.58	3.08	3.04	3.31	3.20	3.63	3.34	3.28	3.26	3.43

* $p<0.05$
** $p<0.01$
*** $p<0.001$
(Range on all variables is 1–7)

considered above were intercorrelated with eight factors measuring more general social attitude syndromes as well as attitudes to other social issues.

These eight factors were based on earlier factor analytic work to develop these measures (Davis *et al.*, 1977) and were replicated in the present study. The names of the eight factors are listed below:

1   *Religiosity*
2   *Trust in People*
3   *Outgroup Prejudice*
4   *Life Satisfaction*
5   *Anomia*
6   *Economic Optimism*
7   *Support for Censorship*
8   *Pro Legalisation of Contraception and Divorce*

Three of the eight factors measure the same constructs as reported in Chapter 4, namely Religiosity, Trust in People and Life Satisfaction. However, in this chapter we also report on five new constructs: Outgroup Prejudice, Anomia, Economic Optimism, Support for Censorship and Pro Legalisation of Contraception and Divorce.[2]

Factor analytic results, presenting a complete list of the items loading on each of the eight factors, are shown in Table 5.4. While most of the constructs are self-explanatory, an explanation in relation to Factor IV, *Outgroup Prejudice* (Anti-Itinerant Stereotype) is in order. Under the general heading of authoritarianism (Adorno *et al.*, 1950) fall many sub-constructs, one of which is outgroup prejudice. In order to measure this syndrome in Ireland, it would not have been reasonable to include, for example, items measuring anti-Negro attitudes or anti-Semitic attitudes, since blacks and Jews do not constitute significant minority groups in this culture. Thus, on the basis of the belief that outgroup prejudice is a gener-alisable phenomenon and that the out-group which becomes a target of prejudice is a function of the culture in question, a set of items measuring anti-Semitism (Levinson and Sanford, 1944) was adapted to the Irish context. It was hypothesised that itinerants might possibly constitute such an outgroup in this society. Thus, in adapting the items, the word "Jew" or "Jewish" was replaced with the word "itinerant", with the more colloquial term "tinker" in parentheses the first time the word itinerant appeared. Both of these terms – itinerant and tinker – were more commonly used at the time the study was carried out. Now the more commonly used term is "Traveller". All of these items which had to do with itinerants (or Travel-lers) loaded on one factor in the earlier factor analytic work (Davis *et al.*, 1977) and this factor was replicated in the present study.

Intercorrelations between measures of attitudes toward the role of women and other social attitudes and beliefs are presented in Table 5.5. As this table shows, there are meaningful patterns among the various

Table 5.4 Factor analysis of 28 Likert items measuring social-psychological attitudes and beliefs (N = 1,862)

Items	Varimax rotated loading
Factor I: Religiosity	
1. One's religious commitment gives life a certain purpose which it would not otherwise have.	0.70
2. Prayer is something which is very important in my life.	0.75
3. How often do you attend mass or other worship services? (1 = never; 7 = daily)	0.67
4. Obedience and respect for authority are the most important virtues children can learn.	0.49
% Variance: 14.6 Cumulative % Variance: 14.6	
Factor II: Life Satisfaction	
1. I am just as happy or happier now than when I was younger.	0.80
2. Taking all things together I would say I'm very happy these days.	0.79
3. In general, I find that the way I'm spending my life these days is not very satisfying.	-0.72
4. I have got fewer breaks in life than most of the people I know.	-0.40
% Variance: 11.0 Cumulative % Variance: 25.6	
Factor III: Trust in People	
1. You can trust most people.	-0.61
2. If you don't watch yourself, people will take advantage of you.	0.72
3. These days a person doesn't really know who he can count on.	0.78
4. Most people are more inclined to look out for themselves than to help others.	0.60
% Variance: 8.0 Cumulative % Variance: 33.6	
Factor IV: Outgroup Prejudice (Anti-Itinerant Stereotype)	
1. There are a few exceptions, but in general, itinerants (tinkers) are pretty much alike.	0.74
2. The trouble with letting itinerants into a nice neighbourhood is that they gradually give it an itinerant atmosphere.	0.80
3. Itinerants seem to have an aversion to plain hard work; they prefer to live off other people.	0.77
% Variance: 5.7 Cumulative % Variance: 39.3	

Factor V: Pro Contraception and Divorce

1. I would be in favour of changing our laws to allow divorce. — 0.69
2. The sale of contraceptives should be legalised in Ireland. — 0.76
3. Contraceptives should be available to married people who want to plan the size of their family. — 0.78

% Variance: 5.0   Cumulative % Variance: 44.3

Factor VI: Support for Censorship

1. Most censorship of books and movies is a violation of individual rights and should be abolished. — -0.73
2. If we did not have censorship in this country, we'd become just like other countries and lose our moral values. — 0.70
3. It is in the best interests of our young people that the Censorship Board decide what is fit for them to read and see at the cinema. — 0.70

% Variance: 4.2   Cumulative % Variance: 48.5

Factor VII: Economic Optimism

1. Generally speaking, I think I will be worse off financially next year than I was this year. — -0.77
2. All in all, I think that I will be at least as well off financially next year as I am this year. — 0.77
3. I would support a pay pause in the present economic difficulties. — 0.44

% Variance: 4.1   Cumulative % Variance: 52.6

Factor VIII: Anomia

1. One good strong leader would be far better for our economy than the present political system. — 0.67
2. It is useless to plan for tomorrow, all we can do is live for the present. — 0.59
3. In spite of what some people say, the life of the average person is getting worse, not better. — 0.46
4. There are some problems which can never be solved by democratic methods. — 0.42

% Variance: 3.8   Cumulative % Variance: 56.4

Table 5.5 Interrelationships among attitudes toward the role of women and other social-psychological attitudes and beliefs in a nation-wide representative Irish sample (N=1,862)

	Sample Mean[1]	1 Trad. sex role	2 Higher tax	3 Matern. employ.	1 Relig.	2 Trust	3 Prej.	4 Life sat.	5 Anomia	6 Econ. opt.	7 Censor.	8 Contra. div
Attitudes toward the role of women												
1. Trad. sex role orientation with perception of female inferiority	3.4	—	0.25	−0.36	0.12	−0.18	0.26	−0.14	0.21	0.00	0.14	−0.18
2. Support for higher taxation of married women	3.0		—	−0.33	0.08	−0.11	0.10	−0.05	−0.02	0.10	0.13	−0.20
3. Positive attitude to maternal employment	3.3			—	−0.35	0.16	−0.26	0.00	−0.06	−0.06	−0.29	0.33
Other social-psychological attitudes and beliefs												
1. Religiosity	5.7				—	−0.07	0.26	0.08	0.09	0.03	0.45	−0.37
2. Trust in people	3.2					—	−0.26	0.20	−0.23	0.08	−0.11	−0.04
3. Outgroup prejudice	5.2						—	−0.03	0.11	−0.03	0.22	−0.14
4. Life satisfaction	5.2							—	−0.22	0.27	0.02	0.05
5. Anomia	4.0								—	−0.22	0.06	0.04
6. Economic optimism	4.9									—	0.03	−0.03
7. Support for censorship	4.9										—	−0.40
8. Pro contraception and divorce	4.2											—

Notes

1 Each variable is a composite score of several Likert items, scored 1 (strongly disagree) to 7 (strongly agree). The composite scores thus range from 1 to 7, with a high score being in the direction of the name of the factor. If $r > 0.08$, $p < 0.001$.

attitudes and beliefs. For example, *Religiosity* (as measured by frequency of mass attendance and the importance to the respondent of prayer and religion generally) is strongly correlated with a negative *Attitude to Maternal Employment* ($r=-0.35$; $p<0.001$) as well as to the *Legalisation of Contraception and Divorce* ($r=-0.37$; $p<0.001$) and *Support for Censorship* ($r=0.45$; $p<0.001$). It also tends to be associated – although more weakly – to *Traditional Sex Role Orientation with Perception of Female Inferiority*. These relationships are not that surprising, since the Church has reinforced the traditional role for women and has also opposed contraception and divorce. Nevertheless, the findings illustrate the strong relationship between religious attitudes and practice on the one hand and social attitudes and social policy on the other. While correlational analysis cannot prove causality, the results suggest that the teachings and views of the Church have had a strong influence on social attitudes and thus, indirectly, on social policy. In order to tease out the influence of religiosity on attitudes we carried out a path analysis – presented in Chapter 4 – which illustrated a direct effect of religiosity on traditional sex role attitudes and attitudes to maternal employment.

An unexpected finding was the significant relationship between *Religiosity* and *Outgroup Prejudice* ($r=0.26$; $p<0.001$), as prejudice vis-à-vis minority groups would be contrary to ethical religious teachings. Previous research using a Dublin sample (Davis *et al.*, 1977) also obtained a significant correlation between these two measures ($r=0.34$; $p<0.001$), as did earlier American research (Glock and Stark, 1965), suggesting that this is a fairly stable relationship. While there is some evidence that age and socio-economic status may be acting as moderating variables (Davis *et al.*, 1977), other evidence suggests that these effects are not as strong as the relationships between the attitudinal variables themselves (Fine-Davis, 1979a).

Other aspects of the attitude-belief system involve attitudes and beliefs about other people. Those with high *Trust in People* are more likely to hold liberal sex role attitudes, whereas those low in trust are more likely to hold traditional attitudes and to oppose liberalisation of social policies regarding the status of women. These findings on a nationwide representative sample replicate earlier findings obtained on a stratified Dublin sample (Fine-Davis, 1979a) as illustrated in Chapter 4. Consistent with the above, individuals who express *Outgroup Prejudice* (in this case directed toward itinerants) are also more likely to express traditional sex role ideology, including perceptions of female inferiority ($r=0.26$; $p<0.001$). In fact, in the earlier factor analytic work carried out to develop these measures (Davis *et al.*, 1977) the two factors – *Outgroup Prejudice* and *Traditional Sex Role Orientation* – *converged* onto one factor, when a fewer number of factors were examined, indicating an underlying commonality between attitudes toward women and attitudes toward outgroups.

Further relationships reveal that those holding traditional sex role attitudes and perceiving women as inferior are more likely to express feelings of *Anomia* (embodying feelings of hopelessness and pessimism, together with an alienation from existing democratic institutions). Those with more egalitarian sex role attitudes are less likely to feel alienated and more likely to express high levels of *Life Satisfaction*. The significant relationships involving *Outgroup Prejudice* and *Trust in People* further indicate that healthier personalities (i.e. those more tolerant of minority groups and more trusting of people in general, as well as those more satisfied with their lives and less alienated from the system) are more likely to have egalitarian sex role attitudes, to perceive women as equals, and to favour women's equal participation in all aspects of community life, including the world of work.

The importance of *Religiosity* in the belief system warrants further examination. To what extent is *Religiosity* evenly distributed in the population? To what extent does it predict attitudes independently of demographic variables? As may be seen in Table 5.6, *Religiosity* is significantly higher among females than males ($F=42.86$, $p<0.001$). The female mean of 5.85 out of a possible 7.00 indicates a high level of religious belief and practice among Irish women. While the male-female difference is highly significant, males are also quite religious (mean =5.57).

However, as other results have shown, *Religiosity* is linearly related to age ($F=73.33$; $p<0.001$), with the youngest group (aged 18–24) far less religious (mean=5.16) than the oldest group (55+) (mean=6.01). Rural vs urban residence is also a significant determinant of *Religiosity*, though it is less strong than the effects of age and sex. Predictably, rural respondents are significantly more religious ($F=21.53$; $p<0.001$). There is also a significant effect of social class, but it is far less pronounced than the other effects. A three-way SES break reveals essentially no difference in *Religiosity* among the lower and middle SES groups. The difference is between these two and the highest SES group, which shows lower *Religiosity*.

In a multiple regression analysis with *Religiosity* and demographic variables serving as the predictor variables and a key measure of attitudes toward the role of women (*Positive Attitude to Maternal Employment*) as the dependent variable, *Religiosity* is still highly predictive, even after demographic variables have been entered, being far more significant than any single demographic variable (beta=–0.35; $p<0.001$) – see Table 5.7. The effect of five demographic variables alone yielded a Multiple *R* of 0.26. The addition of *Religiosity* to the equation increases the Multiple *R* to 0.42. These results confirm that *Religiosity* is a key determinant of gender role attitudes in Ireland, with an effect independent of demographic variables.

5.5 Discussion and implications

Attitudes toward the role and status of women are not isolated entities. They were found to be part of a larger set of social attitudes and beliefs.

Table 5.6 Summary of analysis of variance results: source level means and F-ratios for main effects of five independent variables on religiosity (N=1,806)[1]

Religiosity

Sex		Age				Socio-economic status			Marital status		Rural vs urban location	
Male (n=887)	Female (n=919)	18–24 (n=238)	25–39 (n=557)	40–54 (n=433)	55+ (n=578)	Low (n=839)	Medium (n=671)	High (n=296)	Married (n=1,170)	Other (n=636)	Rural (n=1155)	Urban (n=651)
$F=42.86^{***}$		$F=73.33^{***}$				$F=8.53^{***}$			$F=0.33$		$F=21.53^{***}$	
5.57	5.85	5.16	5.44	5.96	6.01	5.73	5.77	5.52	5.72	5.69	5.79	5.58

1 The measure of Religiosity is a composite score based on three factorially pure Likert items. Range is 1–7, with 7 equal to high Religiosity.
*** $p<0.001$

Table 5.7 Multiple regression analysis of predictors of positive attitude to maternal employment (N = 1,862)

	Block 1 (Beta)		Block 2 (Beta)	
Step:				
1. Rural vs urban location	0.08***		0.04	
2. Marital status	−0.01		0.02	
3. Sex	0.06**		0.11***	
4. Socio-economic status	−0.04		−0.02	
5. Age	−0.23***		−0.14***	
6. Religiosity			−0.35***	
	Mult. R	= 0.26	Mult. R	= 0.42
	R^2	= 0.07	R^2	= 0.17
	Adj. R^2	= 0.06	Adj. R^2	= 0.17
	Stand. Error	= 1.27	Stand. Error	= 1.20

** $p < 0.01$
*** $p < 0.001$

The pattern of correlations presented in Table 5.5 contains elements reminiscent of the authoritarian personality syndrome, identified by Adorno *et al.* (1950). In particular, the elements of ethnocentrism and outgroup prejudice, the desire for the good strong leader (see Factor VIII, Anomia), and traditional sex role ideology are found in this data set. Authoritarian Submission, defined by Adorno *et al.* as a "submissive uncritical attitude toward idealized moral authorities of the ingroup" (Adorno *et al.*, 1950, p. 228) would appear to be being tapped in part by the *Religiosity* factor. The attitudes supporting censorship may reflect the authoritarian dimensions of Projectivity ("The disposition to believe that wild and dangerous things go on in the world; the projection outward of unconscious emotional impulses") (ibid., p. 250) and Sex ("exaggerated concern with sexual goings-on") (ibid.).

As may be seen from the overall sample means (Table 5.6), the low levels of trust, high levels of religiosity and high levels of outgroup prejudice go hand in hand with traditional attitudes concerning gender roles and with support for limitations on personal freedom as reflected by the reasonably high levels of support for censorship and low levels of support for contraception and divorce. While contraception was finally legalised in 1979, divorce was rejected by a two-thirds majority in a national referendum in 1986, leaving Ireland among the very few countries in the world which did not permit divorce. This state of affairs remained the same until 1995 when a second referendum on divorce was held and passed by a very small margin. Divorce was legalised in 1996. This issue is discussed in greater detail in Chapter 7. Interestingly enough, the data on life satisfaction presented here show that it was relatively high, indicating that people would seem to have been comfortable with their attitudes, beliefs and way of life, in spite of the fact that there were still many restrictions on personal freedoms which we now take for granted and which were more commonplace in many other countries at that time.

Converse (1964), discussing the nature of belief systems in mass publics, referred to the concept of "constraint" or functional interdependence, which binds the attitudes together. He observed a greater degree of attitudinal consistency or constraint among political elites than among "mass publics" – or samples of the general population. His findings were replicated by Bishop and Frankovic (1981). While the present study did not include a comparative elite sample, it did examine the consistency and functional interdependence of attitudes and beliefs in a representative sample of the Irish population. While most of the relationships are not extremely strong in terms of amount of variance explained (though a few are), the *pattern* of relationships is rather consistent and indicative of a reasonably high level of constraint among this mass public. Furthermore, it should be borne in mind that these factors were extracted using Varimax rotation (Kaiser, 1958), which maximises orthogonality; the resulting significant correlations are all the more noteworthy.

A key element in this belief system is religiosity, which was found to be strongly correlated with disapproval of employment on the part of married women, particularly mothers, and with holding traditional views about appropriate gender roles. Previous research has shown that, even when controlling for demographic variables, such as age, sex, socio-economic status, etc., there is still a *direct* relationship between religiosity and attitudes toward maternal employment (Fine-Davis, 1979a), as shown in Chapter 4. The multiple regression analysis carried out on the present nationwide data set confirms this finding (Table 5.7).

In many countries, but particularly in Ireland, the Church has helped to shape, and has been a prime reinforcer of, traditional roles. The influence of the Judaeo-Christian tradition on the development and perpetuation of traditional sex role attitudes and behaviour has been well documented (e.g. Reuther, 1974; Daly, 1975; Farley, 1976). Flanagan (1975) points to the androcentric structure of the Church itself, as well as to the scriptures, which have provided a justification for women's subordinate role. He asserts that misogynism, which is related to a basic fear of women as evil, has deep roots in the Christian ascetic tradition and touches not only males but females as well, who have come to see themselves as second class citizens. This can be seen in the present data by the convergence of traditional sex role ideology and perceptions of females as inferior. While men were very significantly more likely to hold these views than women, an examination of the male and female means (3.80 and 2.92, respectively) illustrates that even women are subject to these attitudes and perceptions, since a score of "3" indicates only a *slight* disagreement with the statements (with 7=strong agreement and 1=strong disagreement). Our earlier results presented in Chapter 4 showed that the more

religious a woman was, the more likely she was to perceive females as inferior, illustrating the close connection between an exposure to religious
teachings and values and feelings of self-worth and identity among
women.

What implications do these findings have for women? Before continuing, it should be pointed out that the following discussion was written in
the late 1980s (Fine-Davis, 1989) and reflects the situation, the literature
and the author's views at that time. It has been edited ever so slightly to
reflect a more current perspective, but it essentially reflects the *status quo*
and thinking at that time. Subsequent chapters will reflect the changes
that have occurred, both in the actual situation, but also attitudinally in
the 20–25 years since then.

Many previous studies, carried out shortly before these data were collected, as well as shortly afterwards in a variety of countries had demonstrated that employment has very clear benefits for women, in terms of
both their mental and physical well-being. For example, Ferree (1976), in
a study of American women living in a working class neighbourhood,
found that full-time housewives were more dissatisfied than women who
were employed. Their dissatisfaction with housework was found to be
related to a sense of isolation, powerlessness and low self-esteem. In a
study of Irish married women, Fine-Davis (1985) found that employment
status was associated with greater perceived well-being on three measures:
satisfaction with one's health, satisfaction with one's work and life satisfaction. Shaver and Freedman (1976) found American housewives to be
more likely than employed women to report psychological symptoms such
as anxiety, worry, loneliness and feelings of worthlessness. A higher level
of psychiatric symptoms was found by Powell (1977) in the United States
and Cochrane and Stopes-Roe (1981) in Britain to be associated with
being a full-time housewife and Cumming, Lazer and Chisholm (1975)
found Canadian housewives more likely than employed married women to
commit suicide. Cochrane and Stopes-Roe (1981) concluded that "employment offers a protection against depression for women much as it does for
men" (p. 379).

In view of the multiplicity of needs which employment clearly meets for
women, and the apparent benefits which it has for their well-being, it is
particularly disturbing that attitudes of society as a whole were found to be
so negative, and at best ambivalent, toward changing sex role behaviour
and particularly to employment of married women. Such attitudes were
not limited to Ireland around the time this study was carried out. A comparative cross-national study in the European Community similarly found
that 61% of men and 59% of women believed that "in a period of high
unemployment a man has a greater right to work than a woman" (Riffault,
1983, p. 96).

Unless such attitudes were acknowledged and confronted, they would
continue to influence women's access to equal opportunities and status

and thereby would also indirectly affect their health and well-being. Some attitudinal change would be expected as a result of cohort replacement effects and conversions, referred to earlier. Also, the administrative and legislative reforms introduced in Ireland in the 1970s were likely to move attitudes in a more liberal direction. However, the economic recession of the 1980s, bringing with it high levels of unemployment, threatened the gains made to date, since in times of insecurity people need to find a scapegoat. Women were vulnerable to becoming such a scapegoat, since there was already a culturally entrenched and pervasive attitude that men were more *entitled* to jobs than women. As a result, there was an even greater need for enlightened leadership from Government to encourage continued progress toward equality.

It is clear that the Church has played a very important role in shaping attitudes toward the role of women in Ireland. Given the nature of the role specification promulgated by the Church, it is ironic that more of its adherents are female than male. However, there is evidence that the high levels of church attendance in Ireland are beginning to decrease, especially among the young. Also, employment on the part of married women has been shown to be associated with lower levels of religiosity (Fine-Davis, 1979b). The fact that employment of married women has been increasing at a very rapid rate should, therefore, contribute to decreasing religiosity among women. These trends threaten the considerable influence and authority which the Catholic Church has historically enjoyed in Ireland. Unless the Church shifts in its attitude toward women's role, it is to be expected that women, particularly younger ones, will increasingly reject Church teachings.

It is, therefore, of some interest to note that within the Church itself, there was increasing discussion and debate concerning the role of women around the time of the data collection, including the key issue of whether or not women should be allowed to become priests. There was also, significantly, a growing recognition of the right of all individuals to work. The 1981 Papal Encyclical on Human Work, while clearly emphasising the importance of the woman's role as mother, nevertheless also recognises her right to equal employment opportunities (Pope John Paul II, 1981, p. 71). More recently, in an apparent response to increasing demands for a greater role for women with the Church, the Pope issued a letter to priests for Holy Thursday regarding the role of women. In it he said they must "discover in a new way the question of the dignity and vocation of women both in the Church and in today's world" ("Pope stresses theme of women", *The Irish Times*, 30 March 1988, p. 8). These public statements were indicative of the beginning of a process of reassessment of religious teachings pertaining to gender roles in light of changing social values and behaviours. Such reassessment within the Church was and is inevitable if it wishes to retain its influence, particularly on its women members.

However, regardless of the response of the Catholic Church to changing social attitudes and behaviour, it is clear that social change has been occurring in Ireland at a very rapid rate over the past decade and is likely to continue to do so. Contraception has been introduced, thereby facilitating women's employment. The birth rate which had been the highest in Europe is dropping fast (Sexton and Dillon, 1984) and married women's labour force participation is accelerating at a rapid rate. Legal impediments to women's equality of employment have been removed. The kinds of issues that still remain to be fought for are those which are being fought for even in more progressive societies, such as the United States, namely, childcare facilities and greater flexibility in employment. In Ireland, of course, the battles for divorce and, possibly, abortion, were still to be re-enacted at future points.

The obstacles which women in Ireland face as they attempt to affect the *status quo* are particularly difficult because they are invisible, yet are part of a deeply entrenched belief system about the way the world is and ought to be. However, even this is being challenged, because as part of the European Community and subject to its directives, Ireland is no longer an island unto itself.

Notes

1 Since the 1977 Employment Equality Act there have since been several subsequent Acts, including the Employment Equality Act 1998 and the Employment Equality Act 2004.

2 In Chapters 3 and 4 we also reported on a related factor, Positive Attitude to Contraception, but this was part of the set of factors measuring attitudes to the role of women.

6 Attitude change: 1975–2005

6.1 Changing gender role attitudes cross-culturally

As we have discussed in detail in Chapter 1, changing gender roles are a cross-cultural phenomenon. Gender roles and gender role attitudes have been shifting in Western societies since the late 1960s. Social scientists have attempted to measure these changes through attitudinal studies carried out over time. Most of the early work in this area was carried out in the US (e.g. Mason *et al.*, 1976; Thornton and Freedman, 1979) but studies were also carried out in Scandinavia (e.g. Haavio-Mannila, 1972). Some of these earlier studies captured the initial effects of the women's movement; for example, Haavio-Mannila's study captured attitude change in Finland over the period 1966–70. Mason *et al.* (1976) looked at US women's sex role attitudes over the decade 1964–74, while Thornton and Freedman (1979) looked at changes in the sex role attitudes of women, 1962–77. Interest in changes in gender role attitudes continued, as demonstrated by Thornton and Young-DeMarco's (2001) article on four decades of trends in attitudes toward family issues in the United States – the 1960s through the 1990s. Cotter *et al.* (2011) explored the period in the US from 1977 to 2008. Interest in these issues was not restricted to the US. The Australian investigators, van Egmond *et al.* (2010) examined gender role attitudes in Australia over the period 1986–2005. Several authors observed more rapid attitude change in the earlier period, with a plateau effect in the 1990s (Thornton and Young-DeMarco, 2001; van Egmond *et al.*, 2010; Cotter *et al.*, 2011). Some of these authors explored the reasons for the slowing down of change and asked if perhaps there was a backlash effect, as Faludi (1991) had suggested. Braun and Scott (2009) explored cross-cultural data to see if the apparent reversal of the trend was real and they concluded that observed changes in gender role attitudes over time did not support the backlash interpretation. Instead they interpreted the trends as providing evidence of "egalitarianism reaching a peak and retreat" (pp. 365–366). All of the international research in the US, Europe and Australia has found that gender role attitudes have become significantly less traditional over time (e.g. Mason *et al.*, 1976; Thornton and Freedman, 1979; Fine-Davis, 1988a; Mason and Lu, 1988; Whelan and Fahey, 1994; Hinds and Jarvis, 2000; Thornton and Young-DeMarco, 2001; Scott, 2006, 2008; O'Sullivan, 2007, 2012; van Egmond *et al.*, 2010; Cotter *et al.*, 2011). One of the main foci in this cross-cultural train of research has been attitudes to maternal employment and most studies have found that attitudes have become more accepting (e.g. Fine-Davis, 1988a; Mason and Lu, 1988; Thornton and Young-DeMarco, 2001; O'Sullivan, 2007, 2012). Yet, several of the studies have shown that men continue to hold more traditional attitudes than women (e.g. Fine-Davis, 1988a; Treas and Widmer, 2000; Fine-Davis *et al.*, 2005). Some studies have found that opposition to maternal employment is more covertly expressed through concern about its effects on children (e.g. Mason and Lu, 1988; Treas and Widmer, 2000; Fine-Davis, 2011).

6.2 The Irish context for social and attitude change

It is in this international context that we present an examination of changing gender role attitudes in Ireland over the period 1975–2005, covering a 30-year period, which overlaps with many of the studies referred to above. While there are common issues examined in all of the studies referred to above and the present series of studies in Ireland – particularly global gender role attitudes and attitudes to maternal employment – the present studies also include the psychological measure, *Perception of Females as Inferior*, which adds a further dimension to our understanding of traditional gender role attitudes. In addition our series of studies includes several measures of attitudes to social policy issues relevant to the status of women and documents attitude change in the context of legislative and policy changes which took place in Ireland during a period of rapid social change beginning in the early 1970s.

For many reasons social and attitudinal change concerning women's roles began somewhat later than it did in other Western societies. To begin with, Ireland had been a traditional society with a strong rural agricultural tradition. Its industrialisation did not begin until the 1960s and hence its social development began much later than that of the other Western countries examined in the research cited above; hence social change in women's roles also began somewhat later. Added to these factors was the strong influence of the Catholic Church which had a strong effect on the norms and attitudes of the society, particularly concerning issues related to women's roles. The influence of Church teachings on the norms and values of the society were until recently complemented by laws of the State (such as in the case of contraception and divorce) and are still largely consistent concerning the issue of abortion. Furthermore, they are underpinned by passages in the Irish Constitution concerning the role of women (Constitution of Ireland, 1937, Article 41.2). Attitudes toward the role of women in Ireland have been shown in our studies to be part of a larger belief system in which religiosity is a central component (Fine-Davis, 1979a, 1989) and which also contains other elements reminiscent of the authoritarian personality syndrome (ibid.; Adorno *et al.*, 1950).

In spite of the fact that Ireland was a more traditional society relative to many other Western countries, the process of change from the mid 1970s was very rapid. The influence of various factors, including Ireland's economic development, the women's movement – both internationally and in Ireland itself – and the impact of the European Community from 1973 onwards acted as catalysts to stimulate attitude change. In the decade of the 1970s several key administrative and legislative changes were enacted which had sweeping effects on the role and status of women. The first of these was the removal of the marriage bar (1973) – which had prevented married women from being employed in the public service. Legislation concerning equal pay and equal employment were direct results of EU membership, as they followed EU directives. Ireland's membership of the European Community from 1973 onwards meant that it had to enact legislation agreed by the EU, including equal pay legislation, which was passed in 1974 and implemented in 1975. This led to an increase in women's earnings. Women's average hourly earnings in manufacturing were just 58% of men's in 1967, but rose to 68% by 1987 (Callender and Meenan, 1994). By 1998 women's average hourly earnings had increased to 73% (Hannon and Sinclair, 1999; Ruane and Sutherland, 1999) and by 2005 were 86% of men's (CSO, 2007). Thus, the effects of the equal pay legislation of 1975, while not immediate, have been incremental, resulting in major change since its enactment.

Equal pay legislation was followed swiftly by legislation in 1977 in the area of employment equality. This made it unlawful to discriminate on the basis of gender or marital status and also provided for the establishment of the Employment Equality Agency, whose mandate it was to make sure that the equality legislation was enforced. In addition it also set a standard for equality and raised awareness about equality issues in the society. In contrast to social legislation in the area of interpersonal and sexual behaviour and morality (e.g. contraception, divorce and abortion), social legislation in the equality area has been very progressive and led to significant improvements in women's status in the workplace (Callender and Meenan, 1994). In 1998 Ireland passed the Employment Equality Act which further extended the legislation concerning gender equality to nine grounds, including gender, marital status, family status, sexual orientation, religion, age, disability, race and membership of the Traveller community; the Equal Status Acts 2000 to 2004 extended the legislation beyond the workplace and also provided for positive action to promote equality of opportunity. As a result of this legislation Ireland is seen as being in the forefront of equality legislation.

The fight to legalise contraception began in the early 1970s and the first success towards its legalisation came in 1973 with the McGee case, which provided for the importation of contraceptives for personal use. In terms of legislation in the Dáil, the first act to legalise contraception came in 1979, although this law had restrictions and was not liberalised until 1985 and then again in 1992.

Taxation of married women was also a key issue during this period. The income of married women had been aggregated with that of their husbands and taxed at his highest marginal rate. This could be as high as 70% in the higher income brackets, and with a surcharge of 10% could lead to a taxation rate of 77%. Clearly this was a deterrent to married women working. A case was brought to the High Court by a married couple, both teachers, with the support of the Married Persons Tax Reform Association. One of the barristers for this case was Yvonne Scannell, Professor of Law at Trinity College. She has documented the story of this case in Scannell (2000). The 1975 data from the present study showing that the current tax laws were a deterrent to married women working were part of the evidence presented by her in the High Court. The State lost the case but appealed the decision in the Supreme Court. However, it lost again and legislation was subsequently passed in 1980 changing the tax law so that employed married women were no longer discriminated against by the tax code. Further significant changes followed, including the legalisation of divorce (1996), following two national referenda in 1986 and 1995, the latter successful by a very small margin (Adshead, 1996; O'Connor, 1998).

All of these developments had a profound effect on the position of women in Ireland and in many cases removed concrete barriers to their equal participation in the society. This led to an influx of married women into the labour force from the 1970s onwards (Callan and Farrell, 1991) and the retention of women in the labour force upon marriage. While married women's labour force was negligible in the early 1960s (5.2%) and early 1970s (7.5%), by 1977 the latter figure had doubled and in the two decades from 1989 to 2009, a period of economic growth, it increased from 23.7% to 54%, with employment among married women in the childbearing age group much higher at 72.6% (CSO, 2009a).

6.3 A time series analysis of attitudes in Ireland 1975–2005

In this chapter we examine how attitudes concerning the role of women and social issues central to gender roles and women's lives changed over the 30-year period from 1975 to 2005 – a period of major social change in the society. Results of four separate surveys are presented, with comparable measures of attitudes to gender roles and related social issues, conducted at four points in time: 1975, 1978, 1986 and 2005. The chapter thus presents a time series analysis of how attitudes have evolved over the last 30 years and shows how attitude change has been linked to social change and the evolution of public policy during this period. In the course of this presentation we will also address some of the following issues:

1   To what extent did attitudes to gender roles change over the 30-year period from 1975 to 2005 and was this change of equal or different magnitude during the early period (the mid 1970s to the mid 1980s) and the later period (the mid 1980s to 2005)? We ask this question since the early period was one of particular importance given that so much key legislation had been passed with import for women's status. We are also interested in this question from a cross-cultural point of view, since other investigators in other countries have noted that the earlier period was one of greater change.

2   How were attitudes related to legislative change? Did attitudes to equal pay, equal opportunity, contraception and taxation of married women become less liberal, more liberal or stay the same following legislation in these areas? Did more liberal attitudes come before legislative change or after it?

3   Do we see differences between various groups in the population? Did certain sub-groups in the population change at different rates? What did this mean?

The variables in the four datasets include measures of gender role attitudes and stereotypes as well as attitudes to several of the major social policy issues of the day: maternal employment, equal pay, equal opportunity, taxation of married women, and contraception. These issues resulted in developments in public policy over this period, including in many cases to legislation. The availability of comparable attitudinal data at several points in time over this key period of social change enables us see to what extent attitudes may have stimulated legislation and public policy and to what extent changes in legislation and public policy may have in turn facilitated further attitude change. The passage of legislation concerning equal pay (implemented in 1975), employment equality (1977), contraception (1979) and taxation of married women (1980) after collection of baseline data in 1975 offers a unique natural experiment which makes it possible to examine attitudes towards these issues both before the legislation and at two points afterwards. While we cannot definitively attribute causation here, we can assume that public attitudes contributed to a readiness to enact legislation and changes in legislation and related public policies were likely in turn to have facilitated further attitude change.

The four datasets have several methodological advantages over much previous empirical research. First, the measures were based, in part, on earlier, more comprehensive measures developed in the US (Kirkpatrick, 1936; Levinson and Huffman, 1955; Spence and Helmreich, 1972) as well as on issues specifically relevant to the Irish context. These new measures were developed using factor analysis (Fine-Davis,1983a), yielding composite scores which are more robust and reliable than individual items. Finally, the set of measures tap a wider range of attitudes and issues than many previous studies in the area of gender role attitudes do. However, because the main set of items replicates the original items from 1975, it only includes policy issues which were salient in 1975, as well as global attitudes to women and gender roles. The advantage of having a differentiated set of items from the early period is that it provides a baseline against which to measure the effects of key legislation relating to gender equality which was passed in the period 1975–1980 in the immediate aftermath and also allows for the measurement of change over time.

6.4 Method

The methodology used in the various studies has been presented more fully in Chapter 2. We summarise the key features of the methodology of each of the studies below and also outline the nature of the comparisons between the various datasets.

6.4.1 Development of measures

Preliminary work on the first of the studies included an in-depth pilot study and instrument pre-test (Fine-Davis, 1976, 1983a). The pre-test data were factor analysed to examine the dimensionality of the attitudes as well as for purposes of data reduction. Factor analysis was also carried out in the main 1975 study (ibid.) and in subsequent studies. Most of the factors were found to be quite robust and have been replicated over time (e.g. Fine-Davis, 1989; Fine-Davis *et al.*, 2005). The original set of eight factors obtained in the 1975 study was presented in Chapter 3. The 33 original items were included in both the 1975 and 1986 studies. Twelve items of this group were included in the 1978 survey and 14 in the 2005 survey.

6.4.2 Datasets

6.4.2.1 1975 data set

The earliest data set was collected in 1975 in the context of a study of attitudes toward the role and status of women (Fine-Davis, 1976, 1979a, 1979b, 1983a). This was based on a stratified sample of 420 Dublin adults, aged 18–65. Names and addresses from high and low SES neighbourhoods, randomly selected from the Dublin Electoral Register, were used as starting points, in order to optimise randomness. The sample was stratified on the basis of sex, age, socio-economic status and marital status. It included an oversampling of married women who were further stratified by employment status and presence or absence of dependent children.

6.4.2.2 1978 data set

The key items and factors from the original 1975 study were replicated in a larger nationwide study (N=1,862) carried out in 1978 (Fine-Davis,

1983b). The sample was selected using a computer-based system which employs the Electoral Register as the sampling frame and also relies on supplementary information about the population in order to improve the efficiency of the estimates derived from the sample (Whelan, 1977, 1979).

6.4.2.3 1986 Data set

The original 1975 study was replicated and extended in 1986 (Fine-Davis, 1988a, 1988b, 1988c). We shall focus here on the items which were replicated (Fine-Davis, 1988a). The sample included 600 respondents, 300 from Dublin and 300 from rural areas. The sampling procedures replicated those of the 1975 Dublin study and a rural sample was added. When percentage results for the total sample (N=600) are presented they have been re-weighted so as to reflect the precise proportions of the groups as they existed in the population.

6.4.2.4 2005 data set

The data from 2005 are from a nationwide representative survey of the adult Irish population (N=1,212) (Fine-Davis *et al.*, 2005). This study replicated the key gender role items from the 1975, 1978 and 1986 studies.

6.5 Comparisons of datasets

6.5.1 Dublin sample: 1975–1986

The first set of comparisons is for Dublin only. It includes the 1975 data for Dublin (N=420) and the 1986 data for Dublin only (N=300). These samples are comparable and while they are based on stratified sampling, they include the most complete sets of variables, covering the full gamut of social policy issues relevant to gender equality at the time as well as measures of traditional vs non-traditional gender roles, perception of females as inferior and perceptions of limitations in the housewife role. They provide a comparison over an 11-year period at the first stage of social change.

6.5.2 Nationwide samples: 1978, 1986 and 2005

The second set of comparisons is for the country as a whole. It includes the datasets from 1978, 1986 and 2005. The 1978 (N=1,862) and 2005 (N=1,212) datasets are based on representative nationwide samples selected using probability sampling. The 1986 data for Dublin and rural Ireland (N=600) were re-weighted to reflect the proportions of the groups studied in the country as a whole. While the 1986 sample is not strictly comparable to the 1978 and 2005 datasets, it is a national sample which provides a third comparison point between 1978 and 2005. The advantage of the comparison between these three datasets is that it is of the country as a whole, and in the case of the 1978 and 2005 surveys, the comparison is of representative nationwide samples. However, the sets of variables are more limited in the case of the 1978 and 2005 datasets. Data from these three points in time allow for an examination of attitude change over a 27-year period in two phases – the earlier phase (1978–1986) and the later phase (1986–2005).

6.6 Changing attitudes: Dublin 1975–1986

Table 6.1 presents comparisons between the 1975 and 1986 samples from Dublin on the eight factors measuring attitudes toward the role and status of women. Percentages for each item on each of the eight factors are compared and the amount of shift over time is also presented.

All of the six items in the first factor, *Traditional Sex Role Orientation*, showed sizeable shifts from 1975 to 1986 in the egalitarian direction. The item showing the greatest shift was "Being a wife and mother are the most fulfilling roles any woman could want"; 70% of the sample agreed in 1975, while only 39% did so in 1986 – a shift of 31%. Another large shift concerned a husband's right to expect his wife to be "obliging and dutiful at all times". While this item appears out of date today, quite a high proportion (52%) agreed with it in 1975; the level of agreement fell to 25% by 1986. Consistent with this, close to half of the 1975 sample felt that "... by and large the husband ought to have the main say in family matters". This fell to less than one-quarter in 1986. It was widely believed in 1975 that if equal job opportunities were opened to women, this would take away jobs from men who needed them more. This belief also changed radically over the decade, from 51% agreement in 1975 to 28% in 1986.

Attitudes to Contraception also changed over this period, though not nearly as much as some of the other attitudes. In 1975 68.5% of the Dublin sample believed that "the sale of contraceptives should be legalised in Ireland". By 1986 75.6% said that "I think the legalisation of the sale of contraceptives in Ireland was a good idea". The item showing the greatest shift on this factor concerned birth control as a basic human right. A large majority (71%) had endorsed this in 1975, which reflected a readiness on the part of the population for contraception to be available. By 1986 this level of support had increased substantially to 84%. These shifts undoubtedly reflected the legalisation of the sale of contraception in 1979 as well as the extensive discussion of this issue in the media.

It is interesting to contrast these levels of support in Dublin samples with data from a nationwide representative survey carried out in 1977 (Davis and Fine-Davis, 1979). In this case just 55.4% agreed that "the sale of contraceptives should be legalised in Ireland". This study found significantly greater support for contraception among urban dwellers than among rurals ($F=26.42$; $p<0.001$; mean for rurals 4.06; mean for urbans 4.73).

Table 6.1 Responses to items measuring attitudes toward the role and status of women, grouped by factor: percentage distributions for Dublin samples 1975–1986 (total N=720)

		Disagree			DK etc.	Agree			% Shift 1975–1986
		Strong	Moderate	Slight		Slight	Moderate	Strong	
Factor 1: Traditional Sex Role Orientation									
1. Some equality in marriage is a good thing, but by and large the husband ought to have the main say in family[1] matters.	1975 (N=420)[1]	25.0	13.5	12.0	3.2	9.7	14.7	22.0	
			(50.5%)				**(46.4%)**		
	1986 (N=300)[1]	42.3	20.7	12.0	0.3	7.0	9.7	8.0	**21.7**
			(75.0%)				**(24.7%)**		
2. A husband has the right to expect that his wife will be obliging and dutiful at all times.	1975	21.0	12.7	10.0	4.0	12.7	18.2	21.5	
			(43.7%)				**(52.4%)**		
	1986	48.5	16.1	10.0	0.3	11.4	5.4	8.4	**27.2**
			(74.6%)				**(25.2%)**		
3. Being a wife and mother are the most fulfilling roles any woman could want.	1975	7.7	11.8	7.0	3.5	10.2	19.7	40.2	
			(26.5%)				**(70.1%)**		
	1986	22.3	19.0	18.3	1.3	12.3	14.7	12.0	**31.1**
			(59.6%)				**(39.0%)**		
4. If equal job opportunities are opened to women, this will just take away jobs from men who need them more.	1975	20.0	17.2	10.3	0.8	20.3	16.5	14.5	
			(47.5%)				**(51.3%)**		
	1986	34.8	20.1	17.1	0.3	17.4	5.4	5.0	23.5
			(72.0%)				**(27.8%)**		
5. The political and business leadership of a community should be largely in the hands of men.	1975	33.2	21.7	9.7	1.2	8.7	10.2	15.5	
			(64.6%)				**(34.4%)**		
	1986	47.0	19.8	11.7	–	6.7	9.4	5.4	12.9
			(78.5%)				**(21.5%)**		

Note:

The percentages in bold indicate summary agree and disagree responses.

1 There were 420 respondents in the 1975 sample, all of whom were from Dublin, and 300 respondents from Dublin in the 1986 sample. The composition of the samples was identical except that in 1975 there were 240 married women, whereas in 1986 there were 120. To correct for this, the responses of the married women in the 1975 sample were weighted by 0.5. The data presented in this table for the two time periods is thus completely comparable.

continued

Table 6.1 Continued

		Disagree			DK etc.	Agree			% Shift 1975–1986
		Strong	Moderate	Slight		Slight	Moderate	Strong	
6. Most women need and want the kind of protection and support that men have traditionally given them.	1975	7.0	4.5 **(18.0%)**	6.5	0.5	10.3	32.8 **(81.4%)**	38.3	18.2
	1986	16.7	11.4 **(36.8%)**	8.7	–	15.1	27.4 **(63.2%)**	20.7	
Factor II: Positive Attitude to Contraception									
1. a) The sale of contraceptives should be legalised in Ireland.	1975	17.0	5.2 **(29.2%)**	7.0	2.3	8.0	12.7 **(68.5%)**	47.8	
b) I think the legalisation of the sale of contraceptives in Ireland was a good idea.	1986	13.0	5.0 **(23.7%)**	5.7	0.7	10.7	19.1 **(75.6%)**	45.8	**7.1**
2. It is a basic human right to be able to control whether or not one has a child through the use of contraceptives.	1975	15.3	5.5 **(24.0%)**	3.2	5.0	8.2	16.5 **(71.0%)**	46.3	**13.0**
	1986	8.7	3.7 **(16.1%)**	3.7	–	5.7	16.4 **(84.0%)**	61.9	
3. It is perfectly healthy and natural for couples to have sexual intercourse, even if they don't want to conceive a child.	1975	5.7	0.8 **(7.5%)**	1.0	6.0	9.5	17.7 **(86.5%)**	59.3	**4.9**
	1986	4.3	1.7 **(8.3%)**	2.3	0.3	3.7	14.0 **(91.4%)**	73.7	
4. There would probably be more communication and understanding later on if boys and girls got to know each other earlier by going to the same schools.	1975	4.5	2.8 **(13.3%)**	6.0	–	9.0	17.8 **(86.6%)**	59.8	**0.0**
	1986	4.3	5.0 **(13.3%)**	4.0	–	13.4	24.4 **(86.6%)**	48.8	
Factor III: Belief in Equal Opportunity									
1. People should be employed and promoted strictly on the basis of ability, regardless of sex.	1975	3.3	2.3 **(6.3%)**	0.7	–	6.0	18.7 **(93.7%)**	69.0	**3.3**
	1986	1.0	0.7 **(3.0%)**	1.3	–	4.7	16.0 **(97.0%)**	76.3	
2. The daughters in a family should have the same privileges and opportunities as the sons.	1975	1.3	2.0 **(4.8%)**	1.5	–	4.2	16.3 **(95.2%)**	74.7	**2.7**
	1986	1.0	0.3	0.7	–	1.3	11.3	85.3	

Factor IV: Positive Attitude to Maternal Employment

1. A woman who has a job she enjoys is likely to be a better wife and mother because she has an interest and some fulfilment outside the home.	1975	6.8	8.3 **(22.4%)**	7.3	1.0	13.5	26.5 **(76.5%)**	36.5	
	1986	5.7	6.4 **(24.9%)**	12.8	1.0	20.2	23.9 **(74.1%)**	30.0	**-2.4**
2. Women with children should not work outside the home if they don't need the money.	1975	15.3	16.7 **(45.0%)**	13.0	0.3	9.5	13.8 **(54.6%)**	31.3	
	1986	22.5	12.4 **(50.7%)**	15.8	0.7	13.8	14.1 **(48.7%)**	20.8	**5.9**
3. It is bad for young children if their mothers go out and work, even if they are well taken care of by another adult.	1975	10.7	13.7 **(31.2%)**	6.8	0.5	11.0	17.2 **(68.4%)**	40.2	
	1986	24.0	14.7 **(53.7%)**	15.0	0.7	11.3	19.7 **(45.7%)**	14.7	**22.7**
4. Women should be more concerned with house-keeping and bringing up their children than with desires for careers.	1975	15.8	15.2 **(40.2%)**	9.2	1.3	14.2	19.8 **(58.5%)**	24.5	
	1986	26.6	18.2 **(61.3%)**	16.5	1.0	16.5	11.8 **(37.7%)**	9.4	**20.8**
5. When there is high unemployment, married women should be discouraged from working.	1975	13.5	11.2 **(33.7%)**	9.0	1.3	18.8	19.2 **(65.0%)**	27.0	
	1986	13.1	13.8 **(48.7%)**	21.8	0.3	11.1	14.8 **(51.1%)**	25.2	**13.9**

Note

The percentages in bold indicate summary agree and disagree responses.

1 The word "immediately" appeared in 1975, but not in 1986 since the equal pay legislation had not been implemented until a few months after the 1975 survey, but was in effect in 1986.

continued

Table 6.1 Continued

		Disagree			DK etc.	Agree			% Shift 1975–1986
		Strong	Moderate	Slight		Slight	Moderate	Strong	
Factor V: Belief in Equal Pay									
1. Even if it means financial difficulties for some companies, equal pay for equal work should be given (immediately).[1]	1975	7.7	8.7 (24.6%)	8.2	1.5	10.2	20.0 (74.0%)	43.8	
	1986	2.3	2.7 (7.0%)	2.0	–	8.3	14.7 (93.0%)	70.0	**19.0**
2. A married man should be paid more than a woman for performing the same job.	1975	39.5	12.3 (57.6%)	5.8	1.0	8.5	14.7 (41.4%)	18.2	
	1986	57.7	14.7 (81.4%)	9.0	–	6.3	5.3 (18.6%)	7.0	**22.8**
3. It is only fair that male workers should receive more pay than women even for identical work.	1975	47.3	18.7 (70.3%)	4.3	0.7	5.8	9.2 (29.0%)	14.0	
	1986	65.3	11.3 (88.6%)	12.0	–	3.0	3.7 (11.4%)	4.7	**17.6**
Factor VI: Belief in Higher Tax for Married Women									
1. It is only fair that a married couple (both working) pay more tax than two single people.	1975	36.3	21.2 (62.8%)	5.3	1.2	9.3	13.2 (36.0%)	13.5	
	1986	46.3	9.7 (70.3%)	14.3	1.3	14.3	5.3 (28.3%)	8.7	**7.7**
2. Married women should be taxed more than single women.	1975	46.7	20.0 (73.4%)	6.7	0.8	6.7	10.2 (25.9%)	9.0	
	1986	53.5	15.1 (77.6%)	9.0	0.3	10.4	5.4 (22.2%)	6.4	**3.7**
Factor VII: Perception of Females as Inferior									
Generally speaking, women think less clearly than men.	1975	48.2	21.3 (77.5%)	8.0	–	7.5	8.7 (22.5%)	6.3	
	1986	52.8	23.4 (85.9%)	9.7	0.3	6.7	3.3 (13.7%)	3.7	**8.8**

2. Women are, by nature, too highly strung to hold certain jobs.	1975	31.8	19.0 (58.1%)	7.3	1.0	15.0	14.2 (40.9%)	11.7		
	1986	41.7	19.7 (72.4%)	11.0	–	11.0	9.7 (27.7%)	7.0	13.2
3. Female workers, even if qualified and experienced, are in some ways, less reliable, less committed and less serious than men.	1975	39.8	17.7 (65.5%)	8.0	0.3	12.0	14.5 (34.2%)	7.7	
	1986	52.0	20.7 (80.4%)	7.7	0.3	11.0	4.0 (19.3%)	4.3	14.9

Factor VIII: Perception of Limitations in Housewife Role

1. Housework is basically dull and boring.	1975	14.8	17.8 (44.4%)	11.8	0.7	11.8	18.7 (54.8%)	24.3		
	1986	8.3	12.7 (32.0%)	11.0	0.3	18.0	18.0 (67.7%)	31.7	12.9
2. Being at home with children all day can very often be boring for a woman.	1975	7.8	7.3 (20.6%)	5.5	1.2	17.3	28.7 (78.2%)	32.2	
	1986	7.0	8.7 (22.1%)	6.4	1.7	25.5	22.8 (76.2%)	27.9	–2.0

Belief in Equal Opportunity was widespread in 1975, with 94–95% endorsing the items on this factor. There was little room for shift, yet some did take place in the direction of greater support. While the overall shifts were only about 3%, within the agreement side of the continuum 7–10% shifted from moderate to strong support for equal opportunity. The high levels of support at both points in time suggest that the measure was largely tapping a social desirability response set, since other items tapped more resistance to equal opportunity.

The issue of *Maternal Employment* was controversial in 1975 and remained so in 1986. In spite of this there were large shifts in attitude in a more accepting direction. In 1975 68.4% believed that it was bad for young children if their mothers went out to work, even if well taken care of by another adult. By 1986 the level of agreement had fallen to 45.7%. There was a strong belief in 1975 that "in times of high unemployment, married women should be discouraged from working" (65% agreement). While approximately half of the sample still held this view in 1986, the level of support had fallen by close to 14%, in spite of the fact that the level of unemployment was even higher than in 1975.

Attitudes to Equal Pay also showed major change over this period. Although a majority favoured equal pay in 1975, this increased by 1986. In 1975 41.4% believed that "a married man should be paid more than a woman for performing the same job". This fell to just 18.6% in 1986. Three-quarters of the 1975 sample believed that "even if it means financial difficulties for some companies, equal pay should be given immediately". This increased by 19% to 93% by 1986, a decade after the implementation of the Anti-Discrimination (Pay) Act. These shifts illustrate how attitudes changed to become consistent with new norms of social behaviour behaviour. As cognitive dissonance theory (Festinger, 1957) would predict, if the individual holds attitudes which are inconsistent with prevailing norms and practices, this will produce cognitive dissonance and such dissonance is uncomfortable for the individual. If attitudes are out of sync with new policies and procedures, they generally change to be congruent with the new situation. As Deutsch and Collins (1958) pointed out many years ago, in the context of research on race relations in the US: "The implication of our study is that official policy executed without equivocation, can result in large changes in behaviour and attitudes despite initial resistance to that policy" (p. 622). The case of the equal pay legislation is a clear example of how legislation can affect attitudes. Other examples in the data also reflect this effect: support for higher taxation of married women was stronger in 1975 prior to the 1980 High Court case (Murphy vs the Attorney General), the decision of which was upheld in the 1980 Supreme Court decision (see Scannell, 2000). In 1986, some six years later, there was less support for this policy since it was no longer the de facto situation, although it should be pointed out that even in 1975 a majority was opposed to the then current tax policy, which no doubt helped to set the stage for the High Court case itself. These findings suggest that social attitudes can pave the way for changes in legislation and legislation can in turn further affect attitudes and behaviour.

Because of the centrality of the *Perception of Female Inferiority* to traditional gender role ideology, several items were included in the original study and replicated in 1986. They were found to form an identifiable cluster which was correlated with traditional gender role attitudes and opposition to social policies related to equality (Fine-Davis, 1983a). All three items on this factor showed shifts from 1975 to 1986 in the direction of a decreasing likelihood of perceiving women as inferior. While in no case did a majority agree with any of the statements even in 1975, the percentages agreeing were far from negligible. It could be argued that the only unequivocally egalitarian response would be "strongly disagree". It may be seen from the responses that attitudes which a respondent may find socially unacceptable to express too strongly, are expressed in a milder, yet still explicit, way. In 1975 22.5% endorsed the statement: "Generally speaking, women think less clearly than men". This level of agreement fell to 13.7% in 1986. However, only 52.8% strongly disagreed with the statement; 47.2% still harboured a residue of this stereotype even in 1986. The other items in this factor also reflect this pattern. In 1975 40.9% believed that "women are too highly strung to hold certain jobs". The percentage endorsing this fell to 27.7% in 1986. However, only 41.7% strongly rejected the statement while 58.3% did not.

Factor VIII measured *Perception of Limitations in the Housewife Role*. In 1975 over half of the sample (54.8%) endorsed the view that "housework is basically dull and boring". This rose to 67.7% in 1986. By 1986 over two-thirds of the sample perceived limitations in the housewife role – a further indication that people's attitudes concerning what constituted appropriate gender roles were shifting. As women's role in the labour force was increasing, the housewife role was becoming less valued.

6.7 Attitude shifts among groups: Dublin 1975–1986

While there were significant shifts across the board in the attitudes of Dubliners during the period 1975–1986, there were also significant differences between groups. We compared the attitudes of five groups (employed and non-employed married women, employed single women, and employed single and married men) at two points in time on composite scores for the eight attitudinal factors referred to above (Table 6.2). The comparison of these five key groups enables us to examine 1) the effect of gender, while holding employment status constant; 2) the effect of employment status on married women's attitudes; 3) the effect of women's marital status on their attitudes, while holding their employment status constant; and 4) the effect of men's marital status on their attitudes, while holding their employment status constant.

Table 6.2 Measures of attitude change, 1975–1986: mean scores on eight factors measuring attitudes toward the role and status of women for five sub-groups of Dublin adults (N=720)

Factor I: Traditional Sex Role Orientation

	1975 (N=420) Mean	1986 (N=300) Mean	t-value
Employed Married Women (1975 n=120; 1986 n=60)	4.01	2.88	5.88***
Non-Empl. Married Women (1975 n=120; 1986 n=60)	4.45	2.97	7.72***
Single Women (1975 n=120; 1986 n=60)	3.96	2.87	4.12***
Married Men (1975 n=60; 1986 n=60)	4.5	3.42	4.33***
Single Men (1975 n=60; 1986 n=60)	4.69	3.42	5.25***

Factor V: Belief in Equal Pay

	1975 Mean	1986 Mean	t-value
Employed Married Women	5.41	6.38	-4.99***
Non-Empl. Married Women	4.93	5.98	-4.33***
Single Women	5.44	6.17	-2.89**
Married Men	4.89	6.15	-4.49***
Single Men	4.45	5.53	-3.75***

Factor II: Positive Attitude to Contraception

	1975 Mean	1986 Mean	t-value
Employed Married Women	5.61	6.07	-2.08*
Non-Empl. Married Women	5.35	6.1	-3.34***
Single Women	4.88	5.43	-1.63
Married Men	5.73	5.86	-0.49
Single Men	5.62	5.77	-0.51

Factor VI: Belief in Higher Tax for Married Women

	1975 Mean	1986 Mean	t-value
Employed Married Women	2.17	2.27	-0.37
Non-Empl. Married Women	2.86	2.43	1.55
Single Women	3.63	2.82	2.45*
Married Men	2.83	2.63	0.58
Single Men	3.17	2.83	0.95

Factor III: Belief in Equal Opportunity

	1975 Mean	1986 Mean	t-value
Employed Married Women	6.52	6.8	-2.73**
Non-Empl. Married Women	6.54	6.85	-3.34***
Single Women	6.58	6.62	-0.21
Married Men	6.15	6.58	-2.09*
Single Men	6.37	6.53	-1.00

Factor IV: Positive Attitude to Maternal Employment

	1975 Mean	1986 Mean	t-value
Employed Married Women	4.71	5.15	-1.99*
Non-Empl. Married Women	3.5	4.14	-2.87**
Single Women	3.67	4.52	-3.07**
Married Men	3.77	4.19	-1.52
Single Men	3.20	3.93	-2.80**

Factor VII: Perception of Females as Inferior

	1975 Mean	1986 Mean	t-value
Employed Married Women	2.44	1.88	3.08**
Non-Empl. Married Women	2.83	2.01	4.10***
Single Women	2.63	2.38	0.83
Married Men	3.25	2.51	2.69**
Single Men	3.63	3.12	1.69

Factor VIII: Perception of Limitations in Housewife Role

	1975 Mean	1986 Mean	t-value
Employed Married Women	4.83	4.95	-0.46
Non-Empl. Married Women	4.33	5.04	-2.58*
Single Women	3.97	4.69	-2.19*
Married Men	5.6	5.17	1.57
Single Men	5.22	5.05	0.63

Potential Range of Mean Scores: 1–7
* $p < 0.05$
** $p < 0.01$
*** $p < 0.001$

Significant shifts in an egalitarian direction were observed for all five groups on the global measure, *Traditional Sex Role Orientation*. Those with the least traditional attitudes in 1975 were employed women, both married and single. In contrast, non-employed married women were almost as traditional as married men, while single men were the most traditional of all. Non-employed married women showed the greatest shift. Men also shifted, but a gender gap still remained.

Married women's attitudes to contraception (Factor II) also shifted from 1975 to 1986, with the non-employed shifting more than the employed. Both groups had been slightly to moderately positive to contraception in 1975, but became even more so. Men had been more in favour of contraception than women in 1975, which may have been related to their lesser religiosity. While their attitudes became somewhat more positive over time, the shifts did not reach significance and by 1986 their attitudes were less supportive than those of married women.

Maternal employment has been a particularly emotive issue in the Irish context, given the traditional attitudes to women's roles generally and the strong influence of the Catholic Church, coupled with periods of high unemployment and the prevalent view that men were more entitled to have a job than women. Not surprisingly, employed married women were significantly more positive to maternal employment (Factor IV) than other groups in 1975, a time when the proportion of married working was still very low. While there were moderate shifts on this factor from 1975 to 1986 for four out of the five groups, employed married women still stood out from the others, although their mean score only reflects slight agreement with the items in this factor, indicating that even they shared some of the ambivalent attitudes prevalent in the society at large.

Equal pay legislation came into effect in late 1975, a few months after data collection. The 1975 respondents would have thus been aware of equal pay, but would not yet have observed or experienced it, as would have been the case by 1986. The results show quite marked shifts for all groups in their *Belief in Equal Pay* from 1975 to 1986. Employed women were most supportive in 1975 and were also amongst the most supportive in 1986. However, married men – who were somewhat less supportive than employed women in 1975 – became essentially as supportive in 1986 as employed single women. Single men also shifted considerably, yet they had the lowest scores of all groups at both points in time.

There were no shifts on the factor measuring *Belief in Higher Taxes for Married Women*, except on the part of employed single women. This group had been the most strongly in favour of higher taxes for married women in 1975 – a phenomenon which may have reflected an underlying feeling of jealousy of women who had both a job and a husband. However, by 1986 their attitudes were more in line with those of other groups. This may well have been influenced by the 1980 High Court case concerning the constitutionality of the existing higher rate of taxation for married women (Scannell, 2000). This policy was found by the Supreme Court to be unconstitutional and the tax laws were changed. Public opinion generally had been opposed to higher taxation of married women, as evident both in the 1975 Dublin data and the 1978 nationwide data. The effect of the case therefore did not have any substantial effect on attitudes generally, except on those of employed single women which became more in line with existing legislation and the attitudes of the rest of society. Single women may have experienced cognitive dissonance, which then stimulated attitude change on their part. Theories of attitude change would posit that attitudes change to become more congruent with behaviour (Heider, 1946; Festinger, 1957; Triandis, 1971). Once single women were required to accept equality in taxation, it was likely that their attitudes would follow suit.

Factor VII, *Perception of Females as Inferior*, has been shown to be a key element underpinning inegalitarian gender role attitudes and attitudes concerning policies relevant to women (Fine-Davis, 1983a). While in no case did majorities endorse items concerning female inferiority, notable minorities did. As may be seen in Table 6.2, three out of the five groups shifted in an egalitarian direction over the period 1975–1986. Employed married women had been least likely to perceive females as inferior in 1975 and continued to be in 1986. This may have reflected greater self-esteem and sense of agency which led them to participate in the labour force in the first place at a time when it was not common to do so. Non-employed married women had been more likely than employed to perceive women as inferior in 1975, but by 1986 their scores were close to those of the employed married women, reflecting the greatest shift of any group on this measure. This shift suggests an increase in self-esteem, which may have been indirectly influenced by the effects of the women's movement and social legislation in the area of equality. Men had notably higher scores than women on this factor in 1975. However, those of married men shifted significantly by 1986. Single men, though showing a slight shift, continued to manifest attitudes which were considerably more discriminatory than those of other groups.

Attitudes towards the housewife role also reflected change over this period. In 1975 men, particularly married men, were the group most likely to perceive *Limitations in the Housewife Role* (Factor VIII). Married women were less likely to do so, with the employed somewhat more likely to than the non-employed, the latter of whom were in the role full-time themselves. Employed single women were *least* likely to perceive limitations in the housewife role, which may reflect an idealisation of marriage by the non-married, a phenomenon referred to by Bailyn (1964) as the "traditional dream". The fact that non-employed married women shifted to the level of employed married women is noteworthy and indicated a prelude to future exiting out of the full-time housewife role into the labour force. The fact that this group also manifested large shifts in attitudes on several other factors indicates that they were no longer a passive, traditional group, content with a more delimited role, but were becoming attitudinally quite similar to their employed counterparts. The social implications of this were considerable and in fact these attitudes presaged the enormous influx of married women into the labour market in the 1970s, 1980s and beyond.

6.8 Changing attitudes: nationwide samples – 1978, 1986, 2005

To what extent did attitudes continue to change following the key period of social legislation of the mid to late 1970s to early 1980s? Did they remain at levels seen in 1986 or was there continuing change? We present in Table 6.3 comparative data from three national samples spanning a 27-year period from 1978 to 2005.

Comparative data from 1978, 1986 and 2005 are available for three of the original items on the global factor, *Traditional Sex Role Orientation*. In all cases there was a sizable attitudinal shift from 1978 to 2005. While in 1978 a majority (56.3%) gave lip service to equality in marriage, they ultimately supported male dominance in the home ("Some equality in marriage is a good thing, but by and large the husband ought to have the main say in family matters"). Agreement with this item fell to 27.7% in 1986 and to 19.0% in 2005. The greatest degree of change took place in the first eight years from 1978 to 1986 (28.6%), with only a further 8.7% taking place in the following 19 years from 1986 to 2005.

In 1978 a large majority (78.1%) endorsed the view that "being a wife and mother are the most fulfilling roles any woman could want". By 1986 this fell to 54.5% agreement. However, by 2005 the level of agreement increased again to 63%. Thus, the overall shift from 1978 to 2005 was only 15.1%. This item is unique in showing a partial reversion to earlier levels, rather than a linear decrease over time, a phenomenon which has more frequently been observed in other countries (Scott, 2008; Cotter *et al.*, 2011).

The third item with three comparison points concerned participation in the public sphere: "the political and business leadership of a community should be largely in the hands of men". A total shift of 30.4% took place between 1978 and 2005. In 1978 38.9% of the sample agreed with the statement, whereas in 2005 only 8.5% did. Most of the attitude change took place from 1978 to 1986 (17.8%) and less from 1986 to 2005 (12.6%).

Three comparable items on Factor II, *Positive Attitude to Maternal Employment*, show shifts in a similar direction. Two of the items concern the effect of maternal employment on children. In 1978 more than two-thirds of the population (69.7%) believed that "It is bad for young children if their mothers go out and work, even if they are well taken care of by another adult." This state of affairs changed dramatically over the next two and a half decades. By 2005 only 37.5% agreed with the statement – a shift of approximately 32%. The shift from 1978 to 1986 was 12.4% and from 1986 to 2005, 19.8%. Thus, attitudes to maternal employment continued to undergo significant change over the three decades, with even greater change in the latter period. The strength of the attitude shift in the latter period in the area of maternal employment is corroborated by results of the ISSP surveys carried out in Ireland in 1988 and 2002 (O'Sullivan, 2012). A similar item ("A preschool child is likely to suffer if his or her mother works") elicited 51.4% agreement in 1988 and just 33.7% agreement in 2002 – a shift of 17.7%.

In spite of attitude change in this area, ambivalence toward maternal employment was still apparent. While a majority of the population (64%) in 1978 believed that "A woman who has a job she enjoys is likely to be a better wife and mother, because she has an interest and some fulfilment outside the home", a majority (69.7%) also believed that it was "bad for young children" if their mothers worked. In 2005, support for the first item increased to 86.9% – a shift of 22.9%. In contrast to the shifts observed on other factors, it is noteworthy that most of the shift took place from 1986 to 2005 (20.1%). The overall magnitude of the agree response in 2005 indicates that there was now widespread appreciation of the positive effects which employment could have for women and even an awareness that this could have positive spillover effects for her family. Attitude change in this area was also exemplified by shifts on the item, "When there is high unemployment married women should be discouraged from working." In 1978, when there was very high unemployment in Ireland, support for this view was very strong, with over two-thirds (70.6%) of the population endorsing it. In the bleak economic situation at that time there was a widespread view that men and "school leavers" had a greater right to a job than married women. It was subsequently discovered that married women and school leavers were not actually competing for the same jobs. Moreover, it was found that women's labour force participation, particularly that of married women, in fact helped to stimulate the economy and fuel the "Celtic Tiger" (Fahey and FitzGerald, 1997). By 2005, attitudes in this area had changed dramatically and only 17.7% endorsed the view that married women should be discouraged from working in times of high unemployment. There was an overall shift of 53% from 1978 to 2005, with two-thirds of the shift taking place from 1986 to 2005, indicating that attitude change concerning maternal employment had gained further momentum even after the initial changes of the 1970s. This trend showing a greater shift in attitudes to maternal employment in the later period is in contrast to trends seen in other countries (van Egmond *et al.*, 2010; Cotter *et al.*, 2011). However, as Scott (2008) points out, attitudinal shift patterns may differ depending on the issue.

Table 6.3 Percentage responses to items measuring attitudes toward the role and status of women, grouped by factor, for 1978, 1986 and 2005 (total N=3,674)

	Disagree			D.K. etc.	Agree			% Shift	
	Strong	Moderate	Slight		Slight	Moderate	Strong	1978–1986 / 1986–2005	1978–2005

Factor 1: Traditional Sex Role Orientation

1. Some equality in marriage is a good thing, but by and large the husband ought to have the main say in family matters.

1978 (N=1,862)	19.3	13.2 **(43.1%)**	10.6	0.6	16.5	19.6 **(56.3%)**	20.2	28.6%	36.2%
1986 (N=600)	39.7	19.0 **(71.9%)**	13.2	0.2	10.3	7.9 **(27.7%)**	9.5	7.6%	
2005 (N=1,212)	50.6	17.2 **(78.2%)**	10.4	1.7	9.1	5.2 **(20.1%)**	5.8		

2. A husband has the right to expect that his wife will be obliging and dutiful at all times.

1986	43.0	17.9 **(73.2%)**	12.3	0.7	12.5	3.9 **(26.2%)**	9.8	8.3%	
2005	58.5	12.9 **(79.9%)**	8.5	2.3	9.0	4.3 **(17.9%)**	4.6		

3. Being a wife and mother are the most fulfilling roles any woman could want.

1978	4.9	7.1 **(20.8%)**	8.8	1.0	15.6	23.3 **(78.1%)**	39.2	23.6%	12.1%
1986	13.1	14.5 **(44.6%)**	17.0	0.8	18.0	17.9 **(54.5%)**	18.6	11.5%	
2005	10.8	10.3 **(32.5%)**	11.4	1.4	19.3	19.9 **(66.0%)**	26.8		

4. If equal job opportunities are opened to women, this will just take away jobs from men who need them more.

1986	33.2	18.7 **(71.6%)**	19.7	0.1	18.9	6.1 **(28.2%)**	3.2	15.3%	
2005	51.8	22.8 **(86.9%)**	12.3	0.3	6.4	3.7 **(12.9%)**	2.8		

5. The political and business leadership of a community should be largely in the hands of men.	1978	26.6	–	20.1	(60.7%)	14.0	0.5	12.4	–	13.1	(38.9%)	13.4	17.8%
	1986	40.7	–	16.3	(78.4%)	21.4	0.4	9.6	–	7.3	(21.1%)	4.2	11.8%	29.6%
	2005	62.1	–	18.0	(90.1%)	10.0	0.5	5.0	–	2.3	(9.3%)	2.0	
6. Most women need and want the kind of protection and support that men have traditionally given them.	1986	10.1	–	8.9	(24.4%)	5.4	0.2	20.6	–	32.7	(75.4%)	22.1	8.2%
	2005	11.7	–	10.2	(31.7%)	9.8	0.9	19.9	–	21.6	(67.2%)	25.7	

Factor II: Positive Attitude to Maternal Employment

1. A woman who has a job she enjoys is likely to be a better wife and mother, because she has an interest and some fulfillment outside the home.	1978	9.0	–	12.3	(34.3%)	13.0	1.6	21.6	–	21.0	(64.0%)	21.4	2.8%
	1986	6.7	–	5.9	(31.2%)	18.6	2.1	23.4	–	19.0	(66.8%)	24.4	22.4%
	2005	3.5	–	3.1	(12.5%)	5.9	1.2	16.5	–	28.8	(86.4%)	41.1	19.6%
2. Women with children should not work outside the home if they don't need the money.	1986	17.6	–	9.1	(41.0%)	14.3	**0.7**	22.0	–	13.8	(58.2%)	22.4	26.8%
	2005	34.7	–	21.1	(67.9%)	12.1	**0.7**	11.7	–	7.5	(31.4%)	12.2	
3. It is bad for young children if their mothers go out and work, even if they are well taken care of by another adult.	1978	10.3	–	11.4	(29.8%)	8.1	0.6	13.3	–	20.7	(69.7%)	35.7	12.4%
	1986	13.3	–	14.4	(41.9%)	14.2	0.9	20.5	–	18.2	(57.3%)	18.6	30.6%
	2005	28.0	–	18.4	(60.3%)	13.9	0.7	18.6	–	9.4	(39.1%)	11.1	18.2%

continued

Table 6.3 Continued

		Disagree			D.K. etc.	Agree			% Shift	
		Strong	Moderate	Slight		Slight	Moderate	Strong	1978–1986 1986–2005	1978–2005
4. Women should be more concerned with housekeeping and bringing up their children than with desires for careers.	1986	21.1 –	17.4 (58.1%)	19.6 –	0.5	20.0 –	12.0 (41.3%)	9.3 –	} 22.8%	
	2005	52.5 –	18.0 (80.6%)	10.1 –	0.9	9.6 –	4.2 (18.5%)	4.7 –		
5. When there is high unemployment married women should be discouraged from working.	1978	10.7 –	9.6 (29.0%)	8.7 –	0.4	18.7 –	20.8 (70.6%)	31.1 –	} 15.3%	} 53.0%
	1986	19.3 –	11.6 (44.4%)	13.5 –	0.2	28.2 –	12.5 (55.3%)	14.6 –	} 37.7%	
	2005	47.7 –	22.3 (82.2%)	12.2 –	0.3	9.3 –	4.5 (17.6%)	3.8 –		
Factor III: Belief in higher tax for married women										
1. It is only fair that a married couple (both working) pay more tax than two single people.	1978	31.4 –	18.0 (61.0%)	11.6 –	1.4	13.0 –	11.3 (37.7%)	13.4 –	} 8.0%	
	1986	39.6 –	13.1 (69.7%)	17.0 –	0.7	14.6 –	8.1 (29.7%)	7.0 –		
2. Married women should be taxed more than single women.	1978	40.6 –	20.6 (72.4%)	11.2 –	1.0	10.4 –	8.1 (26.6%)	8.1 –	} 1.8%	
	1986	45.8 –	12.7 (74.1%)	15.6 –	1.1	14.0 –	4.8 (24.8%)	6.0 –		

Factor IV: Perception of Females as Inferior

Statement	Year								{ %	{ %
1. Generally speaking women think less clearly than men.	1978	36.6 / –	22.0 (**73.5%**)	14.9 / –	0.8	12.9 / –	7.8 (**25.7%**)	5.0 / –	14.8%	16.7%
	1986	54.3 / –	19.6 (**88.3%**)	14.4 / –	0.7	5.8 / –	2.7 (**10.9%**)	2.4 / –	1.9%	
	2005	64.6 / –	16.2 (**90.7%**)	9.9 / –	0.4	4.4 / –	2.2 (**9.0%**)	2.4 / –		
2. Women are, by nature, too highly strung to hold certain jobs.	1978	24.8 / –	19.2 (**56.9%**)	12.9 / –	0.8	19.8 / –	13.8 (**42.4%**)	8.8 / –	17.5%	26.3%
	1986	42.6 / –	18.7 (**74.9%**)	13.6 / –	0.2	14.8 / –	4.8 (**24.9%**)	5.3 / –	8.8%	
	2005	58.0 / –	14.9 (**83.0%**)	10.1 / –	0.8	8.7 / –	3.7 (**16.1%**)	3.7 / –		
3. Female workers, even if qualified and experienced, are in some ways less reliable, less committed and less serious than men.	1978	36.2 / –	21.9 (**71.8%**)	13.6 / –	0.6	12.8 / –	9.9 (**27.6%**)	4.9 / –	13.2%	15.5%
	1986	50.0 / –	21.0 (**85.0%**)	14.0 / –	0.5	7.1 / –	4.9 (**14.4%**)	2.4 / –	2.3%	
	2005	59.6 / –	18.9 (**87.5%**)	9.0 / –	0.5	5.0 / –	4.0 (**12.1%**)	3.1 / –		

Note

1986 – refers to the 1986 sample re-weighted so that each group in the sample was given the weight which it has in the actual population.

The factor *Perception of Females as Inferior* emerged in the original 1975 study and was found to be a distinct dimension, although in some subsequent factor analyses it merged with Factor I, *Traditional Sex Role Orientation*, indicating its close connection to traditional sex role ideology (Davis *et al.*, 1977; Fine-Davis, 1989; Fine-Davis *et al.*, 2005). At no time did a majority endorse these items, though notable percentages did and furthermore only small percentages rejected them utterly with the response of "strongly disagree", a phenomenon which we observed in the Dublin data. Thus it may be assumed that a significant proportion of the population harboured such attitudes to one degree or another. The item "generally speaking women think less clearly than men" elicited 25.7% agreement in 1978. The item "women are, by nature, too highly strung to hold certain jobs" elicited even more agreement – 42.4%. The item "female workers, even if qualified and experienced, are in some ways less reliable, less committed and less serious than men" elicited 27.6% agreement. To what extent did such attitudes persist over three decades of change? Did greater gender equality have an effect on such basic perceptions of women? An inspection of the data from 2005 shows that in all three cases *Perceptions of Female Inferiority* decreased from earlier levels. The trends on this factor reveal that the greatest amount of attitude change took place from 1978 to 1986 and less so from 1986 to 2005. The shifts on this factor are all the more notable since it is measuring stereotypes, which tend to be more resistant to change (Williams and Best, 1986).

6.9 Effects of demographic characteristics on attitudes over time

While attitudes have changed over time, the influence of demographic characteristics on attitudes has been relatively consistent. The strongest and most consistent predictor of attitudes has been gender. In the 1978 nationwide study the effect of gender on a combined factor *Traditional Sex Role Orientation with Perception of Female Inferiority* was highly significant ($F=201.42$; $p<0.001$), with males almost a full scale point higher than females (Table 6.4).

The strength of the gender difference was still apparent in the 2005 data on this combined factor ($F=98.73$; $p<0.001$), even though the male and female means decreased from their earlier levels.

Age was also a significant predictor of attitudes at both points in time. There was a linear effect of age in 1978 with conservative attitudes increasing with age ($F=19.27$; $p<0.001$). The significant age effect held in 2005, but all groups held less traditional views at this time point. It was also notable that only the oldest group (55+) held views different from the younger three age groups. An examination of the different age cohorts in the two different time periods indicates that there were strong period effects as well as strong cohort effects.

Table 6.4 Summary of analysis of variance results for 1978 and 2005: source level means and F-ratios for main effects of five independent demographic variables on two composite scores measuring attitudes to the role and status of women (N, 1978=1,803; N, 2005=1,150)

Attitudes toward the status of women		Sex		Age				Socio-economic status			Marital status		Rural vs urban location	
		Male	Female	18–24	25–39	40–54	55+	Low	Med.	High	Married	Other	Rural	Urban
		(n=886)	(n=917)	(n=238)	(n=557)	(n=433)	(n=575)	(n=839)	(n=668)	(n=296)	(n=1169)	(n=634)	(n=1152)	(n=651)
		(n=551)	(n=599)	(n=104)	(n=306)	(n=306)	(n=434)	(n=463)	(n=337)	(n=350)	(n=706)	(n=444)	(n=585)	(n=565)
1. Traditional sex role orientation with perception of female inferiority	1978	$F=201.42^{***}$ 3.8	2.92	$F=19.27^{***}$ 2.93	3.18	3.44	3.62	$F=12.72^{***}$ 3.43	3.41	3.00	$F=4.54^{*}$ 3.30	3.45	$F=15.70^{***}$ 3.44	3.18
	2005	$F=98.73^{***}$ 2.48	1.69	$F=5.13^{**}$ 2.00	1.93	1.93	2.28	$F=17.97^{***}$ 2.41	1.92	1.76	$F=2.00$ 2.05	2.10	$F=0.95$ 2.06	2.08
2. Positive attitude to maternal employment	1978	$F=10.18^{***}$ 3.22	3.41	$F=34.54^{***}$ 3.82	3.58	3.08	3.04	$F=11.76^{***}$ 3.31	3.20	3.63	$F=0.99$ 3.34	3.28	$F=7.58^{**}$ 3.26	3.43
	2005	$F=10.86^{***}$ 4.52	4.87	$F=32.43^{***}$ 5.20	5.00	4.84	4.27	$F=19.60^{***}$ 4.38	4.78	5.05	$F=2.91$ 4.66	4.73	$F=0.21$ 4.65	4.75

* $p<0.05$
** $p<0.01$
*** $p<0.001$
(Range on all variables is 1–7)

Socio-economic status (SES) was also consistently associated with gender role attitudes in the direction of lower SES being more closely associated with traditional attitudes. In the 1978 study the most traditional attitudes were held by lower and middle SES individuals and least by those of higher SES ($F = 12.72$; $p < 0.001$). In 2005 a significant SES effect remained ($F = 17.97$; $p < 0.001$); however, there was more differentiation this time between the two lower SES groups, with the lowest group being out on its own with more traditional attitudes, whereas the middle group was more similar to the highest SES group in this sample. Marital status was a significant predictor of attitudes in 1978, with married respondents holding less traditional views than others, though this was not highly significant. By 2005 marital status was no longer a significant predictor of attitudes. Similarly, while rural/urban location was a significant predictor in 1978, with rurals holding more traditional attitudes, this effect no longer held in 2005.

Attitudes to Maternal Employment became more positive from 1978 to 2005, yet a gender gap persisted. In both cases this was highly significant, though the magnitude of the difference was not as great as in the case of Factor I. The effect of age was similar to that seen on Factor I, with younger people having more positive attitudes to maternal employment and older people more conservative attitudes. It is evident that all age groups shifted in their attitudes in a more positive direction. Again the data reveal strong period effects as well as strong cohort effects. The SES distinctions remained on Factor II, showing a linear pattern, and as on Factor I, there was no significant main effect for marital status or rural vs urban distinctions. This shows a dramatic change in the nature of Irish society, which had notably been more traditional in rural areas. These data indicate that there is now more homogeneity throughout the country in the area of gender role attitudes.

The fact that attitudes had changed in rural areas was already evident in the 1986 data, which compared Dublin and rural areas. As may be seen in Table 6.5, there were significant rural/urban differences on six of the eight original factors, with rural expressing more conservative views, although the strength of the differences was not great in the case of *Contraception* (Factor II), *Equal Opportunity* (Factor III), Factor IV (*Maternal Employment*) or Factor VII (*Perception of Females as Inferior*), with the differences only significant at the $p < 0.05$ level. Rural/urban differences were greatest on Factor I (*Traditional Sex Role Orientation*) ($p < 0.001$) and Factor VIII (*Perception of Limitations in the Housewife Role*) ($p < 0.01$). There were no significant rural/urban differences on two of the factors, Factor V (*Belief in Equal Pay*) and Factor VI (*Belief in Higher Tax for Married Women*).

In order to explore the nature of rural/urban attitude change during this early period a comparison was made between the 1978 nationwide sample and the 1986 nationwide sample. For the purpose of this comparison, the 1978 nationwide representative sample was modified so as to be

Balbriggan
Library
Ph: 8704401

Table 6.5 The effects of five demographic characteristics on eight factors measuring attitudes toward the role and status of women: 1986 (N=600)

	Sex		Age		Socio-economic status		Marital status		Location	
	Female (n=360)	Male (n=240)	18–34 (n=300)	35–65 (n=300)	Low (n=300)	High (n=300)	Married (n=360)	Single (n=240)	Rural (n=300)	Dublin (n=300)
1. Traditional Sex Role Orientation	$F=30.75$*** 3.06	3.62	$F=13.77$*** 3.10	3.46	$F=9.89$** 3.43	3.13	3.26	3.31	$F=12.09$*** 3.45	3.11
2. Positive Attitude to Contraception	5.67	5.74	$F=61.59$*** 6.16	5.24	5.68	5.72	$F=22.28$*** 5.93	5.36	$F=5.60$* 5.56	5.84
3. Belief in Equal Opportunity	$F=8.41$** 6.69	6.49	6.61	6.61	$F=4.13$* 6.54	6.68	6.64	6.57	$F=4.55$* 6.54	6.68
4. Positive Attitude to Maternal Employment	$F=16.23$*** 4.45	3.97	$F=20.54$*** 4.52	4.00	$F=6.20$* 4.12	4.40	4.35	4.13	$F=3.93$* 4.14	4.38
5. Belief in Equal Pay	$F=17.79$*** 6.24	5.83	$F=13.87$*** 6.25	5.91	$F=4.78$* 5.98	6.18	6.15	5.97	6.12	6.04
6. Belief in Higher Tax for Married Women	$F=4.21$* 2.53	2.81	$F=11.84$*** 2.41	2.87	$F=9.41$** 2.85	2.43	$F=8.37$** 2.48	2.88	2.69	2.59
7. Perception of Females as Inferior	$F=59.17$*** 1.94	2.74	2.17	2.35	$F=8.20$** 2.40	2.12	$F=11.21$*** 2.12	2.47	$F=5.40$* 2.14	2.38
8. Perception of Limitations in Housewife Role	$F=9.26$** 4.63	5.04	4.86	4.71	4.75	4.83	4.87	4.68	$F=9.67$** 4.59	4.99

* $p<0.05$
** $p<0.01$
*** $p<0.001$

comparable to the 1986 sample, i.e. it was limited to Dublin and rural Ireland, to individuals 18–65 and to respondents in the five categories studied in the 1986 survey. For this analysis the weighted version of the 1986 sample was used, which re-weighted each category of respondents in terms of their actual proportions in the population. These procedures enabled us to carry out comparisons on the 1978 and 1986 data which were completely comparable and thus any measures of change detected are reliable for the populations and areas studied.

The 1978 survey contained 11 items in common with the 1986 survey. These 11 consisted of three items on each of three of the attitude factors and two on a fourth factor. New composite scores were created based on these common items, which are either completely identical to those factors examined previously or slightly abbreviated versions of the same factors.

The effect of year (1978 versus 1986) was examined, while controlling for the effects of five demographic variables: sex, age, socio-economic status, marital status and rural vs urban location. Table 6.6 presents the main results of this analysis. The data of primary interest is that for year. It may be seen that there were highly significant shifts from 1978 to 1986 for rural areas as well as for Dublin on three of the four factors:

1   *Traditional Sex Role Orientation*
2   *Positive Attitude to Maternal Employment,* and
3   *Perception of Females as Inferior*

There was also a shift, but of much lesser magnitude on the factor, *Belief in Higher Tax for Married Women.*

It may be seen that rural respondents became less traditional by 0.99 scale points, moving from 4.42 to 3.43. Dubliners moved essentially the same amount (0.96 scale points) over the same time period. Rurals were somewhat more traditional than Dubliners in 1978 and they remained somewhat more traditional in 1986, yet their attitudes shifted as much as did those of Dubliners during this period. It is also interesting to note that rural respondents became less traditional by 1986 than Dubliners were in 1978 (Table 6.7).

A similar pattern can be observed in relation to attitudes to maternal employment (Table 6.8). Both rurals and Dubliners became more positive toward maternal employment during this period (a movement of 0.55 for rurals and 0.45 for Dubliners) and hence the gap between rural dwellers and Dubliners of 0.33 in 1978 closed slightly by 1986 to just 0.23.

On the factor, *Belief in Higher Tax for Married Women* a different pattern is evident. As may be seen from Table 6.9 below, rural respondents became even more opposed to higher taxation of married women than they had been in 1978, whereas Dublin respondents became slightly less

Table 6.6 An examination of the effect of year on four factors measuring attitudes toward the role and status of women, while controlling for five demographic variables:[1] weighted national samples for 1978 and 1986[2] (N = 1,766)

Four factors measuring attitudes toward the role and status of women	Year		Sex		Age		Socio-economic status		Marital status		Location	
	1978	1986	Male	Female	18–34	35–65	Low	High	Married	Single	Rural	Dublin
	(n=1,169)	(n=597)	(n=859)	(n=907)	(n=796)	(n=969)	(n=925)	(n=841)	(n=1,252)	(n=514)	(n=1,185)	(n=581)
1. Traditional Sex Role Orientation	$F=178.93$***		$F=77.51$***		$F=42.54$***						$F=33.95$***	
	4.26	3.29	4.24	3.64	3.67	4.19	3.93	3.93	3.91	3.97	4.07	3.64
2. Positive Attitude to Maternal Employment	$F=46.61$***		$F=15.01$***		$F=45.49$***		$F=4.15$*				$F=9.69$**	
	3.64	4.14	3.67	3.94	4.09	3.58	3.74	3.89	3.82	3.78	3.73	3.97
3. Belief in Higher Tax for Married Women	$F=4.43$*		$F=4.34$*		$F=30.75$***		$F=7.19$**		$F=18.18$***		$F=25.69$***	
	2.99	2.80	3.02	2.84	2.65	3.16	3.04	2.81	2.80	3.24	3.08	2.62
4. Perception of Females as Inferior	$F=95.21$***		$F=215.57$***		$F=6.44$**							
	2.97	2.30	3.23	2.28	2.64	2.82	2.74	2.74	2.70	2.84	2.78	2.65

Notes

1 Six-way analysis of variance was used. Mean scores and significant F-ratios for main effects are presented.

2 The 1986 sample was re-weighted to reflect the proportions of the respondents sampled as they exist in the population. The 1978 nationwide representative sample (with an original N of 1,862) was modified so as to be completely comparable to the 1986 sample.

* p < 0.05
** p < 0.01
*** p < 0.001

Table 6.7 Comparison of means – Factor I: traditional sex role orientation

	Rural	Dublin
1978	4.42	3.94
1986	3.43	2.94

Table 6.8 Comparison of means – Factor IV: positive attitude to maternal employment

	Rural	Dublin
1978	3.53	3.86
1986	4.08	4.31

opposed. Although the rural respondents remained slightly more supportive than Dubliners of higher taxation of married women in 1986, this difference was negligible. What is interesting is that rurals moved in a more liberal direction, whereas urbans moved in a less liberal direction. What may have been happening here is that attitudes were reaching a common level nationally following the Supreme Court case in 1980 which removed the discrimination against working married women from the tax code (Scannell, 2000).

Factor IV, *Perception of Females as Inferior,* also shows a very interesting pattern. It indicates that rural dwellers shifted even more than Dubliners and were slightly less likely to perceive females as inferior than were Dublin respondents in 1986 (Table 6.10).

The rural/urban distinction was clearly no longer apparent. Whereas rurals shifted 0.83 scale points, Dubliners shifted only 0.48 scale points on this factor. It is not clear what influences caused this egalitarian shift in rural views, but what is clear is that the rural/urban divide on gender role attitudes was beginning to disappear.

A more detailed analysis of where the rural shifts on this factor occurred is illustrated in the means below which illustrate a significant four-way interaction effect between sex, age, rural vs urban location and year (Table 6.11):

It may be seen that rural women, particularly younger ones, manifested dramatic shifts on this factor, being significantly less likely to see women as inferior in 1986 than they did in 1978. In fact the score for young rural women in 1986 of 1.57 was lower than that of any other group in the sample. Young rural males also showed a large shift (from 3.57 to 2.84) but the gap between young rural men and women was still large and slightly widened from 1.17 to 1.27 on this dimension, indicating quite divergent attitudes, suggesting potential conflict between young rural men and women in their perceptions of women. Older rural men and women also shifted in the same direction, but the gap in their attitudes narrowed to just 0.69 points. Thus, while older men and women still had some differences in perception, the discrepancy was not as great as for the younger rurals.

Looking at the urban data, it is interesting to note that young urban women did not move at all on this measure. Their scores were already quite low (1.94) in 1978 but it is somewhat surprising that no movement was registered, whereas other urban groups showed rather noticeable shifts. Young urban males, in particular, showed a rather large shift from 3.59 to 2.67. Thus the very large gap in attitude between young urban men and women of 1.65 scale points, which existed in 1978, diminished to just 0.70 points, which was indicative of greater attitudinal congruence and hence potential harmony.

Table 6.9 Interaction effect between year and rural–urban location on Factor III: belief in higher tax for married women

	Rural	Dublin
1978	3.23	2.49
1986	2.85	2.63

$F=9.92$; $p=0.002$

Table 6.10 Interaction effect between year and rural–urban location on Factor IV: perception of females as inferior

	Rural	Dublin
1978	3.08	2.77
1986	2.25	2.29

$F=7.20$; $p=0.007$

Table 6.11 Four-way interaction effect of sex, age, rural–urban location and year on Factor IV: perception of females as inferior: cell means

	Young Rurals (Aged 18–34)		Older Rurals (35–65)	
	1978	1986	1978	1986
Males	3.57	2.84	3.56	2.67
Females	2.40	1.57	2.70	1.98

	Young Urbans (Aged 18–34)		Older Urbans (35–65)	
	1978	1986	1978	1986
Males	3.59	2.67	3.22	2.62
Females	1.94	1.97	2.53	2.05

Note
(higher score = greater likelihood of seeing females as inferior) ($F=7.26$; $p=0.007$).

6.10 Discussion and conclusions

It is clear that basic attitudes towards women moved in a more egalitarian direction during this period of rapid social change. Theories of attitude change tell us that attitudes change to become more congruent with behaviour (Heider, 1946; Festinger, 1957; Triandis, 1971). Since women have been engaging more actively in the public sphere – most notably through their increased labour force participation, and to a lesser extent in the political sphere (Galligan and Knight, 2011), it is apparent that basic attitudes towards women have been re-adjusting to take account of this new reality. This has been supported by the enactment of equality legislation in the 1970s providing for gender equality in the areas of pay and equal opportunity and bolstered by contraception legislation in 1979 and tax equity for married women in 1980. Thus, it is not surprising that attitudes would shift to be congruent with prevailing norms and social policies. This too is in line with theories of attitude change which predict that attitudes will change to be congruent with behaviour and also with other attitudes and they will shift in order to reduce cognitive dissonance (Festinger, 1957). Since most people respect the law, if the law endorses equality, then in order to reduce cognitive dissonance, people are likely to shift their attitudes to be consistent with prevailing laws (Deutsch and Collins, 1958; Colombotos, 1969). This illustrates how the law can be a tool to facilitate attitude change in a more egalitarian direction (Raab and Lipset, 1959).

The results comparing attitudes from 1975 to 1986 illustrate that attitudes shifted considerably following legislation in areas related to gender equality. This was particularly clear in the case of attitudes to equal pay. In the Dublin sample there was an average shift of 20% for the three items measuring attitudes to equal pay from 1975 to 1986, and by 1986 an overwhelming majority supported equal pay for men and women. The 1975 data were collected just prior to the implementation of the Anti-Discrimination (Pay) Act in 1975 and the 1986 data were collected 11 years following its implementation. The shift on this issue illustrates clearly how attitudes change to become congruent with social norms and required behaviour. Thus, law may be seen as also having a potential educative effect (Raab and Lipset, 1959), since it

> changes the social situations and community practices which breed prejudiced behaviour and attitudes. Since these situations and practices are the prime learning influences with respect to prejudice, law then must be perceived as a prime educational weapon in combating prejudice.
>
> (Ibid., p. 41 et seq.)

The results also suggest that the Employment Equality Act of 1977, which prohibited discrimination on the grounds of sex or marital status, may have contributed to the increased acceptability of married women working and to the significant decrease in traditional sex role ideology reflected in the changing attitudes from 1975 to 1986 and beyond. The issue of maternal employment was controversial in 1975 and remained so in 1986. Yet in spite of this there were large shifts in attitude in a more accepting direction. The increasing acceptance of maternal employment from the mid 1970s to the mid 1980s echoes the findings of Thornton and Young-DeMarco (2001) in the US who reported greater acceptance of maternal employment in 1985–1986 than in 1977.

While all groups shifted over the decade, women did so to a greater extent than men, and among the women, married women shifted more so than single women. Non-employed married women shifted significantly on more measures than any other group, suggesting that they were particularly affected by the events of the decade of the mid 1970s to mid 1980s. Their increasingly positive attitudes to contraception and to maternal employment would facilitate their re-entry to employment and their increased self-esteem (as measured by a decreased *Perception of Females as Inferior*) would also give them greater confidence to re-enter the labour force. It was clear that by 1986 this group was no longer a passive, traditional one, content with a more limited and defined role. These women had in fact become attitudinally quite similar to their employed counterparts.

Among the men, both married and single became less traditional and more egalitarian in their sex role attitudes and more supportive of the principle of equal pay. Single men became more positive to maternal employment than they had been in 1975, yet they remained the most conservative of all groups on this issue, as they did in the case of equal pay. Married men became more supportive of equal opportunities and less likely to see women as inferior to men; single men did not shift on this dimension and continued to be the group most likely to perceive females as inferior. It may be that by being exposed to women's situation first hand through living with wives and daughters, married men become sympathetic to women's concerns with equality. This process of increasing empathy may have been particularly heightened over the decade in which women themselves became more aware of such issues and hence likely to talk about them. This process would also have been reinforced by media attention to equality issues, as well as by men's exposure to the new legislation in the workplace.

The comparisons of nationwide data for 1978 and 1986 showed that there were significant shifts not only among Dubliners, but also among rural respondents whose attitudes became more liberal over this time and in some cases even more liberal than those of urban dwellers, notably in relation to the factor, *Perception of Females as Inferior*. The data showed less attitudinal congruence between young rural men and women than among urbans.

The shifts in attitudes continued beyond the mid 1980s into the new millennium. Although the time period was longer, the magnitude of the shifts were generally smaller than those seen in the earlier period of 1975–1986. This is consistent with trends observed in the US (Cotter *et al.*, 2011) and Australia (van Egmond *et al.*, 2010) except for attitudes to married women working and to maternal employment, where shifts were greater in the period from 1986 to 2005. This may reflect legislation on parental leave in 1998 which showed further commitment of the Government to employment equality, also following an EU directive, as well as a new focus on work–life balance (e.g. Drew, Humphreys and Murphy, 2003) and childcare (e.g. Expert Working Group on Childcare, 1999) The increasing labour force participation of married women would also have been likely to affect further attitude change in this area. Taken together, the shifts from 1975 to 1986 and 1986 to 2005 represent major attitude change on the part of the Irish population. By 2005 most Irish people endorsed egalitarian attitudes to gender roles. This pattern is similar to that seen in the US in which dramatic shifts occurred through the mid 1980s and continued into the 1990s, even though the levels of egalitarianism reached in the 1980s were already quite high (Thornton and Young-DeMarco, 2001; Cotter *et al.*, 2011). On the basis of the fact that the largest shifts in Ireland took place in the earlier period, it can be concluded that a number of key influences from the early 1970s to the early 1980s had a significant effect on gender role attitudes. These included legislation in the area of contraception, equal pay, equal opportunity and taxation. It is clear that the removal of the marriage bar in 1973, which allowed married women to remain at work and enabled non-employed married women to enter or re-enter the workplace was also a crucial factor. Ireland's entry to the European Community in 1973 was also highly significant, since it had a direct influence on Irish legislation through directives on equal pay and equal opportunity, and subsequently on parental leave, as well as through its more egalitarian ethos, reflecting the more liberal mores of some of the other member states. Thus, it cannot be assumed that attitude change in Ireland paved the way for equal pay and equal opportunity legislation since this legislation came as a result of EC directives. It is more likely that the ensuing attitude change was in fact a result of the effect of the legislation on attitudes and on behaviour, which in turn would be expected to have affected attitudes. This interpretation is supported by the strong period effects evident in the time series data.

Thus, the overall picture is one of dramatic change, yet there is a lingering residue of traditional attitudes concerning gender roles, particularly concerning maternal employment, even though attitudes in this sphere have undergone much change. As Scott (2008) points out, while there is support for equality in gender roles, there is still concern about work–life balance and how this is to be achieved. Men's role in the domestic sphere is still an area of resistance (Fine-Davis *et al.*, 2004; McGinnity and Russell,

2007; Esping-Andersen, 2009). As Scott (2008) suggests, understanding this realm will require research with new attitudinal measures that explore men's roles in future surveys. It will also require further policy responses, ideally based on research, to support the dual roles of men and women (Esping-Andersen, 2009; Fagnani, 2012).

7 Attitudes to divorce

7.1 Introduction

In Celtic times, under the Brehon law, divorce was a legal right. "If a couple decided to part, all they had to do was stand back to back on the hill of Tailteann near Tara and walk away from each other" (Trewhela, 1975, p. 12). In his discourse on women in early Irish society, Ó Corráin (1978) points out that during this early period "the wide-ranging rules in regard to divorce served as a guarantee of extensive women's rights and protected women in a way which was remarkably different from the customs of other European countries" (p. 8).

However, as discussed in Chapter 1, developments in Irish history led to a diminishing of women's status over time. After the Norman invasion of 1169, Ireland was partly conquered and colonised. Thus, for approximately 400 years the Gaels and the Anglo-Normans lived side by side, with two separate legal systems. The Gaels continued to live under the Brehon Laws, although these were modified to some extent in the later period, and the Anglo-Normans lived under the system of English Common Law. Simms (1978) points out that English Common Law, which reflected standard practice in most of Western Europe, was less egalitarian than the Brehon Laws in the rights it accorded to women. Ó Tuathaigh (1978) observes that from the conquest and plantations of the sixteenth and seventeenth centuries by the English until the Great Famine of the mid nineteenth century, women were:

> totally without formal political rights; ...their property and inheritance rights both within and outside of marriage were now governed by English common law, and ... theirs was a subject and subsidiary role to the male, and it was performed, for the most part within a domestic context.
>
> (Ó Tuathaigh, 1978, p. 26)

Prior to the 1937 Constitution, while there was no divorce law, it was theoretically possible to obtain a divorce by means of a private bill in the Irish

Parliament; but this recourse was effectively blocked by an amendment to standing orders introduced in 1925 by the then Taoiseach, W. T. Cosgrave (Whyte, 1971, pp. 36–37). However, in the 1937 Constitution (Article 41.3.2), a prohibition on divorce law was officially enacted. While it was possible to obtain a deed of separation, this did not dissolve the marriage or permit remarriage. It was also possible to obtain a civil divorce *a mensa et thoro*.[1] However, this was actually a legal separation granted by the High Court. It was not, strictly speaking, a divorce, since the parties were not free to remarry. Because it was quite cumbersome and expensive to obtain such a decree, very few cases of this kind were brought. Forty cases were brought in 1970 and 43 in 1975 (Hussey, 1976, p. 14).

There existed two important anomalies with regard to divorce in Ireland. The first is that, while it was possible for an Irish husband, domiciled in Britain, to obtain a divorce there, such divorces were not always recognised by the Irish courts (Commission on the Status of Women, 1972, pp. 182–183). A second anomaly lay in the fact that, while it was possible for members of the Roman Catholic Church to have their marriage annulled by the Church, in which case they were then free to remarry under Canon law, if they did remarry they committed bigamy in the eyes of the State unless they first obtained a civil annulment. However, the grounds for civil annulment were very narrow, as indicated by the fact that only eight cases for civil annulments were brought before the High Court in 1975 (Hussey, 1976, p. 14).

The Irish experience in relation to family law reform was quite different from that of other countries in the post-Second World War period (Burley and Regan, 2002). This was primarily due to the fact that from 1937 onwards divorce was banned under the Irish Constitution. Thus, in order to make divorce available it would first be necessary to hold a referendum to change the Constitution. Given that there were thousands of separated people in Ireland in the early 1980s, many of whom were living in second relationships which were not legalised by marriage, there became a groundswell of public opinion seeking divorce. At the same time there were equally strong forces which wanted to retain the status quo. A referendum to legalise divorce was held in June 1986 and the campaign was strongly fought on both sides. Burley and Regan (2002) point out that despite the large numbers of separated people living in irregular situations, the proposal to introduce divorce was vociferously opposed in the referendum of 1986:

> The opposition to constitutional change was fuelled by anti-divorce campaigns which used fear tactics related to money, children, property and inheritance to argue that divorce would tear apart the fabric of Irish society. The campaigns also claimed that divorce would open the floodgates to marriage breakdown.
>
> (Ibid., p. 202)

Prendiville (1988) concurs with this view in her own analysis of the arguments used in the campaign, some of which emphasised that marriage and "the family unit" were "the cornerstone of society" and as such needed to be protected from threat. Prendiville believes that it was the desire to maintain this status quo "rather than an unquestioned adherence to Roman Catholic dogma" which was the determining factor in the outcome of the referendum (ibid., p. 356). While Prendiville argues that people were generally in favour of legalising divorce, they were not confident that the Government would satisfactorily deal with the socio-economic ramifications. In addition she points to the significance of the Northern Ireland issue in the whole divorce debate – namely that if divorce were legalised in the Republic – thereby making it a more secular state – that this would appeal to the Northern Irish Protestant majority (ibid., pp. 357–358). Other issues which emerged in the campaign were the notion that a caring society would provide a solution for those in an unhappy marriage, that people had the right to a "second chance" at happiness, and that divorce was an "individual right".

Several authors have observed that a striking feature of the campaign was that attitudes to divorce were mainly positive for most of the campaign, but these turned negative in the run up to the vote (e.g. O'Leary, 1987; Darcy and Laver, 1990; Fahey, 2012). Fahey (2012) attributes this to the campaign of Catholic anti-divorce activists "highlighting risks to children and wives abandoned by errant husbands", which was "enough to sway a large number of waverers in the middle ground and bring them into the anti-divorce camp" (p. 246).

Because the issue of divorce is of obvious relevance to the status of women and since it was very much on the political agenda in the 1980s, it was included in the 1986 study (Fine-Davis, 1988c), carried out in September–December 1986, just a few months following the first national referendum on divorce in June 1986, so that people's attitudes and memories of their voting behaviour would have been quite fresh in their minds.

Thus, in the overall context of the broader survey of attitudes to gender roles, the 1986 survey also elicited people's attitudes to divorce, including several of the key issues which emerged in the campaign prior to the referendum, e.g. (1) perceptions of the effects of divorce on children, (2) on the husband's and wife's financial situation and (3) on the institution of marriage itself, including the notion that (4) if divorce were legalised this would "open the floodgates" to marital breakdown and (5) perceptions of the effect divorce would have on the prospects for reconciliation with the North, etc. How respondents had actually voted in the June referendum was also obtained so that attitudes could be examined in relation to actual voting behaviour. Through such analyses, it was hoped to gain a fuller understanding of the attitudes and other characteristics which underlay voting behaviour. The results were re-weighted to make them representative of the population in the groups sampled, thus permitting greater generalisability of the results.

7.2 The 1986 Divorce Referendum: an analysis of attitudes and voting patterns

Up until 1996 Ireland was one of the few remaining countries in the world which did not permit divorce. A national referendum was held in the Republic of Ireland in June 1986 in which the electorate was given the opportunity for the first time to choose to make divorce legally available or to opt for the status quo. The result was a rejection of divorce by significant majority: 36.3% in favour and 63.1% opposed.

7.2.1 *Voting behaviour*

Respondents in our survey were first asked whether or not they had voted in the referendum which had been held a few months previously. The results are presented in Table 7.1.

The figure of 81.8% of our sample who said they voted diverges from the actual turnout of the electorate, which was 62.7%. This may in part reflect the fact that the sample was not a strictly nationwide representative sample. It may also reflect the tendency of people to over-report voting behaviour, since it is a socially desirable behaviour.

Those who said they had voted were asked how they voted and their responses are presented in Table 7.2 – followed by the actual voting pattern of the electorate:

While there are discrepancies of the order of 5–7% between the voting behaviour of the sample and the electorate, they are roughly similar, and the sample certainly offers enough variance to permit the analysis of correlates and determinants of the voting behaviour, which is the primary focus of this aspect of the study.

Table 7.1 Reported voting behaviour in the 1986 Divorce Referendum (N=600)

	(%)
Voted in referendum	81.8
Did not vote	16.8
Don't know/Can't remember/refused	1.5
Total	100.0%

Table 7.2 Comparison of reported voting behaviour with actual voting by the electorate

	Sample (N = 600) (%)	*Actual voting by electorate (%)*
In favour of making divorce available	41.3	36.3
Against making divorce available	56.1	63.1
DK/can't remember/refused	2.6	–
Total	100.0	100.0

All respondents were then asked how they would vote if the same referendum were held tomorrow. As may be seen in Table 7.3 below, a very similar proportion to that voting in favour said they would again vote in favour and approximately 8% fewer said they would vote against than had actually voted against.

7.2.2 *Informational influences on voting*

It is clear that the Church directly and indirectly tried to influence the outcome of the referendum (O'Leary, 1987; Prendiville, 1998; Burley and Regan, 2002; Fahey, 2012). The effect of this influence, together with that of other potential sources, such as the newspaper and television media, on respondents' voting behaviour was assessed (see analysis and discussion of the influence of the media in this referendum by Breen (1998)). In the present study respondents were asked to what extent various sources of information were important in helping them make up their mind how to vote. Responses to this set of questions are presented in Table 7.4 below.

It may be seen that while few people rated any of the four as very important, the overall influence of television and church sermons was greater than that of national newspapers. Provincial newspapers appeared to have less influence on this issue than national newspapers. A total of 41.4% said that television was either "somewhat important", "quite important" or "very important" in helping them make up their mind. Approximately the

Table 7.3 Voting intentions in a similar referendum (N=600)

	(%)
In favour of making divorce available	42.0
Against making divorce available	47.7
Wouldn't vote	4.3
DK/refused	6.0
Total	100.0

Table 7.4 Importance of various influences on voting behaviour (N=600)

	Not at all important (%)	Somewhat important (%)	Quite important (%)	Very important (%)
Television	58.5	21.6	11.0	8.8
		–	(41.4)	–
Church sermons	58.7	20.8	13.9	6.6
		–	(41.3)	–
National newspapers	66.7	23.9	8.6	0.8
		–	(33.3)	–
Provincial newspapers	84.3	12.0	3.7	0.1
		–	(15.8)	–

same proportion said this was true of church sermons. National newspapers were cited by 33.3% and provincial newspapers by 15.8%.

7.2.3 Attitudes to divorce

Prior to asking people if and how they voted in the referendum, etc., a series of ten items concerning divorce was presented, embedded in a larger set of other attitudinal items. These covered the major issues which had been debated and discussed prior to the actual referendum. Five items were phrased in a pro-divorce direction and five were phrased in an anti-divorce direction, so as to provide balancing.

The responses to these items were factor analysed to explore the underlying dimensionality of the items. Factor analysis also makes it possible to create composite, or summary, scores which are statistically more reliable than individual items. Table 7.5 presents the results of this analysis and Table 7.6, following, presents the percentage responses to the individual items for the total sample (re-weighted to reflect the proportions of the respondents as they exist in the population). In addition, the differential responses of those who voted for and against divorce are presented for each item.

We discuss below each of the factors which emerged in the factor analysis of attitudes to divorce.

Factor I, entitled *Concern for Economic and Social Consequences of Divorce for Wife*, shows that the items concerning the potential economic and social consequences of divorce for the wife loaded together and formed one dimension (see Table 7.5). This factor alone explained 35% of the overall variance out of a total of 67.7% explained by these items, indicating that this factor is highly significant in explaining people's attitudes. Eighty-three per cent of the total sample believed that "in most cases the divorced wife would suffer great economic hardship in struggling to support her children and would be likely to end up on social welfare" (see Table 7.6). This view was shared both by the pro and the anti-divorce groups, but was held much more strongly by the anti-divorce group. Half of the total sample believed that divorce was not in the best interests of women, since it was the husband who was more likely to remarry. This view was held by 68% of the anti-divorce group, but by only 30% of the pro-divorce group. The hypothesis that many voted against divorce because they feared it would lead to a woman's losing her "status" and "respectability" in the community was largely not borne out by the results. Only 38.5% of the anti-divorce group held this view and less than half that proportion of the pro-divorce group. The item which most strongly differentiated between the pro and anti groups on this factor was: "If you open the floodgates to divorce you undermine the very nature of marriage as a lifelong commitment." Over 90% of the anti-divorce group agreed with this (47.9% strongly), whereas only 29.6% of the pro-divorce group did. The use of the emotive phrase "open the floodgates" may have played a role in the responses here. Such language appears to have evoked a response more in

Table 7.5 Factor analysis of items measuring attitudes to divorce (N = 600)

	Varimax rotated loading
Factor I: Concern for Economic and Social Consequences of Divorce for Wife	
1. A major reason for not introducing divorce into Ireland is that it would unjustly deprive the wife of her status and respectability.	0.77
2. If you open the floodgates to divorce you undermine the very nature of marriage as a lifelong commitment.	0.70
3. Divorce is not in the best interests of women since it is the husband who is more likely to remarry.	0.66
4. In most cases, a divorced wife would suffer great economic hardship in struggling to support her children and would be likely to end up on social welfare.	0.61
% Variance: 35.0 Cumulative % Variance: 35.0	
Factor II: Concern for Minority Rights, Reconciliation with Northern Ireland and the Victims of Marital Breakdown	
1. Making divorce legal in the Republic would show that we are willing to protect the right of minorities.	0.79
2. Making divorce legal in the Republic would be a step toward reconciliation with Northern Ireland.	0.76
3. By making divorce available, society would show its compassion to those suffering the misery of marital breakdown.	0.74
% Variance: 14.3 Cumulative % Variance: 49.3	
Factor III: Belief that Divorce Leads to Greater Well-Being for Victims of Marital Breakdown	
1. Children suffer greater psychological damage by living with two parents who are in constant conflict than by living with one divorced parent in a stable home.	0.82
2. People have a right to a second chance at happiness, legalised by marriage, if their first marriage has failed.	0.57
% Variance: 9.8 Cumulative % Variance: 59.1	
Factor IV: Concern for Financial Consequences of Divorce for Husband	
1. Divorce places an unbearable financial burden on the husband.	0.97
% Variance: 8.6 Cumulative % Variance: 67.7	

one group than the other. It is also interesting to note from its loading on this factor, that the idea of marriage as "a lifelong commitment" was clearly tied to economic factors, particularly to feelings about a wife's economic and social security, rather than to other feelings such as love, romance or happiness.

Factor II, *Concern for Minority Rights, Reconciliation with Northern Ireland, and the Victims of Marital Breakdown*, contains three items. The first concerns the rationale for divorce as offering protection of minority rights. The second concerns the implications of divorce for reconciliation with Northern Ireland and the third concerns compassion for those suffering the misery of marital breakdown. The items share in common a concern for others (i.e. the victims of marital breakdown and religious minorities such as Protestants, Jews and others who may not share the Catholic beliefs about divorce). It also indicates a desire to move toward greater reconciliation with Northern Ireland and sees the legalisation of divorce in the Republic as a step in that direction. This factor differentiated rather clearly between the pro- and anti-divorce groups. More than three-quarters (77.8%) of the pro-divorce group agreed with the item on minority rights as compared with just 43.7% of the anti-divorce group. Moreover this issue was something the pro-divorce group felt rather strongly about: 33.7% expressed strong agreement, whereas only 6.9% of the anti-divorce group did so. The item concerning reconciliation with Northern Ireland elicited 56.1% support from the pro-divorce group and only 20.5% from the anti-divorce group. Both the pro- and anti-divorce groups agreed that "by making divorce available, society would show its compassion to those suffering the misery of marital breakdown". However, whereas 54% of the anti-divorce group agreed with this, 92.6% of the pro-divorce group did (of whom 49% did so strongly).

Factor III, *Belief that Divorce Leads to Greater Well-Being for Victims of Marital Breakdown*, includes an item concerning the perceived effect of divorce on children. The debate about divorce prior to the referendum presented two points of view. One was that divorce is very disruptive and leads to negative psychological effects for children. The other was that children suffer greater psychological damage by living with two parents who are in constant conflict than by living with one divorced parent in a stable home. The results showed that a majority of the total sample (89%) held the latter view. There was slightly greater support for it among the pro-divorce group (92.6%), but also very high agreement from the anti-divorce group (83.7%). This clearly shows that (1) most people believe that divorce is the lesser of two evils with regard to children when parents are in conflict, and (2) that concern for the welfare of children did not significantly determine the voting in the referendum on the part of the anti-divorce group, since their views on this would have been consistent with voting pro-divorce. The second item on this factor concerns people's right to a "second chance at happiness, legalised by marriage, if their first marriage has failed". Again a majority of both groups supported this, but the

Table 7.6 Percentage responses to items measuring attitudes to divorce, grouped by factor, for total re-weighted sample and by voting behaviour

	Disagree			DK etc.	Agree		
	Strong	Moderate	Slight		Slight	Moderate	Strong

Factor I: Concern for Economic and Social Consequences of Divorce for the Wife

	Disagree Strong	Disagree Moderate	Disagree Slight	DK etc.	Agree Slight	Agree Moderate	Agree Strong
1. A major reason for not introducing divorce into Ireland is that it would unjustly deprive the wife of her status and respectability.							
Total sample (N=600)*	23.4	20.3 (67.6%)	23.9	0.4	13.0	11.1 (32.0%)	7.9
Voted pro-divorce (n=202)	40.1	22.3 (82.2%)	19.8	0.5	9.9	4.0 (17.4%)	3.5
Voted anti-divorce (n=262)	17.6	22.5 (61.1%)	21.0	0.4	12.6	13.7 (38.5%)	12.2
2. If you open the floodgates to divorce you undermine the very nature of marriage as a lifelong commitment.							
Total sample (N=600)	14.4	9.8 (32.7%)	8.6	0.3	16.1	21.1 (66.9%)	29.7
Voted pro-divorce (n=203)	32.0	23.2 (69.0%)	13.8	1.5	11.3	8.9 (29.6%)	9.4
Voted anti-divorce (n=263)	1.9	2.7 (9.5%)	4.9	–	16.7	25.9 (90.5%)	47.9
3. Divorce is not in the best interest of women since it is the divorced husband who is more likely to remarry.							
Total sample (N=600)	20.3	14.9 (48.9%)	13.7	0.5	17.7	16.7 (50.6%)	16.2
Voted pro-divorce (n=203)	36.9	20.2 (69.4%)	12.3	0.5	15.8	8.4 (30.1%)	5.9
Voted anti-divorce (n=263)	9.9	9.5 (30.0%)	10.6	1.5	19.0	24.3 (68.4%)	25.1
4. In most cases, a divorced wife would suffer great economic hardship in struggling to support her children and would be likely to end up on social welfare.							
Total sample (N=600)	5.1	5.0 (16.0%)	5.9	0.4	27.5	29.2 (83.6%)	26.9
Voted pro-divorce (n=202)	7.9	11.4 (29.7%)	10.4	1.0	27.2	23.3 (69.3%)	18.8
Voted anti-divorce (n=264)	3.0	2.3 (9.1%)	3.8	0.4	23.1	30.3 (90.5%)	37.11

Factor II: Concern for Minority Rights, Reconciliation with Northern Ireland and the Victims of Marital Breakdown

1. Making divorce legal in the Republic would show that we are willing to protect the rights of minorities.	Total sample (N=600)	10.4	11.1 (38.5%)	17.0	0.6	24.5	17.1 (60.9%)	19.3
	Voted pro-divorce (n=202)	7.4	5.0 (21.3%)	8.9	1.0	21.8	22.3 (77.8%)	33.7
	Voted anti-divorce (n=261)	15.7	17.2 (55.1%)	22.2	1.1	24.5	12.3 (43.7%)	6.9
2. Making divorce legal in the Republic would be a step toward reconciliation with Northern Ireland.	Total sample (N=600)	30.2	17.8 (67.1%)	19.1	0.1	15.4	9.9 (33.0%)	7.7
	Voted pro-divorce (n=203)	13.8	15.8 (43.9%)	14.3	–	25.1	16.7 (56.1%)	14.3
	Voted anti-divorce (n=263)	41.8	17.1 (79.1%)	20.2	0.4	10.6	6.5 (20.5%)	3.4
3. By making divorce available, society would show its compassion to those suffering the misery of marital breakdown.	Total sample (N=600)	6.8	5.9 (26.6%)	13.9	1.1	30.0	18.0 (72.3%)	24.3
	Voted pro-divorce (n=202)	1.0	2.0 (6.5%)	3.5	1.0	21.8	21.8 (92.6%)	49.0
	Voted anti-divorce (n=261)	13.4	11.5 (44.8%)	19.9	1.1	32.2	13.0 (54.0%)	8.8

continued

Table 7.6 Continued

	Disagree			DK etc.	Agree		
	Strong	Moderate	Slight		Slight	Moderate	Strong

Factor III: Belief that Divorce leads to Greater Well-Being for the Victims of Marital Breakdown

	Strong	Moderate	Slight	DK etc.	Slight	Moderate	Strong
1. Children suffer greater psychological damage by living with two parents who are in constant conflict than by living with one divorced parent in a stable home.* Total sample (N=600)	1.0	3.3 **(10.7%)**	6.4	0.3	25.7	23.6 **(89.0%)**	39.7
Voted pro-divorce (n=203)	2.5	3.0 **(7.5%)**	2.0	–	15.3	24.1 **(92.6%)**	53.2
Voted anti-divorce (n=263)	2.7	4.9 **(15.6%)**	8.0	0.8	27.4	25.5 **(83.7%)**	30.8
2. People have a right to a second chance at happiness, legalised by marriage if their first marriage has failed. Total sample (N=600)	5.2	4.0 **(24.1%)**	14.9	0.2	29.2	14.0 **(75.6%)**	32.4
Voted pro-divorce (n=203)	0.5	– **(3.5%)**	3.0	–	17.7	19.2 **(96.5%)**	59.6
Voted anti-divorce (n=263)	11.5	9.6 **(38.3%)**	17.2	1.1	38.7	9.6 **(60.6%)**	12.3

Factor IV: Concern for Financial Consequences of Divorce for Husband

	Strong	Moderate	Slight	DK etc.	Slight	Moderate	Strong
1. Divorce places an unbearable financial burden on the husband. Total sample (N=600)	9.6	11.5 **(36.1%)**	15.0	1.5	28.7	15.8 **(62.4%)**	17.9
Voted pro-divorce (n=202)	13.9	12.9 **(43.6%)**	16.8	2.0	25.2	15.3 **(54.4%)**	13.9
Voted anti-divorce (n=260)	7.7	10.0 **(30.0%)**	12.3	1.2	31.9	19.2 **(68.8%)**	17.7

* Re-weighted to reflect proportions in the population.

pro-divorce group did so to a far greater extent (96.5% vs 60.6%). Also, this was something the pro-divorce group felt quite strongly about (59.6% strongly agreed with this as opposed to just 12.3% of the anti-divorce group).

Factor IV, *Concern for Financial Consequences of Divorce for Husband*, consisted of only one item – that of the effect of divorce on the financial situation of the husband. This item clearly did not load together with the items concerning the economic effects on the wife, as one might have expected. Rather it was seen by respondents as a distinct dimension. A majority of the sample believed that divorce places "an unbearable financial burden on the husband", but this view was held more strongly by those who opposed divorce (68.8%) than by those who favoured it (54.4%).

7.2.4 Effects of demographic characteristics on attitudes to divorce

An analysis of demographic determinants of these attitudes showed that there were no sex differences on three out of the four factors (Table 7.7). Interestingly enough, women were not more likely to be concerned with the economic and social consequences of divorce on the wife. However, men *were* more concerned about the economic consequences of divorce for the husband. Marital status was significant on one factor and almost reached significance on another of the factors, in an unexpected direction. Single people were much less likely to think that divorce led to greater well-being than did married people (this related to Factor III, which concerned the belief that divorce led to greater well-being for children and those in marital conflict). A significant interaction effect showed that older, single people were much less likely to believe this than were married people ($F=5.49$; $p<0.02$).

Concerning the right to a "second chance at happiness", the results indicate that older, single people were less likely (than married people or younger single people) to believe that people have a right to a second chance at happiness, legalised by marriage, if their first marriage has failed. Since they have not yet married themselves and perhaps think it unlikely that they will do so, they may feel cheated out of even "one chance at happiness", let alone a second one, and thus may feel less generous towards others, who have already had a first "chance at happiness". The results also indicate that older single people – who do not have children – are more likely to think children are better off in a home with conflict than married people are likely to think. Given that married people are more likely to know what marital conflict is like and its effect on children, the discrepant views of older, single people are noteworthy, given that their votes helped to determine the outcome of the referendum. Consistent with this, there was also a trend to the effect that single people were more concerned about the economic effects of divorce on the wife than married people were.

Table 7.7 Effects of five demographic characteristics on four factors measuring attitudes to divorce (N=600)

Attitudes to divorce	Sex		Marital status		Age		Socio-economic status		Location	
	Male (n=240)	Female (n=360)	Married (n=360)	Single (n=240)	18–34 (n=300)	35–65 (n=300)	Low (n=300)	High (n=300)	Rural (n=300)	Urban (n=300)
1. FACTOR I: Concern for Economic and Social Consequences of Divorce for Wife	$F=2.75$; ($p=0.10$) 4.18	4.28	$F=3.66$; $p=0.06$ 4.21	4.43	$F=25.76$*** 4.01	4.59	$F=15.43$*** 4.52	4.08	$F=31.25$*** 4.62	3.98
2. FACTOR II: Concern for Minority Rights, Reconciliation with Northern Ireland and Victims of Marital Breakdown	4.20	4.13	4.24	4.04	$F=18.36$*** 4.43	3.89	4.22	4.10	$F=17.17$*** 3.90	4.42
3. FACTOR III: Belief that Divorce Leads to Greater Well-Being for Victims of Marital Breakdown	5.33	5.45	$F=15.12$*** 5.58	5.13	$F=27.76$*** 5.69	5.11	5.36	5.44	$F=18.35$*** 5.16	5.64
4. FACTOR IV: Concern for Financial Consequences of Divorce for Husband	$F=10.53$*** 4.75	4.23	4.44	4.44	4.30	4.58	4.53	4.35	4.43	4.45

* $p<0.05$
** $p<0.01$
*** $p<0.001$
Range of Scores: 1–7

Age was also a significant independent influence on attitudes to divorce. Older people were significantly more concerned about the economic and social effects of divorce on the wife than were younger people. Young people were more likely to believe that divorce led to greater well-being in cases of conflict than did older people (i.e. Factor III). The young were also more likely to see divorce as facilitating reconciliation with Northern Ireland, with protecting minority rights and showing compassion for those experiencing marital breakdown.

The socio-economic status of respondents did not influence their attitudes to divorce except on Factor I. Those of lower socio-economic background expressed greater concern for the economic and related consequences of divorce on the wife.

Rural vs urban residence was quite significant on three out of the four factors. Rural dwellers were significantly more concerned about the economic and social consequences of divorce on the wife. Urban dwellers were more concerned with the issues of reconciliation with Northern Ireland, minority rights and with compassion for the victims of marital breakdown. They also were more likely to see divorce as leading to greater potential well-being for the victims of marital breakdown.

7.2.5 Attitudes and other characteristics as predictors of voting behaviour in the 1986 Divorce Referendum

We have seen that certain attitudes differentiated between those who voted pro vs anti divorce. We have also seen that demographic variables influenced attitudes to a certain extent. Earlier we examined data concerning the importance to people of the media (television and newspapers) and church sermons in influencing their voting behaviour. We now shall take all of these variables together, in addition to a measure of religiosity,[2] to see which ones were most predictive of respondents' voting behaviour in the divorce referendum.

A multiple regression analysis was carried out, using voting behaviour as the dependent variable. Voting behaviour was treated as a dichotomous variable, with 1 = voted for divorce and 2 = voted against divorce. Demographic characteristics were entered first. Of the seven variables entered, only two were significant predictors of actual voting behaviour (Table 7.8). These were rural/urban location and age. Demographic characteristics accounted for a Multiple R of 0.35 and explained 12% of the variance in voting behaviour.

Religiosity was entered next and it was found to be a highly significant predictor of voting behaviour, much stronger than either age or rural/urban location had been. Its inclusion in the equation increased the Multiple R to 0.50 and the explained variance to 25%.

Informational influences were entered next. Newspapers were found to have had no appreciable influence on voting behaviour, nor had television. Church sermons, on the other hand, were found to have been a significant influence on voting. Those who said that church sermons influenced them were significantly more likely to have voted against divorce. The addition of these influences increased the Multiple R just slightly to 0.53 and the explained variance to 28%.

Finally the ten individual items measuring attitudes to divorce were entered to see which, if any, significantly influenced voting behaviour. It may be seen that of the ten, only three were significant predictors. The strongest was Item 9: "If you open the floodgates to divorce, you undermine the very nature of marriage as a lifelong commitment." Those voting anti-divorce were more likely to hold this belief, whereas those voting for divorce were much less likely to do so. The second strongest predictor was Item 8: "People have a right to a second chance at happiness, legalised by marriage, if their first marriage has failed." For those who voted pro divorce, this belief was a guiding force in their decision. Finally, the item about legalisation of divorce being a step toward reconciliation with Northern Ireland also significantly determined voting behaviour, but at a slightly lower level than the other two items. The addition of attitudes to the equation increased the Multiple R significantly to 0.74 and the explained variance (R^2) to 0.55 or 55%.

What this analysis shows is that while many issues were debated extensively in the media concerning the effects of divorce on the economic situation of the wife and on the psychological state of children, etc., in the final analysis, the key issue which determined voting behaviour was people's underlying attitude about marriage itself – i.e. whether or not they saw it as a lifelong commitment and whether or not they believed people had a right to a second chance at happiness if their first marriage had failed. Religiosity was also a highly significant predictor of voting behaviour. This was reinforced by the evident influence of church sermons. And, of course, people's views about marriage as a lifelong commitment are shaped to a great extent by religious teachings. Thus, the overriding determinant of voting behaviour in the referendum involved a belief in the Catholic view of marriage as a lifelong commitment versus a more secular view that people have a right to a second chance at happiness if their first marriage has failed. However, the results showed that attitudes concerning marriage as a lifelong commitment were closely tied into issues concerning the economic and social consequences of divorce for the wife. Such attitudes were most strongly held by older people and those living in rural areas.

7.3 The 1986 Divorce Referendum: conclusions and implications

This chapter has presented data on the ways that people perceived the divorce issue and also how they voted in the actual referendum on divorce

Table 7.8 Multiple regression analysis of predictors of voting behaviour in divorce referendum (N=600)

	Block 1	Block 2	Block 3	Block 4
	Beta	*Beta*	*Beta*	*Beta*
I Demographic Characteristics				
1. Income	-0.12 ($p<0.06$)	-0.10	-0.07	-0.07
2. Age	0.22***	0.06	0.05	-0.02
3. Sex	-0.00	0.09	0.09	0.03
4. Rural/Urban	-0.22***	-0.13**	-0.10*	-0.00
5. Marital Status	-0.08	-0.07	-0.07	-0.00
6. Education	0.01	0.05	0.03	0.04
7. Occupational Status	0.02	0.02	0.04	0.06
	Multiple R=0.35 R^2=0.12 Adj. R^2=0.11 Stand. Error=0.47			
II Religiosity (Composite Score)		0.42***	0.38***	0.09
		Multiple R=0.50 R^2=0.25 Adj. R^2=0.23 Stand. Error=0.43		
III Reported Importance of Various Influences on Voting Behaviour				
1. Nat. Newspapers			-0.06	-0.07
2. Church Sermons			0.16**	0.08
3. Television			0.05	0.09
4. Prov. Newspapers			0.02	0.04
			Multiple R=0.53 R^2=0.28 Adj. R^2=0.25 Stand. Error=0.43	

continued

Table 7.8 Continued

	Block 1	Block 2	Block 3	Block 4
	Beta	Beta	Beta	Beta
IV Attitudes to Divorce				
1. Divorce places an unbearable financial burden on the husband.				0.00
2. Children suffer greater psychological damage by living with two parents who are in constant conflict than by living with one divorced parent in a stable home.				0.05
3. Making divorce legal in the Republic would show that we are willing to protect the rights of minorities.				−0.08
4. A major reason for not introducing divorce into Ireland is that it would unjustly deprive the wife of her status and respectability.				0.00
5. In most cases, a divorced wife would suffer great economic hardship in struggling to support her children and would be likely to end up on social welfare.				0.01
6. Making divorce legal in the Republic would be a step toward reconciliation with Northern Ireland.				−0.14**
7. Divorce is not in the best interest of women since it is the divorced husband who is more likely to remarry.				0.06

8. People have a right to a second chance at happiness, legalised by marriage if their first marriage has failed.	−0.21***
9. If you open the floodgates to divorce you undermine the very nature of marriage as a lifelong commitment.	0.36**
10. By making divorce available, society would show its compassion to those suffering the misery of marital breakdown.	−0.03

Multiple $R = 0.74$
$R^2 = 0.55$
Adj. $R^2 = 0.53$
Stand. Error $= 0.34$

* $p < 0.05$
** $p < 0.01$
*** $p < 0.001$

which had been held in June 1986, just a few months before the survey was conducted. It also examined the effects of attitudes, informational influences, religiosity and background characteristics on how people voted in the referendum.

An analysis of the effects of background characteristics of respondents on their attitudes to divorce revealed no sex differences on most of the dimensions examined. Interestingly enough, women were not more likely than men to be concerned with the economic and social consequences of divorce on the wife, whereas, in contrast, men *were* more concerned than women about the economic consequences of divorce for the husband. Marital status was also significant, but again, in an unexpected direction. Older single people were much less likely than married people to think that divorce led to greater well-being for children and those in marital conflict. Given that married people are more likely to know about marital conflict and its effect on children, the discrepant views of older, single people are surprising and noteworthy, particularly given that their votes helped to determine the outcome of the referendum. Older, single people were also less likely (than married people or younger single people) to believe that people have a right to "a second chance at happiness", legalised by marriage, if their first marriage has failed. Since they have not yet married themselves and perhaps think it unlikely that they will do so, they may feel cheated out of even "one chance at happiness", let alone a second one, and thus may feel less generous towards others, who have already had a "first chance at happiness". This pattern was also observed in the earlier stages of the research in which older people and single people were found to be more traditional on a wide range of measures related to gender equality ranging from maternal employment to taxation of married women.

Older people (regardless of marital status) were significantly more concerned about the economic and social effects of divorce on the wife than were younger people, whereas younger people were more likely to believe that divorce led to greater well-being in cases of conflict. The young were also more likely to see divorce as facilitating reconciliation with Northern Ireland, with protecting minority rights and showing compassion for those experiencing marital breakdown. The less supportive attitudes of older people may in part be related to their stronger religiosity, as was shown in Chapter 5.

While the attitudes and values of older people prevailed in the 1986 referendum, these results portended that in the years to come the attitudes and values held by the younger people of that time would be likely to play a greater role in future discussions and legislation on this question.

In addition to the effect of age, there were significant rural/urban differences on a majority of the attitudinal factors. Rural dwellers were significantly more concerned than those from urban areas about the economic and social consequences of divorce on the wife. Urban dwellers were more concerned with the issues of reconciliation with Northern Ireland, minority rights and with compassion for the victims of marital breakdown. They also were more likely to see divorce as leading to greater potential well-being for the victims of marital breakdown. The greater concern of rural respondents with the economic consequences for the wife may well have been related to the complicated situation which would ensue in a rural divorce in terms of the family farm. Since property is so central to rural life, this tends to reinforce the need for continuity of marriage. In urban areas, where there are greater opportunities for female employment and property does not have quite the same import as the family farm, the economic consequences of divorce are seen as less important. Thus, the extent to which Ireland remained an agricultural nation vs the extent to which it continued to urbanise would be likely to have an effect on future attitudes on this question.

An analysis of the attitudes of those voting pro- and anti-divorce indicated that the item which most strongly differentiated between these two groups was: "If you open the floodgates to divorce you undermine the very nature of marriage as a lifelong commitment." Over 90% of the anti-divorce group agreed with this (47.9% – strongly), whereas only 29.6% of the pro-divorce group did. The use of the phrase "open the floodgates" may have played a role in the responses here. Such language would appear to have evoked a response more in one group than the other. It was also interesting to note that the idea of marriage as a "lifelong commitment" was clearly seen by respondents to be tied to economic factors, particularly those concerning a wife's economic and social security, rather than to feelings, such as love or happiness.

Other issues which were found to be significantly related to voting behaviour in the referendum included (1) the belief that divorce offered protection of minority rights, (2) the implications of divorce for reconciliation with Northern Ireland and (3) concern for those suffering marital breakdown. The attitudinal items tapping these issues reflect an awareness and concern for the suffering of others (i.e. the victims of marital breakdown and minorities in the Republic, such as Protestants, Jews and others who may not share the Catholic beliefs about divorce). One of the items taps a desire to move toward greater reconciliation with Northern Ireland and sees the legalisation of divorce in the Republic as a step in that direction. This factor differentiated rather clearly between the pro- and anti-divorce groups. Those voting pro-divorce were much more concerned with these issues than were those voting anti-divorce.

The debate prior to the referendum presented two points of view concerning the effects of divorce on children. One was that divorce is very disruptive and leads to negative psychological effects for children. The other was that children suffer greater psychological damage by living with two parents who are in constant conflict, than by living with one divorced parent in a stable home. The results showed that a majority of the total sample (89%) held the latter view. There was slightly greater support for it among the pro-divorce group (92.6%), but also very high agreement from the anti-divorce group (83.7%). This clearly shows, first, that most people believed that divorce was the lesser of two evils with regard to children when parents are in conflict, and (2) that concern for the welfare of children did not significantly determine the voting in the referendum on the part of the anti-divorce group, since their views on this would have been consistent with voting pro-divorce.

While many issues were debated extensively in the media concerning the effects of divorce on the economic situation of the wife and on the psychological state of children, etc., the main issue which, in the final analysis, determined actual voting behaviour was people's underlying attitude about marriage itself – that is, whether or not they saw it as a lifelong commitment or whether they felt people had a right to "a second chance at happiness" if their first marriage had failed. *Religiosity* was also quite a significant predictor important and was reinforced by the importance of church sermons in influencing voting decisions.

Thus, the overriding determinant of voting behaviour in the referendum involved a belief in the Catholic view of marriage as a lifelong commitment versus a more secular view that people have a right to a second chance at happiness if their first marriage has failed. However, the results showed that attitudes concerning marriage as a lifelong commitment were closely tied into concerns about the economic and social consequences of divorce for the wife.

In societies where divorce is quite prevalent (e.g. the US and Great Britain), rates of female labour force participation are far higher than they were in Ireland at the time of the 1986 referendum. Women in these countries are thus more readily able to be economically self-sufficient. When the economic security issue becomes less important, the role which marriage plays in fulfilling emotional needs becomes more important. To the extent that Ireland's rate of married female labour force participation continued to increase it would be expected that marriage would be viewed less in terms of providing economic benefits and more in terms of providing psychological benefits. This trend would be likely to lead to a greater desire on the part of the population for easier dissolution of marriage. Increasing labour force participation of women, together with their decreasing fertility (Sexton and Dillon, 1984) and religious belief (Breslin and Weafer, 1984) were likely to contribute to social conditions which would be more favourable to future passage of divorce legislation.

These factors, together with increasing economic buoyancy in the Celtic Tiger years, contributed to a climate which favoured a second referendum on divorce in 1995.

7.4 The 1995 Divorce Referendum and its impact

Attitudes favouring a solution to the divorce issue did not go away and momentum built which led to a second referendum in 1995. The result of this referendum was very close, with just 50.28% voting in favour and 49.72% against. There was a significant rural/urban divide in voting and Adshead (1996) notes that the 11 Dublin constituencies carried the referendum, with all of them voting in favour. The fifteenth amendment to the Constitution repealed the constitutional prohibition on divorce and was signed into law in 1996.

Several authors have analysed and discussed the 1995 referendum (e.g. Adshead, 1996; Crowley, 2011; Fahey, 2012) including the impact that the legalisation of divorce had on marital breakdown. Both Burley and Regan (2002) and Fahey (2012) agree that the enactment of divorce legislation did not lead to an increase in marital breakdown: "the divorce and family breakdown floodgates have not been opened" (Burley and Regan, 2002, p. 202) and "at least in the first five years, relatively few Irish people applied for divorce" (ibid.). Fahey (2012) argues that by 1995 the nature of the family had changed so much that the legislation did little to facilitate family change other than to make re-marriage possible. Other ways of dealing with marital breakdown had increased before divorce was introduced and hence, when it was, "There was no post-divorce 'spike' in marital breakdown rates which is usually said to have followed the easing of divorce law in other countries" (ibid., p. 244). Fahey further observes that parallel developments in social policy had accommodated non-marital families, which had become more normative, and as a result the status of marriage itself had weakened (Fahey, 2012). These changes were accompanied by an increase in non-marital births, lone parenthood and an increase in cohabitation (Lunn, Fahey and Hannan, 2009).

Apart from its potential effect on marital breakdown, Adshead (1996) observed that the Referendum was noteworthy "for the changes it signaled in other aspects of the Republic's political life" including the position of the Catholic Church:

> Neither the traditionalists nor the modernizers can claim victory in the Irish divorce referendum. Amongst all players, perhaps the Catholic Church was the greatest loser. Despite its best efforts, and in a devoutly Catholic state, it was unable to convince voters of the wisdom of copperfastening their religious beliefs in the Constitution.
>
> (Ibid., p. 142)

Fahey (2012) concurs with this view and notes that passage of divorce legislation was part of an overall liberalisation and secularisation of Ireland which began with passage of contraception legislation in the late 1970s. The other key issue which was part of this transformation of Ireland from a traditional Catholic state to a more modern secular society is that of abortion, which we shall address in the following chapter.

Notes

1 The translation of *a mensa et thoro* from the Latin means "from bed and board".
2 This composite measure, based on the earlier work of Faulkner and De Jong (1965), Glock and Stark (1965) and MacGréil (1974) was developed in Ireland in 1975 (Davis *et al.*, 1977) and subsequently replicated in several other Irish studies (e.g. Fine-Davis, 1979a; Davis, Grube and Morgan, 1984). It contains items measuring religious belief, the importance of prayer to the individual, the importance of religion to the individual and frequency of church attendance.

8   Attitudes to abortion

8.1 The 1983 Abortion Referendum: attitudes and voting patterns

As Randall (1987) observed in the late 1980s, abortion policy in the Republic of Ireland appeared to be moving in an opposite direction to that of most other countries. Citing Francome (1984), Randall pointed out that between 1967 (the year that Britain liberalised abortion provision) and 1982 more than 40 countries had widened the legal grounds for abortion, whereas Ireland, in September 1983, reinforced the existing prohibition against abortion in the 1861 Offences against the Person Act by amending the Constitution following a national referendum. Commenting on this development in the context of other issues which he sees as related to the family – but which could equally be seen as related to the status of women and religiosity – Whelan and Fahey (1994) point out that

> On a number of occasions since the early 1980s, such as the abortion referendum of 1983, the divorce referendum of 1986, and the further three-part referendum on abortion in 1992, public debate has been convulsed by controversy over the "politics of the family". On the surface, the dominant outcome of this conflict has been to reaffirm traditional approaches to family matters. The first two referendums just mentioned, for example, rejected any lessening of the prohibition of divorce in Irish law and installed an anti-abortion clause in the Constitution, thus placing Ireland in an exceptionally conservative position on these matters by comparison with other western countries. However this surface adherence to tradition belies the shifts and uncertainties that have emerged beneath.
>
> (p. 45)

We shall explore some of the attitudinal shifts related to the issue of abortion as we trace the legal and social developments over the period since the 1983 referendum. However, let us begin by looking at the attitudes of the respondents in our sample in 1986, who also told us how they voted in the 1983 referendum, thus enabling us to see how attitudes affected voting behaviour.

8.1.1 Actual voting behaviour

Because abortion was such a sensitive topic in Irish society we did not include it in our initial studies of gender roles in the 1970s. However, given the salience of this issue following the 1983 Referendum, we included it for the first time in the 1986 survey with a series of questions on people's attitudes, as well as their voting behaviour in the 1983 Referendum. Since it is widely believed that the issues were confusing and that even the wording of the referendum may have been confusing to people, particular care was taken to explain the issues clearly to the interviewers in the briefing sessions and to present the questions clearly in the questionnaire. The topic was introduced as follows:

> You may recall that in 1983 there was a referendum on a Constitutional Amendment which acknowledged the "right to life" of the unborn child and thereby made abortion not only illegal, as it already was, but also unconstitutional, thus making it impossible for the Dáil to pass any legislation in the future which would legalise abortion. Could you please tell me if you voted in that referendum?

The responses, contained in Table 8.1, indicate that 70% of the sample reported having voted in the referendum, 18.8% said they had not and 11.2% refused or couldn't remember. The 70% figure is higher than the actual turnout, which was just 54.6%. Reported voting amongst the sample was more prevalent among married people than single and was particularly low among single men.

Those who had voted in the referendum were then asked how they had voted. The overall total (for the re-weighted sample) was 75.1% in favour of the amendment and 23.5% against, which was higher than the actual figure of approximately 66% in favour of the amendment (Table 8.2).

While there was no overall significance in the differences between the groups (Table 8.2), non-employed married women were more likely than any of the other groups to be in favour of the amendment (80%), followed by employed single women (77.6%) and employed single men (76.7%). The least support was expressed by employed married women (70.8%) and men (70.5%), although this level of support still reflects a majority in favour of the amendment in these groups. This pattern of responses is similar to what we have seen in relation to a wide range of gender role attitudes presented earlier, in which employed married women in particular have shown more liberal attitudes to social issues compared with non-employed married women. Single people have consistently shown conservative attitudes on gender issues and married men have shown a tendency to be more supportive of equality.

Table 8.1 Percentage of various groups who reported having voted in the 1983 Abortion Referendum

	Women			Men		Total (N = 600)	Re-weighted total
	Employed married (n = 120)	Non-employed married (n = 120)	Employed single (n = 120)	Employed married (n = 120)	Employed single (n = 120)		
Yes	80.0	75.8	63.3	74.2	50.0	68.7	70.0
No	11.7	15.0	29.2	12.5	35.8	20.8	18.8
Don't know/Can't remember/refused	8.3	9.2	7.5	13.3	14.2	10.5	11.2
Total	100.0	100.0	100.0	100.0	100.0	100.0	100.0

$\chi^2 = 42.24$; df = 8; $p < 0.001$

Table 8.2 Reported voting behaviour of various groups in the 1983 Abortion Referendum

	Women			Men		Total (N = 410)	Re-weighted total
	Employed married (n = 96)	Non-employed married (n = 90)	Employed single (n = 76)	Employed married (n = 88)	Employed single (n = 60)		
In favour of amendment to make abortion unconstitutional	70.8	80.0	77.6	70.5	76.7	74.9	75.1
Against the amendment	22.9	20.0	21.1	28.4	20.0	22.7	23.6
Refused/Don't know	6.3	–	1.3	1.1	3.3	2.4	1.3
Total	100.0	100.0	100.0	100.0	100.0	100.0	100.0

$\chi^2 = 11.81$; df = 8; N.S.

8.1.2 *Potential voting behaviour*

Respondents in the 1986 survey were then asked how they felt about the issue at the present time. If the same referendum were held tomorrow, how did they think they would vote? As Table 8.3 shows, 67.5% of the re-weighted sample said they would vote in favour of the amendment, 22.2% would vote against and 10.3% refused to answer the question or did not know how they would vote. These figures indicate that support for the amendment dropped from 75.1% reported actual voting in 1983 to 67.5% anticipated voting three years later – a drop of 7.6%. Those who would have voted against the amendment stayed about the same, but the proportion of "don't knows" etc. increased. By and large, there were few differences between the sub-groups examined; however there was again a tendency for non-employed married women to be more likely than other groups to be pro the amendment (72.3%) compared with 61–64% of the other groups. Single men were more likely than other groups to either be against the amendment or to not know or refuse to answer. It will be recalled that their voting turnout was the lowest in the sample (50%). This group may have been the least likely to see the issue as relevant to them.

8.2 Attitudes towards abortion under various circumstances

Respondents in the 1986 survey were then asked if they felt abortion should be prohibited under any and all circumstances or did they think there may be certain circumstances under which it might be permissible. It may be seen in Table 8.4 that 37.9% felt that abortion was not permissible under any circumstances, while 58.4% felt it may be permissible under certain circumstances.

All, except those who did not see abortion as permissible under any circumstances, were then shown a list of possible circumstances and asked whether they agreed or disagreed that abortion might be permissible under each of them. The respondents completed this set of questions by themselves so as to facilitate greater privacy. A seven-point agree-disagree response continuum was used in this set of items. Responses to each of the seven items are presented in Table 8.5. Percentages are presented first for all respondents who said abortion may be permissible under certain circumstances or who were not sure (367 respondents or approximately 61% of the sample). Percentages are then presented for those who both voted in the referendum and said that abortion might be permissible under certain circumstances. These are broken down on the basis of voting behaviour (i.e. pro vs anti the amendment). Of the 412 respondents who voted, 400 reported how they voted. Of these, 234 felt abortion might be permissible under certain circumstances: 157 (or 67.1%) of these had voted for the amendment and 77 (or 32.9%) had voted against.

Table 8.3 How respondents said they would vote if abortion referendum were held tomorrow

	Women			Men		Total (N=585)	Re-weighted total
	Employed married (n=115)	Non-employed married (n=119)	Employed single (n=118)	Employed married (n=116)	Employed single (n=117)		
In favour of amendment to make abortion unconstitutional	63.5	72.3	64.4	61.2	62.4	64.8	67.5
Against the amendment	27.8	21.8	22.9	25.9	17.1	23.1	22.2
Refused/Don't know	8.7	5.9	12.7	12.9	20.5	12.1	10.3
Total	100.0	100.0	100.0	100.0	100.0	100.0	100.0

$\chi^2 = 16.62$; df$=8$; $p<0.05$

Table 8.4 Attitudes toward whether abortion should be permissible under certain circumstances

	Total (re-weighted) sample (N = 600) (%)
Not permissible under any circumstances whatsoever	37.9
Permissible under certain circumstances	58.4
Don't know	3.8
Total	100.0

Almost all of those who believed that abortion might be permissible under certain circumstances, believed that such a circumstance was in the case of the pregnancy seriously endangering the life of the mother. Ninety-three per cent agreed with this. How one voted in the referendum made little difference in how people felt about this (97% of those voting anti the amendment and 90% of those voting for the amendment). Extrapolating from these data, it may be seen that more than half (57%) of the total sample (N=600) i.e. 93% of 61% of the sample believed that abortion should be permissible if the pregnancy seriously endangered the life of the woman.

A high percentage (78.8%) also believed that abortion should be permissible if the pregnancy endangered the woman's health. This translates into about 48% of the total sample (N=600). Of those voting for the amendment who believed abortion should be permissible under certain circumstances, 73% believed the health of the mother was one such situation. Close to 91% of those voting against the amendment felt this way.

A slightly higher overall proportion felt that abortion should be permissible if it resulted from rape. Close to 83% felt this way (75% of those voting pro-amendment and 87% of those voting anti-amendment). Extrapolating to the total sample, it would appear that 50.5% of the total sample (i.e. 82.8% of 61%) would consider abortion permissible in cases of rape.

Pregnancy resulting from incest was similarly viewed. Over 84% felt abortion should be permissible in such cases (79.5% of the pro-amendment people felt this way and 85.7% of the anti-amendment people). Extrapolating to the total sample, 51.4% would consider abortion potentially permissible in pregnancy resulting from incest.

Respondents were less inclined to consider potential deformity of the child a potentially acceptable ground for abortion. Fifty per cent felt abortion should be permissible in this situation (43% of pro-amendment voters and 59% of anti-amendment voters). Thus, extrapolating to the total, only 30% of the overall sample would consider this a potentially acceptable reason for abortion.

The remaining two situations – that of a pregnant woman being unmarried and that of a couple being unable to afford another child – elicited far less support than did the previous circumstances. Only 14% could envisage abortion as acceptable in the case of an unmarried woman and only 11% in the case of a couple who could not afford another child.

One of the interesting aspects of these results is the fact that there were no significant sex differences on any of the items. The fact that women were not more permissive is somewhat surprising given that movements to liberalise abortion in other countries, such as Italy and France, have been spearheaded by women (Randall, 1992) and this has also been true to some extent in Ireland (ibid.). It is also surprising given that women are the ones who suffer if they find themselves in a predicament in which abortion seems the only way out. The fact that women did not differ from men on abortion may result in part from the fact that they are significantly more religious than men (MacGréil, 1974; Fine-Davis, 1979a, 1989) and the attitude of the Church on abortion is unequivocal.

What is also extremely interesting about these results is the unexpectedly high degree of consensus between those voting for and against the amendment. The differences in their attitudes were non-significant in the case of the pregnancy endangering the life of the mother, in the cases of rape and incest, and in the case of the unmarried woman. It would seem that even though there was very strong polarity on the issue in the lead-up to the referendum, in certain respects the two groups think alike. However, this is said bearing in mind that a certain percentage did not see abortion as permissible under any circumstances. Nevertheless, these data have revealed that 57% of the total sample considered abortion permissible if the woman's life were in danger, 51.4% in cases where pregnancy resulted from incest, 50.5% in cases resulting from rape and 48% in cases in which the woman's health was in danger.

These results are rather surprising in light of the high proportion of the population which voted in favour of the amendment. However, it has been suggested that the relatively low voter turnout indicated a high degree of confusion on the part of the electorate (e.g. O'Carroll, 1984). Our data in fact indicate that approximately half of the sample – including many who voted for the amendment – believed in 1986, just three years after the amendment, that abortion should be allowed in certain particular circumstances, notably (1) when the woman's life is in danger; (2) when the woman's health is in danger; (3) when the pregnancy results from rape and (4) when the pregnancy results from incest. Moreover, the strength of agreement was quite high, particularly in the cases of the woman's life, rape and incest, as illustrated in Table 8.5.

These findings reflect a trend which was reported earlier by Fogarty, Ryan and Lee (1984), authors of *The Irish Report of the European Value Systems Study*. Based on data collected in 1981, some five years prior to our 1986 study, these authors concluded:

> In Ireland the proportion who thinks abortion may be justifiable on "social grounds" remains tiny, except in the case of the non-religious.

But the proportion who think it may be justified on the two health grounds, especially on that of the mother's health, has been rising steadily.... Among people under 45 a majority think that abortion may be justified when the mother's health is at risk.

(Ibid., p. 47)

Clearly the Irish people do not wish to have abortion on demand. On the other hand, they can contemplate it under certain highly specific and delimited situations. The fact that these issues did not sufficiently emerge prior to the referendum led to a referendum which did not fully take account of people's views on this topic in a more differentiated way. This is usually the nature of referenda, which led the Joint Oireachtas Committee on Women's Rights (1988) to question whether this was the right way to proceed:

In an increasingly complicated world where the rights of minorities must be respected, the Joint Committee feel that legislation should be sufficiently flexible to meet the complexities of modern life. The Constitution, with all its merits, is too blunt an instrument to use to govern such situations because, of its nature, it is too rigid and too difficult to amend to enable it to respond to the needs of a changing society. A person who is called on to answer "yes" or "no" to a single question put in a constitutional referendum cannot have regard to a range of nuances arising from the principal proposition even if they have been exhaustively discussed beforehand. This calls into question the desirability of regulating in the Constitution issues which closely affect women as well as other issues in such a way as to preclude flexibility of approach which is essential if the rights of women are to be preserved.

Despite the results of the referenda in 1983 and 1986, there would seem to be evidence of considerable ambivalence in attitude towards moral questions relating to divorce and abortion. The application of legislative provisions – constitutional or other – depends on the consent of the population at large. If that consent is not forthcoming or there is a considerable body of dissent there is a danger that the law will fall into disrepute or that those who can afford it will be able to circumvent the law while the less well-off will be required to conform. As legislators, the members of the Joint Committee on Women's Rights believe that this is a situation which should be avoided (Second Joint Committee on Women's Rights, 1988, pp. VI–VII).

8.3 Medical implications of the amendment

In discussing the medical implications of a potential amendment prior to the 1983 referendum, doctors pointed out that in the case of certain

Table 8.5 Extent to which abortion was perceived as permissible[1] under different circumstances: percentage distributions for total 1986 sample and by voting behaviour in the 1983 Abortion Referendum

	Disagree			DK etc.	Agree		
	Strong	Moderate	Slight		Slight	Moderate	Strong
1. If the pregnancy seriously endangered the woman's life. Total sample (N=367) χ²=11.06 df=6; N.S.	1.7	1.1 (6.2%)	3.4	0.3	20.5	17.3 (93.4%)	55.6
Voted Pro-Amend[2] (n=157)	2.5	1.3 (8.9%)	5.1	0.6	15.3	18.5 (90.5%)	56.7
Voted Anti-Amend[2] (n=77)	–	1.3 (2.6%)	1.3	–	11.7	9.1 (97.4%)	76.6
2. If the pregnancy seriously endangered the woman's health. Total sample (N=367) χ²=14.65; df=6 p<0.05	3.6	6.6 (21.1%)	10.9	0.1	22.2	19.0 (78.8%)	37.6
Voted Pro-Amend (n=157)	6.4	6.4 (26.2%)	13.4	0.6	19.7	18.5 (73.2%)	35.0
Voted Anti-Amend (n=77)	2.6	5.2 (9.1%)	1.3	–	15.6	24.7 (90.9%)	50.6
3. If the pregnancy is the result of rape. Total sample (N=365) χ²=10.73; df=6; N.S.	4.3	5.8 (16.6%)	6.5	0.7	15.0	13.2 (82.8%)	54.6
Voted Pro-Amend (n=156)	7.7	7.1 (24.4%)	9.6	0.6	15.4	11.5 (75.0%)	48.1
Voted Anti-Amend (n=77)	7.8	3.9 (13.0%)	1.3	–	9.1	14.3 (87.0%)	63.6
4. If the pregnancy is the result of incest. Total sample (N=365) χ²=10.13; df=6; N.S.	3.1	5.3 (15.0%)	6.6	0.8	14.8	12.1 (84.3%)	57.4
Voted Pro-Amend (n=156)	4.5	7.7 (19.9%)	7.7	0.6	13.5	11.5 (79.5%)	54.5
Voted Anti-Amend (n=77)	6.5	7.8 (14.3%)	–	–	9.1	7.8 (85.7%)	68.8

5. If there is evidence that the child will be seriously deformed.	Total sample (N=365)	15.5	10.7 (49.3%)	23.1	0.4	15.4	13.7 (50.2%)	21.1
$\chi^2 = 19.24$; df=6; $p<0.01$	Voted Pro-Amend (n=157)	18.5	12.1 (56.1%)	25.5	0.6	12.1	14.6 (43.3%)	16.6
	Voted Anti-Amend (n=76)	14.5	19.7 (40.8%)	6.6	–	14.5	11.8 (59.2%)	32.9
6. If the woman is not married.	Total sample (N=367)	57.5	14.4 (84.8%)	12.9	1.2	7.0	4.2 (14.0%)	2.8
$\chi^2 = 11.99$; df=6; N.S.	Voted Pro-Amend (n=157)	63.7	12.7 (87.9%)	11.5	–	8.9	1.9 (12.1%)	1.3
	Voted Anti-Amend (n=77)	57.1	13.0 (76.6%)	6.5	1.3	9.1	5.2 (22.1%)	7.8
7. If the couple cannot afford another child.	Total sample (N=367)	65.0	12.2 (88.4%)	11.2	0.8	5.9	3.2 (11.0%)	1.9
$\chi^2 = 14.82$; df=6; $p<0.01$	Voted Pro-Amend (n=157)	68.2	10.8 (90.5%)	11.5	–	7.6	1.9 (9.5%)	–
	Voted Anti-Amend (n=77)	66.2	9.1 (80.5%)	5.2	1.3	9.1	2.6 (18.2%)	6.5

Notes

1 This table only includes respondents who said abortion may be permissible under certain circumstances (i.e. 61.6% of the sample). It excludes those 38.4% of the sample who said it was not permissible under any circumstances. The Total Sample is re-weighted to reflect the proportion of respondents in the population at large.

2 The breakdown by voting behaviour adds up to a smaller number of respondents, since they only include those who voted.

diseases of the mother, most importantly cancer, effective treatment of the patient might damage the foetus and doctors would be faced with dilemmas:

> ... if the woman is pregnant at the time the cancer is diagnosed, an invidious choice may be presented to the medical practitioner.... It may well be that if the amendment has been passed and the foetus has thereby been guaranteed a "right to life", that treatment for the cancer must be delayed until the woman has delivered by which time her chances of successful treatment may have been severely retarded (Doctors Against the Amendment, 1982, pp. 6–7) ... although the standards of medical care for the woman with a potentially life-threatening pregnancy will doubtless improve in the years ahead, the passing of the amendment might well mean that ... the option of an abortion might well be denied to the woman with a life-threatening pregnancy.
>
> (Ibid., pp. 9–10)

In view of such potential medical situations arising, respondents were asked how they thought such situations should be resolved. The question was phrased:

> If a pregnant woman is suffering from a serious illness and treatment could save her life, but would result in the death of her unborn baby, would you:
>
> Favour giving the woman treatment (woman would live, baby would die) or
> Not favour giving the woman the treatment (woman would die, baby would live)

The responses to this question are presented in Table 8.6. There was a high level of consensus among the different groups examined. Overall, about 75% favoured giving the woman the treatment, about 5% did not and about 20% were unsure what should be done in that situation. Single people, particularly single men, tended to be more unsure as to what should be done than married people. Almost 30% of single men said they were "unsure", as opposed to 14% of married women and 23% of single women. The situation is probably one that married women can most readily identify with. Indeed non-employed married women were most sympathetic to the woman's plight. Over 83% of them said treatment should be given and only 3.5% said no treatment should be given. This group of women has, on average, more children than employed married women and may be particularly able to visualise such a situation. Married men were also more sympathetic to the woman's situation than were single

Table 8.6 Attitude toward treatment of pregnant woman with life-threatening disease

	Women				Men				
	Employed married (n = 120)	Non-employed married (n = 115)	Employed single (n = 119)		Employed married (n = 118)	Employed single (n = 118)	Total (N = 500)	Re-weighted total
Give treatment	78.3	83.5	67.2		77.1	66.9	74.6	76.1
No treatment	6.7	3.5	9.2		5.1	3.4	5.6	4.7
Don't know	15.0	13.0	23.5		17.8	29.7	19.8	19.3
Total	100.0%	100.0%	100.0%		100.0%	100.0%	100.0%	100.0%

$\chi^2 = 19.32$; df = 8; $p < 0.02$

Table 8.7 Attitudes toward giving medical treatment in relation to actual voting behaviour in 1983 referendum

	Voting pro-amendment (n = 302)	Voting anti-amendment (n = 92)
Give treatment	72.5	89.1
No treatment	6.3	4.3
Don't know	21.2	6.5
Total	100.0%	100.0%

$\chi^2 = 11.55$; df = 2; $p < 0.005$

men and women. Married men have wives and can also probably imagine what such a situation would feel like.

When responses to this question were examined in relation to the respondents' voting behaviour in the 1983 referendum, the following results emerged (Table 8.7).

Not surprisingly, those who had voted against the amendment were significantly more likely to favour treatment for the woman (89% did so). However, a large majority of those voting pro-amendment also favoured giving the woman treatment (72.5%), although quite a high percentage (21.2%) were not sure what should be done in such a case. These findings clearly illustrate that people did not understand the potential consequences for women of the amendment.

Given that the amendment has passed, such medical situations will arise – and indeed have arisen, as shall be discussed below – in which such difficult decisions will have to be made. There are no clear-cut guidelines for action. As barristers pointed out in the context of the discussion and debate concerning the possible legal consequences of the amendment:

> The vagueness of its drafting makes it impossible to say with precision what the result of such use would be but it appears certain that decisions which are now, *de factum*, private ones could be subjected to legal scrutiny in the attempts to prevent individuals or groups acting in a way of which others disapprove ... any person could appoint himself the spokesman for the foetus...
>
> (Barristers Against the Amendment, 1982, p. 8)

If the course of action is unclear as a result of the amendment, would this affect the treatment which pregnant women now receive? What if a doctor is not sure whether a particular treatment is legal or illegal? We shall return to this issue later in the chapter when we discuss recent events in Ireland where this very question arose in a very significant case.

It was also suggested around the time of the 1983 referendum that another result of it would be that the law would have differential effects on the rich and the poor:

The well off, who can afford to pay for specialist medical care, will be able to choose a doctor who is prepared to continue providing treatment allowed under the (previous) law. Working people, who cannot afford to do this, will be treated by doctors who themselves cannot take the risk of being prosecuted for doing something which might be illegal. Doctors will decide what is legal when the law itself is confused.

(Labour Women's National Council, 1983)

As it turned out, all of these concerns were prescient, as will be discussed.

In view of the potential dilemmas which would arise in medical practice and for couples facing such decisions, a series of questions was put to respondents concerning how much "say" they felt various parties (the woman herself, her husband, her doctor, a priest or clergyman) should have in the decision of whether a pregnant woman with a life-threatening disease could receive treatment, even if this would result in the loss of her foetus.

Responses to these questions are presented in Table 8.8. A majority (79.5%) felt the woman should have the "final say" in such a decision, although 20% felt she should only have "some say", "quite a bit of say" or "a major say". Very few (3.8%) thought that the woman's husband should have the "final say". However, 63.7% thought he should have a "major say". Only 5.4% thought the doctor should have the final say, but over 60% thought he should have anywhere from "some say" to "a major say". No one felt that a priest or clergyman should have the "final say", but 55% felt he should have anywhere from "some say" to "a major say". Those who voted pro-amendment were somewhat more likely to think the priest should have influence in this decision.[1] Thus, while 79.5% felt the woman should have the final say, it is quite clear that three (usually) male figures would also be actively contributing to the decision on her life. Given that she would be in a state of ill health (life-threatening health), she would not be in a position to put up much resistance if others disagreed with her wish to be treated.

Given this situation, it is not surprising that female respondents were significantly more likely to think the woman should have the final say in such a decision, as shown in Table 8.9.

Table 8.8 Amount of "say" various individuals should have when a decision must be made concerning giving or withholding medical treatment to a pregnant woman with a life-threatening disease (N=552)

	No say (%)	Some say (%)	Quite a bit of say (%)	A major say (%)	The final say (%)
The woman herself	–	1.6	2.0	16.9	79.5
The woman's husband	2.0	14.3	16.2	63.7	3.8
The doctor	13.1	24.7	27.3	9.6	5.4
A priest or clergyman	45.1	35.4	14.1	5.4	0.0

Table 8.9 Amount of say the woman should have in such a decision (N=552)

	Males (n = 217) (%)	Females (n = 335) (%)
Some say	0.5	2.4
Quite a bit of say	4.1	1.8
A major say	22.6	13.1
The final say	72.8	82.7
Total	100.0	100.0

$\chi^2 = 14.30$; df = 3; $p < 0.005$

As shown in Table 8.9, while 82.7% of female respondents thought women should have the final say, only 72.8% of male respondents thought women in this situation should have the final say. This gender difference was statistically highly significant ($p < 0.005$).

8.4 Changing attitudes to abortion 1986–2013

Since the time of the 1986 survey several public opinion polls have been conducted which have demonstrated that attitudes to abortion have become more accepting over time. The 1990 European Values Survey (EVS) included questions on abortion and Hornsby-Smith and Whelan (1994) compared attitudes from Ireland with those of Europe as a whole. These authors found that 65% of the Irish sample approved of abortion when the mother's health was at risk. This compared with 92% of the European sample as a whole (see Table 8.10). The figure of 65% reflects an increase from 1986 in which just 48% of the total sample supported abortion in this situation. The figure of 48% support on the health ground was also the level observed in the 1981 European Values Survey (Fahey, Hayes and Sinnott, 2005, Table 6.6, p. 125). Thus the increase in support on this ground would appear to have come between 1986 and 1990, suggesting that continuing debate following the referendum may have contributed to attitude change in this respect.

Attitudinal surveys have consistently shown that there was much less support for abortion when it was likely that the child would be physically handicapped. Only 32% of the Irish sample in the 1990 EVS approved in this case, whereas a much larger proportion of the European sample approved (79%) (Table 8.10). The Irish figure of 32% corresponds to the figure in our 1986 survey of 30% approval in this case. There was extremely little support for abortion in the case of single motherhood (8%). While this condition also elicited little support in Europe as a whole, the support was more than three times that in Ireland.

Fahey *et al.*'s (2005) comparison of attitudes to abortion from the European Values Surveys for 1981, 1990 and 1999 showed that there was little

Table 8.10 Circumstances under which abortion is approved of: comparison of Irish and European views (European Values Survey 1990, 1999)

	Ireland (1990) % approving	*Europe (1990)* % approving	*Ireland (1999)* % approving
1. When the mother's health is at risk by the pregnancy	65	92	–
2. Where is it likely that the child would be physically handicapped	32	79	33
3. Where the mother is not married	8	27	14
4. Where a married couple do not want to have any more children	8	34	12

Sources: Hornsby-Smith and Whelan (1994), Table 2.13, p. 36; Fahey *et al.* (2005), Table 6.6, p. 125.

change in attitudes from 1990 to 1999. It was also clear from comparisons of Ireland with the rest of Europe even as recently as the 1999–2000 wave of the EVS that Ireland is out on its own, together with Malta, in terms of its rejection of abortion (ibid., Figure 6.2B, p. 135).

More recent attitudes were examined in the Irish Contraception and Crisis Pregnancy (ICCP) Studies (Rundle, Leigh, McGee and Layte, 2004), carried out in 2003 and updated in 2010 (McBride, Morgan & McGee, 2012). Both of these surveys, which were carried out using nationwide representative samples of over 3,000 men and women, replicated the key questions used in our 1986 survey. However, the samples were of men and women in the childbearing age group, 18–45, whereas our data were from a sample of men and women 18–65 and thus the results are not strictly comparable.

As may be seen from Table 8.11, the proportion saying abortion was not permissible under any circumstance dropped from 38% in our 1986 study to just 8% in 2003 and remained at about that level in 2010 (9%). The ICCP studies also asked if abortion should be permissible "under all circumstances", to which 51% agreed in 2003 and the remaining 39% said it should be allowable "under some circumstances". In 2010 the proportion saying "all circumstances" dropped somewhat to 45%, but the proportion saying "under some circumstances" increased to 44%. These comparisons reflect major change in attitudes from 1986 to 2003, which have remained fairly stable to 2010. However, as noted, the samples are not entirely comparable since the ICCP studies examined attitudes of people in a younger age cohort. Furthermore, the initial question was not entirely the same as the ICCP question also included the option "abortion permissible in all circumstances".

Table 8.12 presents a comparison of our earlier 1986 data with the ICCP data for 2003 in relation to circumstances in which abortion was perceived as permissible. In both cases the figure given is based on extrapolation to the total sample in each study. It may be seen that whereas our

Table 8.11 Public attitudes to abortion 1986, 2003 and 2010

	1986 (Fine-Davis, 1988b) N = 600 % agreement	2003 (ICCP Study, 2004) N = 3,312 % agreement	2010 (ICCP Study, 2010) N = 3,002 % agreement
Abortion not permissible in any circumstances	38	8	9
Abortion permissible under some circumstances	58	39	44
Abortion permissible in all circumstances	NA	51	45
No opinion/don't know	4	2	2

Sources: Rundle *et al.* (2004) Table 3.24, p. 118 and McBride *et al.* (2012), Figure 10.1, p. 131.

Table 8.12 Public attitudes to circumstances in which a woman should have a choice to have an abortion: comparisons between 1986 and 2003

*Should a woman have a choice to have an abortion in this circumstance?**	*1986* *(Fine-Davis, 1988b)* N = 600 *% agreement*	*2003* *(ICCP Study, 2004)* N = 3,312 *% agreement*
If the pregnancy seriously endangered the woman's life	57	90
If the pregnancy seriously endangered the woman's health	48	86
If the pregnancy is the result of rape	51	86
If the pregnancy is the result of incest	52	86
If there is evidence that the child will be deformed	31	70
If the woman is not married	8	56
If the couple cannot afford another child	7	55

Source: Rundle *et al.* (2004), Table 3.25, p. 119.

Notes

* Replies are calculated from whole sample. Those saying abortion should never be permitted were counted as "no" while those who said abortion should always be permitted were counted as "yes" (asked in 2003 only).

study showed support of 57% in the case of a woman's life being in danger, this rose to 90% in the ICCP study. In the case of the woman's health being in danger, our study found 48% support. This rose to 86% in 2003. Whereas we found just about 50% support in the case of rape and incest, the ICCP study found 86%. There was also increased support for allowing abortion in the case of a deformed foetus. The earlier study found 31% support; this rose to 70% in the ICCP study. While the 1986 study found very little support in the case of a woman not being married or a couple not being able to afford another child, the ICCP study found 55–56% support in these cases, reflecting a very sizeable shift. However, these figures take into account the fact that 51% said that abortion was permissible under *all* circumstances, so that it would appear that this forms a base which contributes to the high level of support. When the figures for those who indicated they supported abortion "under some circumstances only" are examined on their own, the support is lower in the case of a woman not being married and the couple not being able to afford another child (Rundle *et al.*, 2004, Figure 3.22, p. 118).

The ICCP Study of 2010 found that attitudes towards abortion in specific circumstances remained very stable from 2003 to 2010. Thus, in addition to the 45% agreeing that abortion should be permissible in all circumstances, those 44% who said it should be permissible under some circumstances expressed these levels of support: when a woman's life was in danger (96%), when her health was in danger (89%), when the pregnancy was a result of rape (88%) or incest (86%), if the child had a serious abnormality (44%). As before, socio-economic factors obtained much lower support: thus only 14% felt it should be permissible if the couple was not married and 11% in the case of a couple not being able to afford another child (McBride *et al.*, 2012, p. 131).

Because of the different nature of the samples in our 1986 study and the ICCP studies, we have also compared our earlier findings with other surveys using samples with comparable age cohorts to our own. We present here the results of three other public opinion polls which have nationwide representative samples of the adult population in Ireland and which had items which are closely comparable to those used in the 1986 study. The first was carried out by Lansdowne Market Research in 2001, the second by Millward Brown in 2013 and the third by Ipsos/MRBI also in 2013 (Table 8.13). The slight variations in question wording are indicated at the left of the table and the corresponding percentages are to the right for each year in question.

Beginning with the 1986 study, we found that 57% supported abortion in the case of the woman's life being in danger. This fell to 52% in the study carried out by Lansdowne in 2001 but rose to 84% in the 2013 Ipsos/MRBI survey.

In the 2001 study the risk of suicide was included as a separate item, since this had been a key feature of the 1992 X Case and was an issue of debate. There was 37% support in the case of suicide in 2001. By 2013 there was evidence of increased support for abortion on both of these grounds – 53% in the case of suicide and 69% in the case of medical risks other than suicide – in the Millward Brown survey.

There was also increased support over time in the case of the woman's health being at risk. This had had 48% approval in 1986. This fell to 41% in 2001, but rose again in 2013, to 64% in the Millward Brown survey and to 70% in the Ipsos/MRBI survey.

Support for abortion in the case of rape went from 50% in 1986 to 68% in 2013. The figure in 1986 was similar in the case of incest (51%). There was a joint question on these issues in the Lansdowne survey of 2001 and the response was just 47%. A similar joint question in 2013 by Ipsos/MRBI obtained agreement of 78%.

There was a distinctly lower level of support in the case of foetal abnormality. In 1986 the level of support for abortion on this ground was 31%. It fell to 23% in 2001. However, in response to the similar question – a foetus suffering from a disorder which is incompatible with life – 79% said that abortion should be permissible. This significant attitudinal shift would appear to reflect increasingly informed public attitudes, which were exposed to actual cases such as this which were discussed in the media prior to 2013.

Socio-economic factors were significantly less likely to elicit support from respondents as justifiable reasons for abortion, with less than 10% agreeing with these in 1986 and 2001. However, new questions were posed in the 2001 and 2013 surveys which indicated a softening of attitudes. Nineteen per cent felt in 2001 that an abortion was permissible if the woman believed that "for her, abortion is the correct choice to make" and in 2013 30% felt it was "where the mother decides to have an abortion for other reasons".

It is clear from the above that attitudes to abortion have become much more accepting over time (see also Collins, 2013a, 2013b). There is overwhelming support over numerous representative surveys for availability of abortion in the case of a woman's life being in danger from the pregnancy. There is also strong support in the case of a woman's health being in danger. The situation of rape also elicits majority support in the Millward Brown and Ipsos/MRBI surveys of 2013 and the ICCP surveys of 2003 and 2010. There is also evidence of increased support in the case of foetal abnormality (Rundle *et al.*, 2004; McBride *et al.*, 2012; Ipsos/MRBI, 2013). There is clearly much less support for abortion for socio-economic reasons; however, there is notable support under such categories as "where the mother decides to have an abortion for other reasons" (Millward Brown, 2013) and in the ICCP studies which offer the option of abortion "in all circumstances" (Rundle *et al.*, 2004 and McBride *et al.*, 2012).

It is obvious that the 1983 Referendum which asked a "yes"/"no" question did not identify the subtleties of people's views on this complex

Table 8.13 Comparison of attitudes to circumstances in which abortion may be permissible: per cent agreement in 1986, 2001 and 2013

	1986 Fine-Davis (1988b) (N = 600) % agreement	*2001* Lansdowne Market Research (N = 1,200) % agreement	*2013* Millward Brown (N = 979) % agreement	*2013* IrishTimes/Ipsos/MRBI (N = 1,000) % agreement
1. When the woman's life is in danger	57	52	–	84
2. Where there is a medical risk to the mother's life other than suicide	–	–	69	–
3. When the woman is at risk of committing suicide if the pregnancy continues	–	37	53	–
4. When the woman's health is in danger	48	41	64	70
5. In the case of rape	50	–	68	–
6. In the case of incest	51	–	–	–
7. In the case of rape or incest	–	47	–	78
8. If there is evidence that the child will be deformed/foetus is suffering from a disorder which is incompatible with life	31	23	–	79
9. If the woman is not married	8	–	–	–
10. If the couple cannot afford another child/ other socio-economic reasons	7	6	–	–
11. Whenever a woman believes that for her, abortion is the correct choice to make	–	19	30	37

matter, whereas public opinion polls and surveys are able to differentiate between these.

8.5 Cross-cultural comparisons and the influence of religion

Abortion has been a contentious issue not only in Ireland, but also in other countries. However, as Scott (1998), who has examined attitudes to abortion over time in the UK, the US, Germany, Sweden, Poland and Ireland notes, "views concerning the morality of abortion have undergone considerable change over time ... and the majority seem to support a moderate policy that allows legal abortion in some but not all circumstances" (p. 177). On the basis of the British Social Attitudes Survey and the General Social Survey in the US, there has been a clear differentiation between people's approval for medical vs social circumstances (ibid.), as we have seen in Ireland. In comparing the six countries using ISSP data for 1994, Scott found that the youngest cohort of Irish men and women were very similar in their abortion attitudes to the corresponding age group in the US, whereas the oldest Irish cohort was far more disapproving than their American counterparts. Religion and religiosity were also significant in this comparative research, with Catholics more opposed to abortion than Protestants in Britain and West Germany, whereas in the US it was the reverse, with Catholic women more supportive of abortion. However, in all countries, those who attended church more regularly were most opposed to abortion on demand. When Scott looked at particular cohorts, she found, for example that women who were in their 20s in the US in 1965, shortly after the pill was introduced, were among the most favourable to abortion and maintained this stance into their fifties (ibid., p. 180). In Britain, there has been an increase in support for abortion since the mid 1980s, particularly among women. There has been greater attitude change in Britain than in the US and it has been mainly the result of period effects, i.e. attitude change among all groups, rather than among particular cohorts. In Scott's cross-cultural comparison, Irish attitudes were found to be least supportive, whereas East German attitudes (where abortion on demand has been available since the 1970s) and those in Sweden were most liberal, followed by West Germany. Attitudes in Poland, despite it being a Catholic country, were found to be similar to those in the US and Britain. While church attendance was positively associated with opposition to abortion, Scott predicted in 1998 that the Church's influence may decrease in the future as trends towards greater secularisation occur. We have already seen this development in Ireland.

The importance of religion as a determinant of abortion attitudes has been emphasised by numerous authors (e.g. Randall, 1992; Jelen, O'Donnell and Wilcox, 1993; Scott, 1998; Craven, 2006, 2010). Randall (1992) observes that the "moral ascendency" of the Catholic Church was a key factor in the Irish referendum debate and indeed studies of abortion policy elsewhere have repeatedly drawn attention to the resistance of the Catholic Church to abortion reform. Referring to research in 22 non-communist countries (Tatalovich and Daynes, 1981, p. 13), Randall notes that Catholicism was the overriding variable in abortion policy (1992, pp. 126–127). Why then has abortion reform been successful in Catholic countries and even in Italy, where the Pope resides? Randall (1992) attributes this to a "countervailing secular culture" which has developed there. This view is supported by Jelen *et al.* (1993) who, after examining data from the World Values Survey for 11 Western European countries, conclude that "the presence of a large Catholic population appears to occasion a counter-mobilization of non-Catholics in a pro-choice direction" (p. 380). In Ireland, this has been less possible since the overwhelming majority is Catholic. However, even though the Protestant minority is relatively small in Ireland, they do have different attitudes to Catholics on the issue of abortion as well as on other issues concerning gender and religion. Craven (2006, 2010) found significant differences between Catholic and Protestant women's attitudes to abortion, in the direction of greater permissiveness on the part of Protestants (Craven, 2010, Table 5.4.1, p. 142).

8.6 Legal and other developments 1983–2013

Following the referendum in 1983, the Eighth Amendment to the Constitution (Article 40.3.3) was enacted. It states:

> The State acknowledges the right to life of the unborn and, with due regard to the equal right to life of the mother, guarantees in its laws to respect, and, as far as practicable, by its laws to defend and vindicate that right.

Since this time there have been numerous legal developments and cases. The most significant of these was the 1992 (February) Supreme Court case (known as the "X case") concerning the right of a 14-year-old rape victim who was at risk of suicide to obtain an abortion. The Court ruled that a pregnant woman did have the right to obtain an abortion if her life was at risk. Yet this ruling was not given expression in legislation until 2013. The reality is that women seeking abortions must travel abroad, usually to England, to obtain them. Barry (2008) pointed out just a few years ago that "the failure of this State to provide for abortion even under the most minimal circumstances of the 'X' Case … is a definite reminder that women's legal status within this State is uncertain and ambiguous" (p. 24).

There were further referenda in 1992 on the right to travel and the right to information. These followed earlier cases in which the right to information was defended by the Well Woman Centres and Open Door and three student unions against the Society for the Protection of the Unborn Child (SPUC). In 1986 Judge Hamilton ruled that the provision of such information was unconstitutional as it undermined the right to life of the unborn. This was upheld in 1988 by the Supreme Court. However, in 1991 the European Court of Justice ruled that abortion was a service under EU law. All of this led to the Irish Government adding protocols to the Maastricht Treaty removing the issue from the jurisdiction of EC law.

In October 1992 the European Court of Human Rights in an appeal taken by Open Door and the Well Woman Centre ruled that the ban on abortion information was in breach of Article 10 of the European Convention on Human Rights. In November 1992 the referenda on the right to information and the right to travel passed. The Irish Government entered a Declaration to the Protocol saying that they would not use it to restrict travel and information. While this did not legislate for the X case, it was a small step towards greater freedoms for women in this realm. For a detailed coverage of the legal situation and the various cases in Ireland, with cross-cultural comparisons, up to 1997, see Kingston *et al.* (1997).

Following these developments the Government set up in 1996 a Constitution Review Group. The report of this group recommended that legislation should be introduced to implement the decision in the "X" case. This was followed by the publication of a Green Paper on Abortion (1999) and the publication of an All-Party Report in 2000 (All Party Oireachtas Committee on the Constitution, 2000).

A further Governmental response to this issue included the establishment in 2001 of the Crisis Pregnancy Agency. Through a multi-pronged programme involving research, a policy strategy and a communication campaign to promote the greater use of contraception, the Agency aimed to reduce the number of crisis pregnancies in Ireland and hence the number of abortions carried out abroad on Irish women. The work of the Agency has been successful in reducing the number of abortions carried out in England on women with Irish addresses from 6,673 in 2001 to 3,982 in 2012, a decline of 40% over 11 years (HSE Crisis Pregnancy Programme, 2013).

In 2010, another landmark decision was made by the European Court of Human Rights in what is known as the "C case". The court declared that the woman (Ms C's) rights were violated because there was no procedure to enable her to establish whether she qualified for a lawful termination of pregnancy in accordance with Irish law, even though she feared that her pregnancy would cause the recurrence of cancer. The Court stipulated that Ireland had failed to implement properly the constitutional right to abortion where a woman's life is at risk. In response to this decision, the Irish Government established an expert group of medical and legal professionals to examine whether changes to abortion legislation in Ireland were needed to ensure that Ireland complied with the European Convention on Human Rights.

Public debate on this issue continued. Failure to legislate on the X case meant that a woman could not access an abortion even when it was necessary to save her life (O'Halloran, 2010, p. 7). Without legislation doctors did not know what services they could lawfully provide to women.

In October 2012 public opinion was galvanised by a tragic case of a young woman who died after being refused a termination. Savita Halappanavar, who was 17 weeks pregnant, presented with back pain at University Hospital Galway in October 2012. It was clear she was miscarrying. However, the miscarriage was delayed and in the interim she developed severe sepsis. She requested a termination but this was refused since the foetal heartbeat was still present, even though it was clear that the baby would not survive. It has been reported that the doctor was not clear on the legal position, since both mother and unborn baby had equal protection under the Eighth Amendment. Because the 1992 X case had not been legislated for, the doctor was not sure if she would be prosecuted for carrying out an abortion. *The Irish Times* reported that at the inquest, "The consultant obstetrician who treated Savita Halappanavar refused her request for a termination because of 'the legal position in Ireland'" (Cullen and Holland, 2013, p. 1). Following the verdict of the inquest into Ms Halappanavar's death, the jury adopted one of the recommendations of the coroner, i.e. that the Medical Council should revise its guidelines for doctors on the termination of pregnancies (ibid.).

The most recent and very significant legal development came on 30th December 2013 when the Protection of Life in Pregnancy Bill was enacted. This took 21 years from the 1992 Supreme Court decision in the X case. There is little doubt that the public reaction to the Halappanavar case and the Government's belated realisation that something had to be done to prevent this occurring to other women speeded up the legislative process. The Protection of Life in Pregnancy Act (2013) legislates for the X case. However, it does not provide for abortion under any other circumstances. The fact that public opinion is demonstrably supportive of abortion in the case of the woman's health being in danger, in cases of rape and incest and increasingly in cases of severe foetal abnormality, it is obvious that legislation is not keeping pace with the wishes of the population.

Note

1 $\chi^2 = 7.23$; df $= 3$; $p = 0.065$.

9 Attitudes to moral issues

9.1 Background and context

The purpose of the series of studies presented here has been to examine changing gender role attitudes in Ireland, with particular reference to the implications of such attitudes for the role and status of women. We have thus far examined a wide range of gender role attitudes, with particular focus on their implications for discrimination and employment equality. We have also explored attitudes toward divorce and abortion in relation to voting behaviour in two national referenda – the 1983 referendum in relation to abortion and the 1986 referendum in relation to divorce. Abortion and divorce are seen as moral issues to varying extents within the population (Breslin and Weafer, 1983, 1984; Fogarty *et al.*, 1984; Scott, 1989; Ester, Halman and de Moor, 1993; Hornsby-Smith and Whelan, 1994; MacGréil, 1996; McShane, 2010); however, discrimination towards outgroups has not always been included in studies of morality in Ireland or in the European Values Studies, although it was included in the research on religious beliefs and moral attitudes of Breslin and Weafer (1983, 1984) and has been addressed in other Irish studies which do not focus on morality per se (e.g. Davis *et al.*, 1984; MacGréil, 1996). However, even when attitudes towards outgroups are studied, women are not always included, since they are not perceived as an outgroup. Nevertheless, they have experienced and continue to experience discrimination based on their gender (Commission of the European Communities, 1987). For these reasons it seemed a logical next step to examine people's attitudes to these issues in a broader matrix of attitudes to moral issues generally. We did this in the context of the 1986 study (Fine-Davis, 1988c), which examined in depth attitudes to abortion and divorce and was carried out in close proximity to the two initial national referenda on these issues.

However, before embarking on an examination of the data obtained in this area, we must add the caveat that the subject of morality is a vast and complex one and the present study, of necessity, does not go into it in great depth. Other studies have taken this as their primary or major focus and the reader is referred to these for a fuller examination of moral attitudes in Ireland (e.g. Breslin and Weafer, 1983, 1984; Fogarty *et al.*, 1984; Whelan, 1994). The more delimited purpose of the examination of moral attitudes in the present study was to explore their implications for the status of women, a topic which has not generally been dealt with by other studies of moral issues.

9.2 An examination of attitudes to moral issues

9.2.1 Method

Ireland was very much a Catholic country in 1986, with the vast majority of the population identifying themselves as Catholics (Hornsby-Smith and Whelan, 1994). Church attendance is very high by European standards, with 87% of Catholics attending mass once a week (57%) or more (30%) as reported in the 1981 European Values Survey and these rates of church attendance remained relatively stable in 1990 (EVS) (ibid.). This compares to a European average in 1990 of 30% church attendance once a week or more (42% among Catholics), with 11% of Europeans saying they attend once a month and 51% saying "less often". However, by 1999–2000 the EVS showed that among Catholics, regular attenders (weekly or monthly) were 76%, whereas irregular attenders (less than monthly or never) were 24% (Fahey *et al.*, 2005). Thus, while Ireland was largely Catholic at the time of the 1986 survey it was by no means entirely Catholic and even among Catholics not everyone was a devout churchgoer. Hence, it was necessary to frame the questions in terminology meaningful to all of the respondents – Catholics, non-Catholics, religious and non-religious. In the context of moral issues it could be assumed that some respondents would be more inclined to evaluate various moral behaviours in terms of their degree of "sinfulness" and others would be more likely to do so in terms of their "morality" or "immorality". Hence respondents were first asked which of these two frameworks was most relevant for them (Table 9.1). The question was phrased as follows:

> Many people judge certain acts in terms of "sinfulness". Others might prefer to use a term such as "morality" or "immorality", which is based on one's own conscience. Which of these two frameworks do you tend

Table 9.1 Respondents' preference for the concept of "sin" or "morality/immorality"

	Total sample (N = 595) (%)	Re-weighted sample (%)
Believe in concept of "sin"	53.1	56.5
Prefer another concept such as "morality/immorality"	42.2	39.1
Other	3.4	2.5
Don't know/refused	1.3	1.8
Total	100.0	100.0

to use for the most part in judging acts which people engage in? Do you believe in the concept of "sin" and tend to judge people's acts accordingly or are you more comfortable with some other concept such as morality/immorality?

Believe in concept of "sin" 1

Prefer another concept such as "morality/immorality" 2

Other (please specify) 3

Don't know, refused 4

Respondents were, of course, free to refuse to make this distinction, if they found it a difficult choice to make, and to opt for a response of "3" or "4". However, 95.3% of the sample was able to make this choice readily, with only 3.4% choosing "Other" and 1.3% saying they didn't know or refusing to answer the question.

Demographic comparisons were carried out and there were no significant differences obtained. It may be seen in Table 9.1 that slightly more than half of the sample (56.5%) tends to think in terms of sin when judging or evaluating human behaviour and slightly less than half (39.1%) tends to see these acts in terms of morality. Bearing this in mind, respondents were encouraged to use their own framework to judge the moral issues. The series of questions was introduced by the interviewer as follows:

> I'm going to show you a list of things which some people consider to be sinful or immoral and others do not. I'd like you to please indicate how you feel about these things on the scales provided.

Respondents were presented with 15 different moral issues, or behaviours with moral or potentially moral implications (e.g. lying, stealing, murder, etc.). Each issue was followed by a seven-point bi-polar scale, ranging from "Not at all sinful or immoral" to "Extremely sinful or immoral", utilising the well-known Semantic Differential format (Osgood, Suci and Tannenbaum, 1957). Respondents were asked to respond to each scale by themselves to optimise their privacy.

9.2.2 Dimensions of morality

These responses were then factor analysed to see whether people tended to see certain moral issues in a similar way and whether the moral issues divided into clusters with a common thread, i.e. a typology of moral issues. The results of the factor analysis, which are presented in Table 9.2, show that people's responses are indeed guided by an underlying typology. The 15 moral issues fell into five clearly interpretable factors. The first contained the items: (1) Religious Intolerance, (2) Discrimination Against Women, (3) Racial Prejudice and (4) Discrimination Against Itinerants. This factor was called

Table 9.2 Factor analysis of ratings of 15 moral issues in terms of their perceived immorality or sinfulness (N = 600)

	Varimax Rotated Loading
Factor I: Discrimination	
1. Religious Intolerance	0.57
2. Discrimination Against Women	0.69
3. Racial Prejudice	0.50
4. Discrimination Against Itinerants	0.77
% Variance: 24.6 Cumulative % Variance: 24.6	
Factor II: Religiously Proscribed Sex-Related Behaviours – I	
1. Divorce	0.80
2. Using Contraceptives	0.85
3. Pre-Marital Sexual Intercourse	0.74
% Variance: 14.3 Cumulative % Variance: 38.9	
Factor III: Rape and Murder	
1. Rape	0.74
2. Murder	0.82
3. Killings carried out for allegedly political motives	0.57
% Variance: 9.4 Cumulative % Variance: 48.3	
Factor IV: Religiously Proscribed Sex-Related Behaviours – II	
1. Adultery	0.73
2. Abortion	0.59
% Variance: 7.7 Cumulative % Variance: 56.1	
Factor V: Dishonesty	
1. Stealing	0.64
2. Evading Tax	0.81
3. Lying	0.65
% Variance: 6.5 Cumulative % Variance: 62.6	

Discrimination. Factor II contained the items (1) Divorce, (2) Using Contraceptives and (3) Pre-Marital Sexual Intercourse. These items are all related to sex and all are proscribed by the Catholic Church. Factor II was thus named *Religiously Proscribed Sex-Related Behaviours I.* Factor III contained the items (1) Rape, (2) Murder and (3) Killings carried out of allegedly political motives; it was entitled *Rape and Murder.* Factor IV contained the items (1) Abortion and (2) Adultery, which are also related to sexual behaviour and also are proscribed by the Catholic Church. Factor IV was named *Religiously Proscribed Sex-Related Behaviours II.* Factor V contained the items (1) Lying, (2) Stealing and (3) Evading Tax. This last factor was called *Dishonesty.* Percentage responses to the individual items, grouped by factor, are presented in Table 9.3. There is some overlap in dimensions with those identified by Ester *et al.* (1993) using the European Values Survey data, discussed by Hornsby-Smith and Whelan (1994) in relation to Ireland. Ester *et al.* identified a "Permissiveness" dimension, which incorporated adultery, abortion and divorce among other things, and a "Civic Morality" dimension, which included cheating, lying in

Table 9.3 Attitudes toward moral issues, grouped by factor: percentage distributions for total sample[1] (N = 600)

		%	%	%	%	%	%	%	
Factor I: Discrimination (Mean Score For Total Sample = 5.25)									
1. Religious Intolerance	Not at all sinful or immoral	8.2	4.5	5.5	15.9	17.8	20.5	27.7	Extremely sinful or immoral
2. Discrimination Against Women	Not at all sinful or immoral	5.9	3.8	3.7	16.1	20.7	18.9	30.9	Extremely sinful or immoral
3. Racial Prejudice	Not at all sinful or immoral	2.7	2.5	1.5	8.3	12.9	22.6	49.5	Extremely sinful or immoral
4. Discrimination Against Itinerants	Not at all sinful or immoral	4.7	4.4	5.2	15.8	19.5	25.0	25.5	Extremely sinful or immoral
Factor II: Religiously Proscribed Sex-Related Behaviours – I (Mean Score = 3.21)									
1. Divorce	Not at all sinful or immoral	34.2	8.7	4.5	13.7	10.6	14.4	13.9	Extremely sinful or immoral
2. Using Contraceptives	Not at all sinful or immoral	53.5	10.3	6.6	10.5	6.9	4.4	7.8	Extremely sinful or immoral
3. Pre-marital Sexual Intercourse	Not at all sinful or immoral	25.8	7.3	6.5	13.7	10.5	12.0	24.2	Extremely sinful or immoral
Factor III: Murder and Rape (Mean Score = 6.79)									
1. Rape	Not at all sinful or immoral	0.1	0.3	0.1	0.3	2.2	4.2	92.8	Extremely sinful or immoral
2. Murder	Not at all sinful or immoral	–	0.4	0.1	–	1.3	5.4	92.8	Extremely sinful or immoral
3. Killings carried out for allegedly political motives	Not at all sinful or immoral	1.1	0.6	0.4	2.6	3.5	7.7	84.0	Extremely sinful or immoral
Factor IV: Religiously Proscribed Sex-Related Behaviours – II (Mean Score = 6.17)									
1. Adultery	Not at all sinful or immoral	3.3	1.2	1.8	6.1	8.9	17.5	61.2	Extremely sinful or immoral
2. Abortion	Not at all sinful or immoral	3.6	1.9	1.3	5.1	3.5	9.7	74.9	Extremely sinful or immoral
Factor V: Dishonesty (Mean Score = 5.04)									
1. Stealing	Not at all sinful or immoral	2.1	1.6	2.8	9.8	18.2	23.9	41.6	Extremely sinful or immoral
2. Evading Tax	Not at all sinful or immoral	17.1	9.5	5.5	16.3	17.5	15.8	18.4	Extremely sinful or immoral
3. Lying	Not at all sinful or immoral	4.8	6.3	6.7	15.8	21.8	22.1	22.5	Extremely sinful or immoral

Note
1 Re-weighted to reflect proportions in population.

one's own interest, etc. Interestingly political assassination loaded on this factor, whereas in our study it loaded with murder.

9.2.3 Perceptions of relative immorality/sinfulness of various behaviours

Mean (average) scores were computed for each respondent on each of the five moral issue factors. The average scores for the total sample are presented in Table 9.4. These are based on the potential range of 1 (not at all sinful or immoral) to 7 (extremely sinful or immoral).

It may be seen that the most sinful/immoral acts are considered to be those of murder, rape and killings carried out for political motives. The next most serious issues are perceived to be abortion and adultery. Following these are discrimination against women, religious and racial minorities and itinerants. Dishonesty comes next after Discrimination, followed by the other religiously proscribed sex-related behaviours of divorce, contraception and pre-marital sex, which are clearly seen as far less serious than those of abortion and adultery.

If one were to rank order each of the behaviours in terms of their mean (average) scores, the rank order would look as follows (Table 9.5):

Table 9.4 Mean scores for total sample on moral issue factors

Factor I:	Discrimination	5.25
Factor II:	Religiously Proscribed Sex-Related Behaviours – I	3.21
Factor III:	Rape and Murder	6.79
Factor IV:	Religiously Proscribed Sex-Related Behaviours – II	6.17
Factor V:	Dishonesty	5.04

Table 9.5 Perceived sinfulness/immorality* of various behaviours

		Weighted mean score
1	Murder	6.90
2	Rape	6.88
3	Killings Carried out for Political Motives	6.66
4	Abortion	6.32
5	Adultery	6.14
6	Racial Prejudice	5.92
7	Stealing	5.78
8	Discrimination Against Women	5.22
9	Discrimination Against Itinerants	5.18
10	Religious Intolerance	5.03
11	Lying	5.00
12	Evading Tax	4.28
13	Pre-Marital Sexual Intercourse	4.09
14	Divorce	3.57
15	Using Contraceptives	2.51

* Range is 1–7 with 1 = not at all sinful or immoral; 7 = extremely sinful or immoral.

It is apparent from these results that discrimination against women comes fairly down on the list. It is considered less immoral than adultery, racial prejudice or stealing. It is interesting to note that racial prejudice is considered more serious than discrimination on the basis of sex. This is particularly curious since there were so few members of racial minorities living in Ireland at the time this study was carried out, whereas women comprise approximately 51% of the population. Religious intolerance and discrimination against itinerants are seen as even less immoral than discrimination against women, indicating that religious minorities and itinerants are seen as worthy of less respect than women and racial minorities. The high level of prejudice toward itinerants/travellers in Ireland is well documented (Davis *et al.*, 1984; Report of the Task Force on the Travelling Community, 1995).

The data lead one to wonder if it may be easier to see racial prejudice as immoral when it is not on one's own doorstep (but rather in the UK, US or South Africa). Injustices against groups closer to home, such as women and itinerants/travellers – not to mention religious minorities – are apparently easier to overlook.

It is also worthy of consideration to see that the issues of contraception and divorce are the lowest on the list. They are not seen as particularly immoral. One wonders why then they engendered so much debate and controversy leading to legislation on the one hand and a referendum on the other.

An analysis of the determinants and correlates of the perceived sinfulness or immorality of these moral issue factors was then undertaken. Sex of respondent, age, marital status, socio-economic status and rural vs urban location were all examined. On the *Discrimination* factor, those living in rural areas were more likely to find discrimination (against women and minority groups) to be immoral.[1] Members of higher socio-economic groups were also more likely to consider discrimination immoral.[2] There was a trend which approached statistical significance that revealed married men to be most likely to consider discrimination immoral, more so than single men, and also somewhat more than women, as illustrated in Table 9.6. To the extent that this factor deals with discrimination against women, the trend reinforces other results seen previously to the effect that married men show greater empathy toward women than single men do.

Table 9.6 Perceived immorality of Discrimination: interaction effect between sex and marital status

	Married	*Single*
Men	5.47	5.05
Women	5.24	5.22

$F=3.43$; $p=0.064$

Older people and people in rural areas were significantly more likely to see the *Religiously Proscribed Sex-Related Behaviours* of divorce, contraception and pre-marital sex as immoral or sinful than were younger people and those living in Dublin.[3] These differences also held for abortion and adultery,[4] as well as for dishonesty.[5] There was also a rural/urban difference on the *Rape-Murder Factor* in the same direction of greater perceived immorality in rural areas.[6] In relation to lying, stealing and evading tax, single men were less likely than other groups to consider these as immoral.[7]

9.2.4 Relationship between religiosity and perceived immorality/ sinfulness of various behaviours

Because of the obvious relationship between religion and morality, an examination of the intercorrelations between Religiosity and attitudes to moral issues was made. Religiosity was measured by a factor containing several items including religious belief, the importance of prayer to the individual, the importance of religion to the individual and frequency of church attendance.[8] There were many significant relationships (see Table 9.7). It may be seen that the higher the person scored on the Religiosity factor, the more likely he/she was to see the five religiously proscribed sex-related behaviours as sinful or immoral. These relationships were very strong and highly significant in all cases. On the other hand, there was no significant relationship between religiosity and attitudes concerning discrimination against women, itinerants and social and religious minorities, although one might have expected, in view of ethical religious teachings, a significant positive correlation between religiosity and the viewing of these acts as immoral and sinful. Nor was there a significant relationship between religiosity and perceived immorality of rape or murder (other than political killings), or indeed between religiosity and lying, stealing and evading tax. This pattern of findings would suggest that the morality or immorality of certain issues may be stressed in Church more than other issues. These would appear to be the sex-related behaviours.

The Dean of St Patrick's Cathedral, Dublin, The Very Rev. Victor Griffin, pointed out in a paper putting forth the Protestant position prior to the abortion referendum:

> This proposed Amendment is one more example of our sex obsessed society. The idea of sin seems to be confined to the sexual sphere. The moral writ of "right" and "wrong" runs only in the domain of sexual morality. Hence far more emphasis is placed on so-called sexual rectitude than on matters of personal honesty, national righteousness and social justice.
>
> (Griffin, 1983, p. 3)

The present data would appear to bear this out.

Table 9.7 Correlations between Religiosity composite score and perceived sinfulness/immorality of various behaviours (N=600)

Perceived sinfulness/immorality of:	Correlation with religiosity
Factor I: Discrimination	
1. Religious Intolerance	r=0.08
2. Discrimination Against Women	r=−0.05
3. Racial Prejudice	r=−0.00
4. Discrimination Against Itinerants	r=−0.04
Factor II: Religiously Proscribed Sex-Related Behaviours – I	
1. Divorce	r=0.41***
2. Using Contraceptives	r=0.36***
3. Pre-Marital Sexual Intercourse	r=0.45***
Factor III: Rape and Murder	
1. Rape	r=0.01
2. Murder	r=0.07
3. Killings Carried out for Allegedly Political Motives	r=0.19***
Factor IV: Religiously Proscribed Sex-Related Behaviours – II	
1. Abortion	r=0.39***
2. Adultery	r=0.34***
Factor V: Dishonesty	
1. Lying	r=0.09
2. Stealing	r=0.08
3. Evading Tax	r=0.07

9.3 Summary, current attitudes and conclusions

9.3.1 Summary of findings on moral issues

The two preceding chapters – Chapters 7 and 8 – focused on people's attitudes and voting behaviour in two national referenda on divorce (1986) and abortion (1983). As these issues are of particular relevance to women and their status, they were considered an essential part of a study of changing gender role attitudes. A wide range of gender role attitudes have been examined, with particular focus on their implications for discrimination and equal opportunity. Discrimination against women, abortion and divorce are seen as moral issues to varying extents within the population. For this reason, it was considered appropriate to examine people's attitudes to these issues in the broader context of attitudes to moral issues generally.

Our analysis of attitudes to divorce, abortion and moral issues identified the importance of religiosity as a key correlate of attitudes to divorce, attitudes to abortion and attitudes to sex-related behaviours generally. Religiosity, as well as the influence of church sermons, were also significant predictors of voting behaviour in the divorce referendum and the influence of religious groups was considered by many authors (O'Leary,

1987; Prendiville, 1998; Burley and Regan, 2002; Fahey, 2012) to have been a key factor in the divorce referendum (see Chapter 7).

Not surprisingly, it was found that the most sinful/immoral acts were considered to be murder, rape and killings carried out for political motives. While it may not be surprising that abortion was considered the next most sinful or immoral act, since many consider it to be akin to murder, it was less predictable that adultery would be seen as the next most sinful/immoral act. It was considered more sinful or immoral, for example, than racial and religious prejudice, discrimination against women, lying, stealing and evading tax. It was also noteworthy, in the context of the focus of the present study, that discrimination against women was considered less immoral than stealing or than racial prejudice – in addition to its lower rank order after adultery.

The fact that racial prejudice was considered more serious than discrimination on the basis of sex is particularly curious since there are so few members of racial minorities living in Ireland, whereas women comprise approximately 51% of the population. Religious intolerance and discrimination against itinerants/travellers were seen as even less immoral than discrimination against women, indicating that religious minorities and itinerants are seen as worthy of less respect than women and racial minorities. It may be easier to acknowledge the immorality of racial prejudice when it is not on one's own doorstep, whereas injustices against groups closer to home, such as women and itinerants, not to mention religious minorities, may be more comfortable to overlook.

It was also noteworthy that the issues of contraception and divorce were not seen as particularly immoral. In view of this, it is interesting that they engendered so much debate and controversy leading to legislation, on the one hand, and a referendum on the other.

The relationship between religiosity and perceived immorality/sinfulness of these various behaviours was examined. The greater the religiosity, the more likely the person was to see the five religiously proscribed sex-related behaviours (contraception, divorce, pre-marital sex, adultery and abortion) as sinful or immoral. These relationships were very strong and highly statistically significant in all cases. On the other hand, there was no significant relationship between religiosity and attitudes concerning discrimination against women, itinerants and social and religious minorities, although one might have expected, in view of ethical religious teachings, a significant positive correlation between religiosity and the viewing of these acts as immoral and sinful. Nor was there a significant relationship between religiosity and perceived immorality of rape or murder (other than political killings), or indeed between religiosity and lying, stealing and evading tax. This pattern of findings would suggest that the morality or immorality of certain behaviours may be stressed to a greater degree by the Church than other issues. These would clearly appear to be sex-related behaviours. Commenting on the results, the Joint Oireachtas Committee on Women's Rights, in its preface to the study, observed:

The results of the study revealed the close link between religiosity ... and perceived immorality of sex-related behaviours, whereas no link between religious beliefs and perceived morality/immorality of issues concerned with social justice was found. The Joint Committee are concerned that issues of social justice, particularly discrimination against women and other disadvantaged groups, are not widely perceived as moral issues by the population. These are issues which should be incorporated into school curricula and teacher training. This recommendation complements recommendations made in the Joint Committee's Report on Education (Pl. 2671).

(Second Joint Committee on Women's Rights, 1988, p. VI)

The importance of religion in the context of attitudes to abortion has also been highlighted by authors in the United States (e.g. Jelen *et al.*, 1993) and Britain (Scott, 1998). Scott (1998) also discusses the importance of religion cross-culturally in relation to generational changes in attitudes to abortion and the conflicting beliefs people often hold in relation to abortion (Scott, 1989).

The apparent preoccupation with the morality of sex-related behaviours by the Church and the apparent relative under-emphasis of the morality of other issues, such as discrimination, including discrimination against women, has led to a situation in which sex-related issues receive pre-eminent attention in public debates in the Oireachtas and in the media.

Such a state of affairs is unusual by international standards and has not gone unnoticed in international fora. For example, Ireland's attitudes towards women were highlighted in an EU report around the time of this data collection which showed that Ireland was at the bottom of the league in the European Community concerning issues of equality of the sexes (Commission of the European Communities, 1987). The 1988 Supreme Court decision, upholding a 1986 High Court decision to ban access to information concerning abortion was considered so newsworthy as to merit page one status in a major international newspaper:

the public's more traditional preferences have been made clear in the explicit constitutional ban on abortion and, two years ago, in the defeat of a proposal to legalise divorce, a campaign that has left Irish politicians warier than ever of public issues that invite church pronouncements.... Critics citing the divorce and abortion issues, say the republic's politics are steeped in church dogma.

(Clines, 1988, p. 1)

Perhaps in response to media coverage such as this, the Catholic Church has been known to issue statements which attempt to deflect this image as one focused almost entirely on sexual morality to one which is more focused on social justice. One such pronouncement at this time came from the US Roman Catholic Bishops. In a pastoral letter on women, the Bishops "labeled sexism a sin, recommended removing sexist language from the liturgy and urged that positions of authority and leadership be opened to women" (Hyer, 1988, p. 3).

Similar views were expressed in the Conclusion to a Report on "Religious Beliefs, Practice and Moral Attitudes", carried out at the Council for Research and Development, St Patrick's College, Maynooth (Breslin and Weafer, 1984):

> The pastoral response called for would seem to be a pro-active one, by the deliberate espousal of the equal rights of women in all areas of society, including Church-related affairs. The Catholic Church should be, and should be seen to be, in the vanguard of those who seek justice for all oppressed groups in society.
>
> (p. 147)

It will be noted that some 25 years later, the Church still has not deigned to allow women to become priests – in spite of public support for this (McShane, 2010, p. 6).

Regardless of any potential changes of emphasis within the Church, it is the primary role of legislators to legislate for the common good. From the period of the referendums of 1983 and 1986 to the present relatively little progress has been made. Divorce was eventually legalised in 1996 and women's life is now protected if a pregnancy endangers it. This latter development did not become enshrined in legislation until the end of 2013. It has been a notable feature of the Irish social and political landscape, that public opinion frequently precedes political action by a significant margin.

9.3.2 Current attitudes to morality

More recent research carried out in 2010 on attitudes to religion and moral issues indicates that attitudes in this sphere have changed considerably. This research suggests that "most Irish people have adopted a relatively liberal view of sex and sexual practices, in contrast with the traditional Catholic Church teachings on the subject" (McShane, 2010, p. 6). The relative "sinfulness" of various moral issues also differs in some respects from our findings of 1986. While the various moral issues differed to some extent between the two studies, carried out some 24 years apart, it would appear that things like lying, financial fraud, drink driving and tax evasion are viewed in a more negative light than for example sexual infidelity or pre-marital sex. The author notes that people's "moral compass" has become recalibrated and there is now a "significant disjoint between Catholic Church teachings on core issues and views of ordinary Catholics on the same matters" (ibid.). Commenting on the findings, the Editorial in the *Irish Times* observed that:

The decline in the centrality of the Catholic Church and of its moral authority to the lives of the 89 per cent who say they are Catholics has been clear to all for some time, not least in the evidence of empty pews on Sundays – only a third say they attend religious services weekly and only 13 per cent admit to being "strongly religious". But the decline in religiosity has been accompanied by an even more dramatic shift over a generation in terms of willingness to take stands opposed to church teaching.

(Editor, *The Irish Times*, 2010, p. 17)

Gaffney (2010) commenting on the findings observes:

For what was once the most powerful institution in the land, the Catholic Church, the poll results must be deeply disturbing.... And this is on top of the ongoing outrage about the church's response to the scandal of clerical child sexual abuse. There is a comprehensive rejection of the position of the church on matters of personal morality and on how the church itself is governed – the issues it most publicly embraces. Sex outside marriage, cohabitation, women priests, celibacy, attendance at Mass – the majority of us now don't agree with the church on any of these positions, with younger people particularly alienated. There are, of course, subtleties in the response. Many may indeed still regard abortion as morally wrong (the survey did not the probe that), but not so abhorrent that it would prevent about half of us from helping a friend to have an abortion abroad. We may admire celibacy when freely chosen for moral or religious reasons; we may personally value virginity in a potential partner – but we reject these values being turned into dogma. In fact, we don't find the church's position on anything to do with sexuality or women credible. The sexual revolution, the development of effective contraception, the growth of the women's and gay rights movements – all these historical shifts have left the church stranded with an archaic psychology of sexuality (p. 14).

Notes

1 $F = 20.39$; $p < 0.001$
2 $F = 3.86$; $p < 0.05$
3 $F = 63.67$; $p < 0.001$ for age; $F = 109.37$; $p < 0.001$ for rural/urban location.
4 $F = 20.99$; $p < 0.001$ for age; $F = 22.88$; $p < 0.001$ for rural/urban location.
5 $F = 4.94$; $p < 0.05$ for age; $F = 11.70$; $p < 0.001$ for rural/urban location.
6 $F = 5.38$; $p < 0.05$.
7 $F = 5.39$; $p < 0.05$.
8 This composite measure, based on the earlier work of Faulkner and De Jong (1965), Glock and Stark (1965) and MacGréil (1974) was developed in Ireland in 1975 (Davis *et al.*, 1977) and subsequently replicated in several other Irish studies (e.g. Fine-Davis, 1979a; Davis *et al.*, 1984).

10 Current attitudes and policy issues

10.1 Background and context

The major changes in women's roles in Ireland began in the 1970s, a time of great social and legislative change in the area of gender equality. Many of the deterrents to women's employment were removed. One of the most important of these was the removal of the "marriage bar" in 1973 which had prevented married women from working. This was followed by a series of legislative changes concerning equal pay, equal employment opportunity, contraception, and taxation policy. Several of these developments were directly or indirectly a result of Ireland joining the European Community in 1973. Others resulted from legal cases within the country. Most of these advances related to removing barriers to women's participation in the labour market as well as putting their participation more on an equal footing with men's.

In addition to issues affecting women's labour force participation, there have also been three key issues which have dominated political and social debate over the decades since the 1970s. The first of these was contraception. The lack of access to contraception not only constituted a barrier to women's access to the labour force, it also represented an instance of control by the State and the Catholic Church working in synchrony to prevent women from having autonomous control of their own reproductive behaviour and thus their own destinies. The other two issues which engendered heated debate and controversy were divorce and abortion. Both of these were seen as so significant that they were the subject of national referenda prior to legislation and abortion continues to be an important social issue which is likely to be re-visited in the future. As has been discussed in Chapters 7 and 8, the controversies surrounding these two issues were very much related to the role of the Catholic Church and to what extent it would continue to dictate the norms of morality to the society. The fact that these issues were so hotly debated indicated the sensitivity and the significance of the issues on both sides.

As a result of the liberalisation in the areas of gender equality, contraception, divorce and to a very limited extent, abortion, the Ireland of today scarcely resembles the Ireland of the 1970s and 1980s. The secularisation of the society increased and the influence of the Catholic Church, particularly in the area of gender role behaviour, significantly diminished during this time, as women were now able to control their fertility and increasingly move out of the private sphere into the public realm (Inglis, 1987, 1998; O'Connor, 1998; Kennedy, 2001; Ferriter, 2009).

Together with these developments have come major shifts in attitudes. These have included a greater acceptance of women's role outside the home as well as changes in perceptions concerning female equality. There have been significant attitudinal shifts on the sensitive indicator of attitudes to maternal employment as well as on policy issues which directly bear on women's equality – contraception, equal pay and taxation of married women. These attitudinal shifts sometimes presaged legislative reform and in other cases followed this reform. We have also seen that attitudes to the more recently debated sensitive moral issues, notably abortion, have also changed in a less orthodox direction, more reflective of the secular society that Ireland is becoming.

This increasing secularisation, together with the social policy and attitudinal changes, has been accompanied by a major increase in women's labour force participation – one of the most dramatic social shifts of this period, with participation rates which now approximate European norms. Employment of married women was the exception rather than the rule in the early 1960s and 1970s. It was almost negligible in the 1960s, with just 5.2% employed as of the 1961 Census. Even by 1971, the rate was just 7.5%. Yet during the 1970s, 1980s and 1990s this rate continued to grow with increasing momentum. By 2009 the figure had increased ten-fold to 54%. The participation of married women in the prime childbearing age group (25–34) increased at an even more rapid rate – in spite of the difficulty of this group to work, given their high likelihood of having children. By 2009 the participation rate of this group was 72.6%. Women's labour force participation has been facilitated by all of the changes – attitudinal and legislative – that have taken place over the last 35 years. It has also been fuelled by women's increased participation in third level education which now surpasses that of men (Lunn and Fahey, 2011).

10.2 Demographic changes

The last three to four decades have also witnessed significant changes in demographic patterns and the nature of the family. These have included a decline in marriage rates as well as a tendency to postpone marriage (Punch, 2007). The average age at which women marry has gone from 24.7 years in 1980 to 31 years in 2005. This, in turn, has affected the average age at which women are now having their first child. While this was 25 years of age in 1980, it rose to 31 in 2005 (ibid.) and has stabilised at between 30–31 (CSO, 2013). These trends suggest that attitudes toward marriage and norms regarding the appropriate age to get married and have children have changed. These changes also reflect the fact that women are staying in education longer and this is equipping them to participate at a higher level in the labour market.

The lesser prevalence of marriage has been accompanied by a greater variety of living arrangements and the traditional nuclear family is now being replaced in many cases by new family forms (Drew, 1998; Family Support Agency, 2005; Punch, 2007; Fahey and Field, 2008; Lunn *et al.*, 2009; Lunn and Fahey, 2011). While having children used to take place primarily in the context of marriage, it is now becoming more common for childbirth and parenting to take place also outside of marriage – either in the context of cohabitation or single parenthood. Punch (2007) points out that

> the strong link which formerly existed between marriage and fertility has weakened in the last few decades. Up to 1980 births outside marriage accounted for less than 5 per cent of all births. However, during the 1980s and 1990s the percentage increased rapidly reaching a figure of 31.1 per cent by 1999. The figure has since stabilised at around 31 to 32 per cent.
>
> (p. 7)

More recently the rate has increased to 34% (CSO, 2013). Of these, approximately half or 19.4% of total births were to unmarried parents with the same address, indicating births in cohabiting relationships (ibid.).

The fastest growing category of family is that of couples – whether married or not – without children. This group increased 130% in the 20 years from 1986 to 2006. Many of these couples are cohabiting. The increase from 1996 to 2006 was four-fold (Lunn and Fahey, 2011). On the basis of the 2006 Census data it is evident that cohabitees tend to be young – 41% of the males and 53% of cohabiting females were less than 30 years of age (Punch, 2007). However, Punch points out that it is not clear to what extent cohabitation is a *precursor* to marriage or whether it is a more permanent form of relationship replacing marriage. However, Lunn and Fahey (2011), examining microdata for households, found that the likelihood of a couple getting married increased sharply after the birth of a first child.

In addition to these major demographic changes and changes in the nature of the family, there have also been changes in Irish fertility patterns. In the 20 years from 1986 to 2006 the average number of children per family decreased from 2.2 to 1.4 (Punch, 2007). Women and men are therefore choosing to have fewer children than in previous generations. We are also observing another significant demographic change, namely an increase in the proportion of childless women – which now stands at

17.5% (CSO, 2007). Among women born in the 1960s, who may be assumed to have completed their fertility, approximately 20% did not have children as of the 2006 Census (Punch, 2007). More recently, Lunn *et al.* (2009) reported that over 50% of 32-year-old women university graduates were childless, compared with less than 25% of women with lower secondary level or less. This phenomenon of increasing childlessness is one which has also been observed in some other countries. For example in Germany, one-third of the cohort of women born in 1965 is childless (Kohler, Billari and Ortega, 2002). Factors such as attitudes toward marriage and children, family policies and employment patterns are seen as contributing to this trend.

10.3 The relationship between women's labour force participation and fertility

Concomitant with the demographic changes cited above, particularly women's increasing labour force participation, together with the changes in attitudes to gender roles, has come a steep fall in the birth rate in many EU and OECD countries, including Ireland. As may be seen in Table 10.1, Ireland's traditionally high fertility rate fell from a total fertility rate (TFR) of 3.93 children in 1970 to 1.90 in 2000, representing a decrease of over 50% during this period. This trend reflects the downward trend in Europe as a whole, which went from a TFR of 2.38 to 1.50 during this same period. Ireland started from a higher base than most other European countries since the social changes in women's roles began later, in addition to the fact that fertility and gender roles were strongly influenced by the Catholic Church in Ireland at that time which promoted traditional and pronatalist values.

The decrease in fertility in Ireland over the last three decades mirrors the increasing labour force participation of married women during the same period (see Table 10.1). While Ireland currently has the highest total fertility rate in Europe at 2.04 in 2011 (the EU average being 1.57) (CSO,

Table 10.1 Relationship between married women's labour force participation and total fertility rate in Ireland 1960–2009

	1960/ 1961	1970/ 1971	1980/ 1981	1989/ 1990	2000/ 2001	2004	2009
Employment rate All ages	5.2%	7.5%	16.7%	23.7%	46.4%	49.4%	54.0%
Employment rate Ages 25–34	4.8%	8.8%	21.6%	39.0%	64.7%	65.5%	72.6%
Total fertility rate	3.76	3.93	3.25	2.11	1.90	1.99	2.07

Sources: CSO (various) and Eurostat (2006).

2014), this still reflects a significant decrease in fertility in Ireland of approximately 50% over the last four decades. It has been predicted by the Central Statistics Office that this will further decrease (CSO, 1999, 2007) and that Ireland's birth rate is likely to continue to fall in line with European norms unless policies intervene to change this trend. The only countries which have been able to reverse this downward trend in fertility are France and Denmark as a result of the introduction of family policies in the 1990s to support both women's labour force participation and their fertility (Fagnani, 2008).

D'Addio and Mira d'Ercole (2005) concluded that fertility rates below replacement level are likely to be a persistent feature of most OECD countries in the coming years. They attribute this to women's higher educational attainment and their increasing labour force participation, as well as changes in their values, which include increased financial autonomy and a less traditional attitude toward family roles. However, they point to the US, France and the Nordic countries as exceptions to this trend, all of which have fertility rates close to replacement. They say that the factors which contribute to "success" in these countries include policies which contribute to the lower cost of having children, namely direct transfers and tax advantages, but more importantly

> investment in education and childcare facilities, access to a variety of caring arrangement, affordable housing, leave provisions and features of their labour market that do not penalise women for their decision to have children and that facilitate the sharing of family chores and the reconciliation of work and family life for young couples.
>
> (Ibid., p. 70)

10.4 Changing attitudes to gender roles

In light of the major demographic, attitudinal and social changes which have occurred in Ireland over the last three to four decades since the early 1970s, one might ask, where are we now? Have gender role attitudes continued to change? Has women's increased status and representation in the workplace had any effects on gender roles and on male/female relationships? Has there been a male backlash to women's success (see Faludi, 1991)? And what are the current crunch policy issues which the society now faces?

We attempted to answer these questions in our recent study, entitled: "Changing Gender Role Attitudes and Behaviour: Implications for Family Formation in Ireland" (Fine-Davis, 2011, 2014). We were interested in seeing to what extent changing gender roles had impacted on people's relationship formation and childbearing behaviour. The study was carried out against the backdrop of major demographic change in the society, which we have highlighted above. Marriage rates had decreased; cohabitation rates had increased. The proportion of people remaining single had also risen. This was accompanied by smaller family sizes, an increase in single person households, delayed fertility and a decrease in the birth rate (Punch, 2007; Fahey and Field, 2008; Lunn *et al.*, 2009). Could any of these developments have been related to the changing gender role attitudes and behaviour that we have seen?

In order to attempt to answer these questions we knew that we would need to find out how people saw gender roles today. The measures which were relevant in the earlier period were no longer sufficiently sensitive to measure current attitudes to gender roles. Because gender role attitudes and behaviour are changing so rapidly it was necessary to develop new measures which adequately capture how people view these issues at the present time, although some items from earlier research were also included.

We thus embarked on an in-depth qualitative study of people in the childbearing age group (Fine-Davis, 2009). This included a stratified sample of 48 men and women throughout the country who varied by social class and family status. On the basis of the results of this qualitative study, we developed a questionnaire which reflected people's current views and attitudes to gender roles and gender relations, family formation and childbearing as well as attitudes to related social policies and aspects of well-being. The items in the questionnaire reflect the recurring themes which emerged in the qualitative study and they reflect the actual language used by the respondents. We then administered this questionnaire to a representative nationwide sample of 1,404 men and women in the childbearing age group. (See Chapter 2 for a fuller discussion of the methodology employed in this study.)

We shall present here some of the key findings concerning current gender role attitudes as well as some of the highlights from other aspects of the study in order to update our earlier findings concerning evolving gender role attitudes in Ireland.

10.4.1 *Attitudes to gender roles and gender relations*

As before, we employed the technique of factor analysis to identify underlying attitudinal clusters or dimensions. Our analysis of items measuring attitudes to gender roles and gender relations yielded an optimally interpretable set of six factors, which we shall describe briefly below (see Table 10.2).

The first factor concerns women's increasing participation in the labour force. The factor is entitled *Perceived Threat of Women's Career Advancement.* As with naming of all factors, the name is phrased so as to be consistent with the directionality of the majority of the items loading on the factor. However, it must be remembered that the factor also measures the opposite of this, since factors measure a continuum of attitudes from

Table 10.2 Factor analysis of 29 items measuring attitudes to gender roles: items from six Varimax rotated factors (N = 1,404)

Item no.	Varimax rotated loading
Factor I: Perceived Threat of Women's Career Advancement	
7. Some men feel threatened by women's advances in the workplace.	0.74
9. Men don't really like it that much that women are getting higher positions – and climbing the scale.	0.69
17. Career oriented women can be more threatening to men.	0.67
14. Most men would find it intimidating to go out with a woman who has a high-powered job.	0.65
10. There would be a proportion of men who would feel women may be taking their jobs.	0.64
27. Men can be uncomfortable if women are too assertive.	0.64
6. Most men could find it difficult taking orders from women at work.	0.64
*11. Men feel a little redundant because there is so much competition from women.	0.49
*29. Women can be so independent sometimes that it makes men feel like they're not needed anymore.	0.48
% Variance: 15.16 Cumulative % Variance: 15.16 Cronbach Alpha: 0.85	
Factor II: Male Role Ambiguity	
28. With all the changes in gender roles, it's hard to know who's supposed to do what.	0.73
25. A lot of men are confused about their roles because they are less defined than they used to be.	0.71
26. As a result of change in women's roles, men are not sure where they stand.	0.63
12. It's more difficult for a man to find a partner now because women are putting careers ahead of relationships.	0.57
11. Men feel a little redundant because there is so much competition from women.	0.54
8. Women's gains in the workplace have sometimes been at the expense of men.	0.52
29. Women can be so independent sometimes that it makes men feel like they're not needed anymore.	0.49
% Variance: 11.73 Cumulative % Variance: 26.89 Cronbach Alpha: 0.83	
Factor III: Support for Female Economic Independence	
22. It's good for a woman to be financially independent in a relationship.	0.68
21. Most men are happy for women to pay their own way.	0.63
16. I think men nowadays like intelligent women who know what they want out of life.	0.62
4. Both men and women should contribute to the household income.	0.60

19. A woman who has a job she enjoys is likely to be a better wife and mother because she has an interest and some fulfilment outside the home. 0.52

% Variance: 7.43   Cumulative % Variance: 34.32   Cronbach Alpha: 0.61

Factor IV: Belief in Traditional Male Support and Protection

5. Most men need and want to give the kind of protection and support that they have traditionally given to women. 0.76

2. Most women need and want the kind of protection and support that men have traditionally given them. 0.70

1. Being a wife and mother are the most fulfilling roles any woman could want. 0.52

% Variance: 5.79   Cumulative % Variance: 40.11   Cronbach Alpha: 0.50

Factor V: Perceived Male Reluctance to Share Housework

3. There's an awful lot of lip service paid to "sharing responsibilities", but it's still a man's world at the end of the day. 0.62

15. While men recognise that women have to spend less time on housework, they don't recognise that they have to contribute more than they used to. 0.52

13. Men respect women more at work than at home. 0.43

20. If a woman is financially independent it can lead to difficulties in a relationship. 0.41

% Variance: 5.59   Cumulative % Variance: 45.70   Cronbach Alpha: 0.62

Factor VI: Belief that Mothers are Best Nurturers

23. Caring for children is best done by mothers. 0.74

24. Fathers can be as nurturing to children as mothers can. -0.58

18. It's bad for young children if their mothers go out and work, even if they are well taken care of by another adult. 0.47

% Variance: 5.53   Cumulative % Variance: 51.23   Cronbach Alpha: 0.49

Note
* Item not composited on this factor because of split loading on Factor II.

strongly disagree to strongly agree. The high loading items contain statements such as "some men feel threatened by women's advances in the workplace" and "men don't really like it that much that women are getting higher positions – and climbing the ladder". The factor also includes items that suggest that women's increased participation in the workplace may negatively impinge on their relationships with men, for example – "career oriented women can be more threatening to men" and "most men would find it intimidating to go out with a woman who has a high-powered job". The Cronbach alpha for this factor is .85, which is unusually high and indicates that it is a very robust and reliable factor. This is notable, since we are not aware of any similar measures in the literature.

Factor II is entitled *Male Role Ambiguity*. It taps an attitude cluster concerning men's perception of their own role in light of changes in women's roles. Those high on the factor tend to agree that "with all the changes in gender roles, it's hard to know who's supposed to do what". This is consistent with the next statement to the effect that "a lot of men are confused about their roles because they are less defined than they used to be". Those high on the factor tend to agree that "as a result of change in women's roles, men are not sure where they stand". The factor also includes a statement concerning family formation: those high on the factor are more likely to think that "it's more difficult for a man to find a partner now because women are putting careers ahead of relationships". The element of the workplace is clearly represented by the item "women's gains in the workplace have sometimes been at the expense of men" and "men feel a little redundant because there is so much competition from women". Thus male role ambiguity is connected to an increasing lack of definition of gender roles and to women's increasing role in the workplace, which may be perceived as having some negative consequences for men. In addition, the factor suggests that male role ambiguity may in part be related to a feeling of not being needed as a result of women's changing role: "Women can be so independent sometimes that it makes men feel like they're not needed anymore." This factor also has a very high Cronbach alpha of 0.83 indicating it is very robust and reliable. As in the case of the first factor, this factor is also, as far as we are aware, tapping a new dimension in the literature.

Factor III is entitled *Support for Female Economic Independence*. This factor expresses the view that "it's good for a woman to be financially independent in a relationship" and "most men are happy for women to pay their own way". It also contains the belief that "both men and women should contribute to the household income". Linked with support for financial independence appears to be an admiration for women: "I think men nowadays like intelligent women who know what they want out of life". Thus, in contrast to some of the items loading on Factors I and II, this factor expresses a positive view about women's financial independence in the context of relationships. Finally, the factor contains an item about maternal employment which was used in several of the previous studies – "a woman who has a job she enjoys is likely to be a better wife and mother because she has an interest and some fulfilment outside the home". Hence we see that in the context of support for female economic independence we also see support for maternal employment, an issue which in earlier studies had sometimes been an indicator of traditional attitudes, although clearly there has been significant change in this area.

Factor IV is entitled *Belief in Traditional Male Support and Protection*. It contains three items, including two which have been used extensively in previous research on gender roles (e.g. Fine-Davis, 1983a, 1983b, 1988a; Fine-Davis *et al.*, 2005), i.e. "Most women need and want the kind of protection and support that men have traditionally given them" and "being a wife and mother are the most fulfilling roles any woman could want". For the first time a male counterpart to the first item was designed, i.e. "Most men need and want to give the kind of protection and support that they have traditionally given to women." Together, these items measure belief in traditional gender roles, with an emphasis on male support and protection of the female.

Factor V concerns male participation in domestic activities and is entitled *Male Reluctance to Share Housework*. The highest loading item (i.e. most reflective of the factor as a whole) is "There's an awful lot of lip service paid to 'sharing responsibilities', but it's still a man's world at the end of the day." The next highest item is "While men recognise that women have to spend less time on housework, they don't recognise that they have to contribute more than they used to." The factor captures the essence of one of today's most difficult problems, namely how to facilitate sharing of domestic responsibilities in light of women's increasing labour force participation. The two other items on the factor add further nuances to this issue. The item, "Men respect women more at work than at home" suggests that while women are earning greater respect in the workplace, this does not necessarily translate to the private sphere. The final item on the factor "If a woman is financially independent it can lead to difficulties in a relationship" suggests again that women's labour force participation is somehow unsettling the delicate balance of male/female relations, including in the personal sphere.

The sixth and final factor in this set contains items which have to do with nurturing of children. The factor is entitled *Belief that Mothers are Best Nurturers*. Those high on this factor tend to think that "caring for children is best done by mothers". They tend to disagree that "fathers can be as nurturing to children as mothers can" (disagreement indicated by the negative loading of the item). Those high on the factor also tend to feel that "it's bad for young children if their mothers go out and work, even if well taken care of by another adult". Conversely, those low on the factor tend to think fathers can be as nurturing as mothers and tend not to think that maternal employment is detrimental to children. In light of women's increasing labour force participation, men's role in childcare has come to the fore and such attitudes are therefore increasingly important.

10.4.2 Prevalence of attitudes to gender roles and gender relations

To what extent do people hold the attitudes just described? And do men and women differ on these attitudes? Below we shall explore how these new attitudinal dimensions are actually distributed in the population. Table 10.3 presents percentage responses for the weighted sample for each of the items grouped by factor.

While Factor I, *Perceived Threat of Women's Career Advancement,* has an ominous tone, the study found that a majority of the sample actually did agree with most of the items on this factor, indicating that there is a consensus that women's career advancement is perceived to be posing a threat to at least some men. For example, 59% agreed that "some men feel threatened by women's advances in the workplace". This may be related to the fact that "there would be a proportion of men who would feel women may be taking their jobs", a statement to which 62% of the sample also agreed. Almost two-thirds (64%) agreed that "men can be uncomfortable if women are too assertive". The factor indicated that almost half of the sample (45%) felt that "men don't really like it that much that women are getting higher positions – and climbing the scale". In light of the fact women are now more likely to be in supervisory positions, it is noteworthy that over half of the sample (54%) felt that "most men could find it difficult taking order from women at work". The findings also suggest that attitudes to women in the workplace can sometimes spill over into the personal sphere. Close to half of the sample (45%) felt that "most men would find it intimidating to go out with a woman who has a high-powered job" and over half (57%) felt that "career oriented women can be more threatening to men".

What these results are showing is that people feel that men are not entirely comfortable with women's progress in the workplace and for some it poses a distinct threat. Women's success in the workplace may also come with a personal price, since it appears that many think men are intimidated by career oriented women and those with "high-powered jobs". To what extent men and women agree or differ with respect to these perceptions will be examined in the next section. We shall also explore the extent to which such attitudes may be having an effect on attitudes to relationships and family formation.

Factor II, *Male Role Ambiguity,* was the second strongest factor in this set of attitudes to gender roles. The responses to the items on this factor indicate that the sample is quite divided in its views. For example, 42% agree that "with all the changes in gender roles, it's hard to know who's supposed to do what", while 47% disagree. Similarly 44% agree that "a lot of men are confused about their roles because they are less defined than they used to be", while 47% disagree. Two of the items reflect a feeling of "redundancy" on the part of men. In one case changes in the workplace have left men feeling "a little redundant because there is so much competition from women"; 40% agreed that this was the case, while 52% disagreed. This notion of redundancy was echoed in another item which seems to relate to the personal sphere: "women can be so independent sometimes that it makes men feel like they're not needed anymore". It is notable that a majority (52%) agreed with this. This suggests that an element in male role ambiguity resulting from changing gender roles may relate to a feeling on men's part that they are not needed. This would seem to be an important psychological element in this overall cluster of attitudes.

Factor III, *Support for Female Economic Independence*, shows a high level of agreement with all of the items on this factor, indicating strong support for women's financial independence. The vast majority of the sample (90%) agreed that "It's good for a woman to be financially independent in a relationship." There was also very strong agreement (88%) that "both men and women should contribute to the household income". Most people (79%) thought that "men are happy for women to pay their own way". A majority (74%) endorsed the view that "a woman who has a job she enjoys is likely to be a better wife and mother because she has an interest and some fulfilment outside the home". The juxtaposition of this item with items about financial independence indicates the emergence of integrated thinking about women's fulfilment, child welfare and the economic well-being of the family unit, something which was certainly not evident in the earlier studies in which maternal employment was seen as a controversial issue solely concerned with children's welfare (see Chapters 3, 4 and 6). The factor further extends to the personal sphere in the sense that women's economic independence is associated with other positive characteristics: e.g. 82% agreed that "men nowadays like intelligent women who know what they want out of life".

Thus it is apparent from Factor III that there is strong support for female economic independence yet there is also recognition on the part of the sample that female economic independence is having an effect on some men's sense of security in the workplace, as reflected in Factor I, and may be generating a degree of male role ambiguity, as indicated by the responses to items in Factor II.

Factor IV, *Belief in Traditional Male Support and Protection*, contains three items, all of which would appear to tap into traditional gender roles. A large majority (73%) agree that "most women need and want the kind of protection and support that men have traditionally given them". This item has been used in several Irish studies over the last 35 years and has been found to be quite stable. For example, in 1975 81.4% of Dublin adults agreed with this statement, as did 75.4% of a national sample in 1986 (Fine-Davis, 1988a) and 67.2% in 2005 (Fine-Davis *et al.*, 2005),

Table 10.3 Percentage distributions of attitudes to gender roles and gender relations, grouped by factor (N = 1,404)

Item no.	Disagree			DK etc.	Agree		
	Strong	Moderate	Slight		Slight	Moderate	Strong

Factor I: Perceived Threat of Women's Career Advancement

Item no.	Strong	Moderate	Slight	DK etc.	Slight	Moderate	Strong
7. Some men feel threatened by women's advances in the workplace.	10	9 (34%)	15	8	33	17 (59%)	9
9. Men don't really like it that much that women are getting higher positions – and climbing the scale.	12	13 (44%)	19	9	23	15 (45%)	7
17. Career oriented women can be more threatening to men.	11	8 (37%)	18	6	32	15 (57%)	10
14. Most men would find it intimidating to go out with a woman who has a high-powered job.	15	14 (49%)	20	6	24	14 (45%)	7
10. There would be a proportion of men who would feel women may be taking their jobs.	8	10 (31%)	13	8	37	18 (62%)	7
27. Men can be uncomfortable if women are too assertive.	8	9 (30%)	13	6	33	21 (64%)	10
6. Most men could find it difficult taking orders from women at work.	10	12 (39%)	17	7	24	17 (54%)	13

Factor II: Male Role Ambiguity

No.	Statement							
28.	With all the changes in gender roles, it's hard to know who's supposed to do what.	14 –	14 **(47%)**	19 –	11 –	23 –	13 **(42%)**	6 –
25.	A lot of men are confused about their roles because they are less defined than they used to be.	15 –	12 **(47%)**	20 –	10 –	25 –	14 **(44%)**	5 –
26.	As a result of change in women's roles, men are not sure where they stand.	15 –	14 **(52%)**	23 –	9 –	24 –	10 **(39%)**	5 –
12.	It's more difficult for a man to find a partner now because women are putting careers ahead of relationships.	12 –	12 **(43%)**	19 –	8 –	26 –	16 **(48%)**	6 –
11.	Men feel a little redundant because there is so much competition from women.	15 –	14 **(52%)**	23 –	9 –	23 –	13 **(40%)**	4 –
8.	Women's gains in the workplace have sometimes been at the expense of men.	14 –	12 **(44%)**	18 –	11 –	26 –	13 **(44%)**	5 –
29.	Women can be so independent sometimes that it makes men feel like they're not needed anymore.	12	11	19	7	29	15	8

Factor III: Support for Female Economic Independence

No.	Statement							
22.	It's good for a woman to be financially independent in a relationship.	1 –	2 **(6%)**	3 –	4 –	21 –	31 **(90%)**	38 –
21.	Most men are happy for women to pay their own way.	2 –	4 **(15%)**	9 –	7 –	26 –	30 **(79%)**	23 –
16.	I think men nowadays like intelligent women who know what they want out of life.	3 –	4 **(12%)**	5 –	6 –	31 –	31 **(82%)**	20 –

Note:
The percentages in bold indicate summary agree and disagree responses.

continued

Table 10.3 Continued

Item no.	Disagree			DK etc.	Agree		
	Strong	Moderate	Slight		Slight	Moderate	Strong
4. Both men and women should contribute to the household income.	2 –	2 (8%)	4 –	5	18 –	26 (88%)	44 –
19. A woman who has a job she enjoys is likely to be a better wife and mother because she has an interest and some fulfilment outside the home.	4 –	5 (17%)	8 –	8	26 –	26 (74%)	22 –
Factor IV: Belief in Traditional Male Support and Protection							
5. Most men need and want to give the kind of protection and support that they have traditionally given to women.	3 –	3 (14%)	8 –	7	33 –	30 (79%)	16 –
2. Most women need and want the kind of protection and support that men have traditionally given them.	4 –	6 (21%)	11 –	7	31 –	27 (73%)	15 –
1. Being a wife and mother are the most fulfilling roles any woman could want.	10 –	8 (35%)	17 –	13	21 –	18 (52%)	13 –
Factor V: Perceived Male Reluctance to Share Housework							
3. There's an awful lot of lip service paid to "sharing responsibilities", but it's still a man's world at the end of the day.	13 –	11 (40%)	16 –	8	23 –	15 (52%)	14 –
15. While men recognise that women have to spend less time on housework, they don't recognise that they have to contribute more than they used to.	7 –	9 (31%)	15 –	8	29 –	19 (60%)	12 –
13. Men respect women more at work than at home.	17 –	17 (55%)	21 –	13	16 –	11 (33%)	6 –

20. If a woman is financially independent it can lead to difficulties in a relationship.	23 —	20 (64%)	21 —	7	14 —	10 (28%)	4 —
Factor VI: Belief that Mothers are Best Nurturers							
23. Caring for children is best done by mothers.	15 —	11 (41%)	15 —	7	21 —	17 (52%)	14 —
24. Fathers can be as nurturing to children as mothers can.	2 —	2 (10%)	6 —	3	19 —	31 (87%)	37 —
18. It's bad for young children if their mothers go out and work, even if they are well taken care of by another adult.	26 —	18 (63%)	19 —	7	17 —	7 (30%)	6 —

as discussed in Chapter 6. While other measures of gender role attitudes have changed dramatically over time, this item has remained at a high level. This suggests that it may be tapping into a psychological need, rather than into gender roles per se. As noted above, we added for the first time a male counterpart item; an almost identical proportion (73%) agreed that "most men need and want to give the kind of protection and support that they have traditionally given to women". There is also a reasonably high level of agreement (52%) with the item "being a wife and mother are the most fulfilling roles any woman could want". In a nationwide study in 1978 78.1% agreed with this statement (Fine-Davis, 1988a). The level of support dropped to 54.5% in 1986 (ibid.). However, in 2005 the agreement increased to 66% (Fine-Davis *et al.*, 2005) – see Chapter 6. While some of this difference may be attributed to slight differences in the samples, what is notable is that relatively large proportions in all studies agreed with the item over time, whereas other items showed larger changes in a less traditional direction. This suggests that this item, as well as the item concerning the need for protection and support, is tapping into basic needs and beliefs concerning male/female relations and motherhood which are not changing to any great degree as a result of social changes in gender roles. At the same time, it must be acknowledged that 48% did *not* agree with the item, "Being a wife and mother are the most fulfilling roles any woman could want", indicating that almost half of the sample think that women can be fulfilled in other ways.

Factor V, *Perceived Male Reluctance to Share Housework*, is a new factor which taps attitudes towards sharing domestic work. There is majority agreement (60%) that "while men recognise that women have to spend less time on housework, they don't recognise that they have to contribute more than they used to". This is supported by responses to the item, "there's an awful lot of lip service paid to 'sharing responsibilities', but it's still a man's world at the end of the day", to which 52% agreed and 40% disagreed. The issue of housework is linked in people's minds with men's respect for women, suggesting that lack of helping may be related to a lack of respect. While most people (55%) disagreed that "men respect women more at work than at home", 33% supported this view.

The fact that the vast majority of the sample favours women's economic independence is supported by the responses to the item: "If a woman is financially independent it can lead to difficulties in a relationship." Only 28% of the sample agreed that this was the case, while the vast majority (64%) disagreed. However, the fact that this item loads in the same direction as the other items (see factor analysis, Table 10.2, above) indicates that those who tend to agree that women's financial independence may lead to difficulties in a relationship also tend to agree that men do not contribute sufficiently to housework. It may be that some of the difficulties in a relationship arising from women working may relate to frustrations about unequal sharing of housework.

Factor VI, *Belief that Mothers are Best Nurturers,* shows that the vast majority of the sample (87%) thinks that "fathers can be as nurturing to children as mothers can", yet approximately half (52%) of the sample thinks that "caring for children is best done by mothers". While this shows an increasing support for male caring, it still reflects an underlying ambivalence and vestiges of traditional views of caring. The item on the effects of maternal employment on children ("it's bad for young children if their mothers go out and work, even if they are well taken care of by another adult") which elicited little support (30%) and majority disagreement (63%) shows that attitudes in this area have clearly changed in recent years, as comparisons with earlier studies will show (see Chapter 6).

10.4.3 Attitudes to gender roles: effects of demographic characteristics

While the percentage responses of the total sample tell us about the prevalence of the attitudes in the population, they do not tell us whether men and women feel the same or whether single people feel the same as married or cohabiting people. Nor do they tell us about social class differences, etc. So the next step was to carry out an analysis which looked at the simultaneous effects of sex, age, family status, presence or absence of a child and socio-economic status on the six factors measuring attitudes to gender roles. We carried out a five-way analysis of variance with these five independent demographic variables, and used the six composite scores based on the factors as the dependent measures. Table 10.4 presents a summary of these results.

On Factor I, *Perceived Threat of Women's Career Advancement,* we see that there is a highly significant main effect of gender ($F=86.89$; $p<0.001$). Contrary to what might have been expected, women were significantly more likely than men to think that men are threatened by women's advancement in the workplace. The fact that men's scores on this factor are lower than women's (mean for men$=3.84$; mean for women$=4.51$) indicates that women may be over-estimating the extent to which men are actually threatened by women's career advancement. This is illustrated in Figure 10.1, which shows the differential percentage responses of men and women on the items in this factor. For example, 59% agreed with the statement, "some men feel threatened by women's advances in the workplace"; however, women were more likely to think this was the case than men were: 67% of women, as compared with 50% of men, agreed with this statement. Similarly, 56% of women think that "men don't really like it that much that women are getting higher positions – and climbing the scale", yet only 36% of men said this was the case. In light of the fact women are now more likely to be in supervisory positions, it is noteworthy that over half of the sample (54%) felt that "most men could find it difficult taking orders from women at work". However, a closer inspection of the results shows that while 43% of men feel this way, a far greater proportion (66%) of women think they do.

Table 10.4 Analysis of variance: effects of five demographic characteristics on six factors measuring attitudes to gender roles (N = 1,404)

Six factors measuring attitudes toward gender roles	Sex		Age (years)		Family status			Child status		Socio-economic Status		
	Male (n = 706)	Female (n = 698)	20–34 (n = 759)	35–49 (n = 645)	Sing (n = 625)	Marr (n = 619)	Cohab (n = 160)	Without child (n = 753)	With child (n = 651)	Skilled/ Unskilled manual (n = 578)	Non-manual (n = 303)	Prof./ Manager/ Technical (n = 523)
1. Perceived Threat of Women's Career Advancement	$F = 86.89$*** 3.84	4.51	$F = 9.95$** 4.13	4.22	$F = 3.94$* 4.28	4.10	4.15	$F = 3.27$ 4.17	4.18	$F = 2.90$ 4.25	4.14	4.13
2. Male Role Ambiguity	$F = 2.50$ 3.75	3.85	$F = 10.46$*** 3.74	3.86	$F = 4.78$** 3.96	3.73	3.72	$F = 5.26$* 3.74	3.86	$F = 5.02$** 3.94	3.75	3.71
3. Support for Female Economic Independence	$F = 0.26$ 5.53	5.53	$F = 1.64$ 5.53	5.53	$F = 3.03$* 5.59	5.47	5.53	$F = 12.79$*** 5.61	5.45	$F = 4.37$* 5.40	5.60	5.59
4. Belief in Traditional Male Support and Protection	$F = 2.54$ 4.83	4.73	$F = 12.06$*** 4.90	4.66	$F = 10.04$*** 4.56	4.98	4.78	$F = 4.38$* 4.70	4.85	$F = 4.92$* 4.85	4.80	4.68
5. Perceived Male Reluctance to Share Housework	$F = 103.94$*** 3.46	4.17	$F = 19.51$*** 3.73	3.90	$F = 19.92$*** 4.08	3.55	3.81	$F = 16.48$*** 3.71	3.92	$F = 3.82$* 3.86	3.84	3.73
6. Belief that Mothers are Best Nurturers	$F = 0.21$ 3.26	3.23	$F = 10.65$*** 3.17	3.32	$F = 1.22$ 3.28	3.27	3.18	$F = 0.52$ 3.22	3.27	$F = 5.31$** 3.33	3.31	3.09

(Range of mean scores: 1–7) (Range of mean scores: 1–7)

* $p < 0.05$
** $p < 0.01$
*** $p < 0.001$

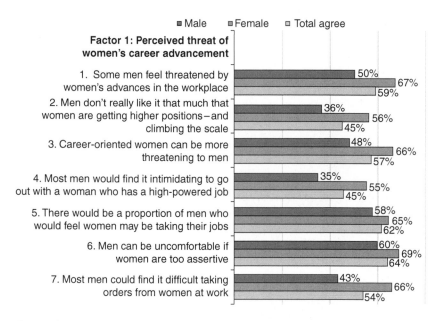

Figure 10.1 Summary agree and disagree responses by gender to items on factor I, perceived threat of women's career advancement (N = 1,404).

There was a significant interaction effect between gender and social class indicating that working class men were more likely to perceive the threat of women's career advancement than men in the middle and higher SES groups, as illustrated below in Figure 10.2. This interaction effect also shows that there is a greater gap between men and women in the middle and higher SES groups than in the lowest SES group, indicating that women in the two higher groups may have more anxiety about the perceived threat of women's career advancement and less reason to do so it would seem from the male scores in these groups.

Returning to an examination of the main effects of demographic characteristics (Table 10.4), we see that there is also a slight tendency for older people to be more likely to think that men are threatened by women's career advancement. An effect for family status indicates that single people are somewhat more likely than married and cohabiting people to think men are threatened by women's career advancement. Taking the main effects together, this would suggest that single women in the age group 35–49 are the most likely to think that men are threatened by women's career advancement. Married and cohabiting women are less likely to think so, perhaps because they are more secure in their relationship and do not fear that their own career advancement would threaten their relationship. Single women, on the other hand, particularly older ones who may be having difficulty forming a permanent

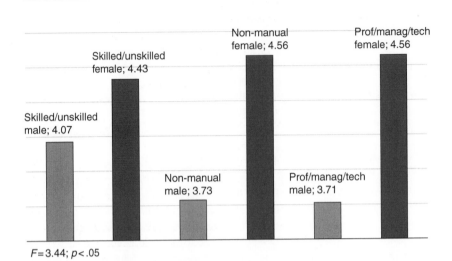

$F=3.44; p<.05$

Figure 10.2 Perceived threat of women's career advancement: means for significant
interaction effect of gender and socio-economic status.

relationship may be more fearful that men will be threatened if they are
too successful in the workplace. This is illustrated by the responses to the
item on this factor, "Most men would find it intimidating to go out with
a woman who has a high-powered job." The proportion of women who
agreed with this statement was 55%, whereas only 35% of men agreed
(Figure 10.1). Thus, some of women's fears concerning the potential
negative effects of their success in the workplace would appear to be
unfounded.

The second factor, *Male Role Ambiguity*, does not show a significant
gender effect, as might have been expected, meaning that men and
women both have similar views on this, with means just under 4, the theoretical midpoint. There is a significant effect for age with older people
being somewhat more likely to think that men's roles are more ambiguous
than they used to be ($F=10.46; p<0.01$). This suggests that younger men
and women (aged 20–34) are more comfortable with changing gender
roles, whereas older people (35–49) may find these changes lead to
greater role ambiguity.

There were also significant effects for family status, presence of children and SES, though these were less strong than the effect for age. These
show that single people are somewhat more likely to perceive male role
ambiguity than married or cohabiting people; people with children are
more likely to perceive male role ambiguity than those without children;
and finally manual workers (unskilled, semi-skilled and skilled) are more

likely to perceive male role ambiguity than are professional/managerial and technical workers or manual workers.

The third factor, *Support for Female Economic Independence*, also does not have a gender effect, as one might have expected. The results show that men and women have similar views on this, with both having mean scores of approximately 5.5 out of 7, indicating mild to moderate support for female financial independence. The strongest effect on this factor is for presence of children. Those without children are more likely than those with children to support female financial independence ($F=12.79$; $p<0.001$). The other two significant main effects are less strong ($p<0.05$ in both cases), showing that single and cohabiting people are somewhat more supportive of female financial independence than are married people and those in working class occupations are less supportive, while those in the middle and higher occupational groups are more supportive. These findings mirror those found for the second factor, *Male Role Ambiguity*. These findings taken together suggest that married people, those with children and those in the lower socio-economic group have more traditional views about gender roles and as a result are finding changes in gender roles, such as greater female economic independence, are leading to greater male role ambiguity.

Married people were the most likely to express a strong *Belief in Traditional Support and Protection* (Factor IV), whereas single people expressed the least support and cohabiting people were in between ($F=10.04$; $p<0.001$). There was also a significant effect of age in the counter-intuitive direction of younger people being more likely to believe in male protection and support ($F=12.06$; $p<0.001$). Those with children and those in the lowest and middle SES groups were also more likely to espouse traditional beliefs concerning male protection and support ($p<0.05$ in both cases).

Factor V, concerning *Perceived Male Reluctance to Share Housework* showed a very strong effect of gender ($F=103.94$; $p<0.001$), with women significantly more likely to perceive a male reluctance to share housework. These differences are illustrated for each item in Figure 10.3. There was a particularly large gender gap on the second item in the factor, "While men recognise that women have to spend less time on housework, they don't recognise that they have to contribute more than they used to", to which 73% of women agreed while just 48% of men did.

There was also a significant effect of family status on this factor, indicating that single people were most likely to perceive male reluctance to do housework, followed by cohabiting people. Married people were least likely to be high on this factor. This is somewhat surprising since housework is often an area of dissension among men and women, especially if both partners are working. We have seen in previous factors that married people have more traditional attitudes towards gender roles and this may explain their views on this factor relative to other groups. In spite of this, the

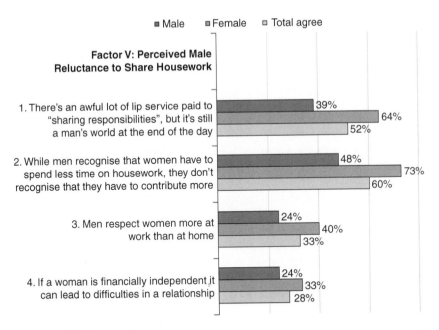

Figure 10.3 Summary agree and disagree responses by gender to items on Factor V, Perceived Male Reluctance to Share Housework (N = 1,404).

extremely strong effect of gender would of course pertain to married people as well and would indicate that married women would still be more likely to perceive male reluctance to share housework than would married men. There was also a significant main effect for children ($F = 16.48$; $p < 0.001$) indicating that those with children were significantly more likely to perceive male reluctance to share housework (Table 10.4). When there are children in the household there is more work to do so that the issue of sharing of domestic responsibilities would clearly be more salient. A significant interaction effect between gender and presence of children shows that it is women with children who are the most likely to perceive a male reluctance to do housework ($F = 5.92$; $p < 0.015$ – see Figure 10.4).

Attitudes toward who should care for children seem to be in flux, as reflected in the responses to Factor VI, *Belief that Mothers are Best Nurturers*. A significant effect of age showed that younger people were less likely to think mothers were the best nurturers, suggesting that attitudes are changing and among younger people men and women are both likely to be seen as equally good nurturers. There is also an effect for social class, indicating that those in the lower two SES groups are somewhat more likely to think that mothers are the best nurturers for children, whereas those in the highest SES group are least likely to perceive gender differences in the

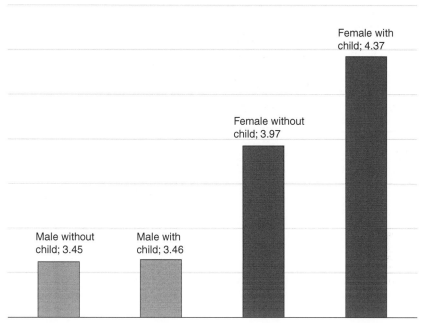

$F=5.92; p<.015$

Figure 10.4 Perceived male reluctance to share housework: means for significant interaction effect between gender and presence of children.

case of nurturing. This finding supports some of the other findings showing more traditional attitudes among lower socio-economic groups.

10.5 Implications of changing gender role attitudes

10.5.1 Summary and implications of main trends

Several positive trends emerged from our recent research on gender role attitudes. The first was the fact that there is now strong support among both men and women for women's economic independence. The overwhelming majority endorsed the view that it is good for a woman to be financially independent in a relationship and that both men and women should contribute to the household income. Associated with this were very positive attitudes to maternal employment. The findings revealed the emergence of more integrated thinking in which maternal employment is now seen as contributing to women's fulfilment and the economic well-being of the family unit, as well as to the well-being of children, rather than merely as something which may or may not affect the well-being of children. These attitudes reflect significant change in people's perceptions of male and female roles.

In spite of the widespread support for women's economic independence, their progress in the workplace was perceived by more than half of the sample as posing a threat to some men. In view of the fact women are now more likely to be in supervisory positions, it is noteworthy that over half of the sample felt that "most men could find it difficult taking orders from women at work". Such perceptions indicate that there is still some way to go to achieving full equality in the workplace, since it would appear that attitudes have not entirely kept pace with equality legislation and with actual changes in behaviour. A comparison of gender differences surprisingly revealed that women were more likely to hold these views than men were. While 56% of women thought that "men don't really like it that much that women are getting higher positions and climbing the scale", only 36% of men actually felt that way. Similarly, while two-thirds of women thought that most men could find it difficult being supervised by a woman, only 43% of men actually felt this way. These findings suggest that while there clearly is a problem, women are exaggerating its magnitude and are super-sensitive to it. This in itself constitutes a further barrier to women's full entrée to all levels of the world of work. It will also have reverberations in the personal sphere, as the data have shown.

The results showed that perceptions of women in the workplace are related to attitudes concerning male/female relations on a personal level. Close to half of the sample (45%) felt that "most men would find it intimidating to go out with a woman who has a high-powered job" and more than half (57%) felt that "career oriented women can be more threatening to men". These findings suggest that women's achievements in the workplace may come at a personal price and it is evident that many women fear there will be a personal backlash to their success. Yet a comparison of men's and women's views reveals that while such fears are partly justified, they are not entirely so. While more than half of women (55%) felt that most men would find it intimidating to go out with a woman who had a high powered job, only 35% of men felt this was the case. Similarly, two-thirds of women felt that career oriented women could be more threatening to men, yet only 48% of men agreed this was the case. While women are clearly over-estimating these attitudes, they are still sufficiently prevalent to be of concern. Working class men were more likely to perceive a threat of women's career advancement than men in the middle and higher socio-economic groups. The study found that women in the higher socio-economic groups had more anxiety about the effect of their role in the workplace and less reason to do so, as their male counterparts were not particularly concerned with this. While clearly a proportion of men are threatened by women's advancement in the workplace, women are significantly over-estimating the extent to which this is the case.

In spite of the support for female economic independence, there was still evidence of support for traditional roles in terms of a wish for men to provide "the kind of support that men have traditionally given them". There was also a belief on the part of half of the sample that "being a wife and mother are the most fulfilling roles any woman could want", yet this attitude is far less strong than it was 30 years ago, when 78% believed it to be the case (Fine-Davis, 1988a). Those most likely to endorse traditional views about male protection and support were married people and people with children. Thus, on the one hand there is widespread support for women's role in the labour force, while at the same time some support for traditional gender roles, at least in a psychological sense. It is clear that gender role behaviour is undergoing change and this was reflected in a degree of male role ambiguity. Forty-two per cent of the sample felt that "with all the changes in gender roles, it's hard to know who's supposed to do what". A similar proportion felt that "a lot of men are confused about their roles because they are less defined than they used to be".

Men's participation in the domestic sphere was a key component of current gender role attitudes. More egalitarian attitudes concerning caring were evident: the vast majority thought that fathers could be as nurturing as mothers could, though half still thought that caring for children was best done by mothers, indicating an underlying ambivalence about who should do the caring. This ambivalence also extended to the area of housework. Most respondents felt that while men recognise that women have less time to spend on housework, they don't recognise that they (men) have to contribute more than they used to. Women were much more likely than men to feel this way (73% of women versus 48% of men) and mothers – who are most likely to bear the burden of housework – were most likely to do so. These findings support research on time use of Irish men and women which found that women – and particularly mothers – spend significantly more time on housework and childcare than men do (McGinnity and Russell, 2007). Men's role in the domestic sphere is clearly still an area of resistance, as was shown in a cross-cultural study of working parents in four European countries (Fine-Davis *et al.*, 2004). In this study women were found to carry out more of the household tasks and there was a great discrepancy between men and women's perceptions of who actually carried out this work, with men tending to perceive that they did more than women perceived to be the case. The issue of housework was linked in the present study with perceptions of men's respect for women, with one-third of the sample thinking that men respect women more at work than at home. As Scott (2008) has pointed out, understanding this realm will require further research which explores men's roles in greater detail and with new measures. We have gone some way towards developing some new measures in this sphere, but there is clearly further work to be done, particularly in understanding the barriers to men's greater participation in domestic life. More than 25 years ago Mason and Lu (1988) concluded that "for many men, support for equal family roles is highly qualified" (p. 46). This could still be said to be true today in spite of the gains that have clearly been made.

Several authors across the world have come to the conclusion that gender role attitude change "stalled" or "plateaued" by the 1990s (Thornton and Young-DeMarco, 2001; van Egmond *et al.*, 2010; Cotter *et al.*, 2011). Braun and Scott (2009), looking at cross-cultural data, also explored if the trend reversal was real, pointing to possible measurement issues in comparative research, and concluded that observed changes in gender role attitudes over time do not support "a story of revolutionary change and backlash", but they do find some evidence of "egalitarianism reaching a peak and retreat" (pp. 365–366). We did not find this in our Irish data going up to 2005. We found that attitudes continued to change in a more egalitarian direction, particularly in the area of maternal employment. We see in the new measures of gender role attitudes that there is continuing support for women's role in the labour force and continued support for male caring, yet we also see some attitudinal resistance to women's success in the labour market and this plays out to some extent in the personal sphere. We also see continuing resistance on the part of men to sharing housework. The four-country study referred to above (Fine-Davis *et al.*, 2004) found that fathers contributed most to playing with children, but were less likely to do things like shopping, cooking and cleaning. While it could be argued that their interaction with their children is the most important thing they could do, there is clearly resentment on the part of their female partners that the "helping" behaviour is not more multi-faceted. Commenting on the results of this study, Esping-Andersen (2004) had this to say:

> The societal revolution that latter-day women are bringing about is mainly spurred by radical change in women's own life course behaviour. When one studies the life course behaviour of Europeans over the past 30–40 years, one is struck by an amazing asymmetry: beginning with educated women and eventually extending to most, we detect a clear masculinisation of female biographies. Women are converging with men in educational attainment, in participation rates and, especially, in life-long employment. The amazing thing is that women have done all the changing while men stubbornly cling to a life course model that closely resembles that of their fathers and grandfathers. What *Fathers and Mothers* helps us realize is that no workable social equilibrium can materialise unless we somehow begin to also reconstruct the male life course.
>
> (p. vi)

10.5.2 *Other key findings from recent study*

The 2010 study also explored other related aspects to gender role attitudes – in particular attitudes to relationship formation and childbearing and the well-being of people in different statuses – single, cohabiting and married.

10.5.2.1 *Attitudes to being single*

The study found that it is now more acceptable to be single than it used to be. There was a general perception that people are staying single longer because they are more selective about relationships. This may help to explain the later age at marriage evident in the latest Census results. This greater selectivity in looking for the ideal partner may relate to the greater freedom people have, including sexual freedom, and the greater options available to them, including educational opportunities, as well as the possibility to cohabit. There is, in addition, a greater acceptance of single parenthood.

While there was widespread acceptance of being single, there was also some ambivalence towards this status. Almost two-thirds of the sample said, "I don't think anybody chooses to be single and on their own if they are really honest." It was also evident that there was a feeling of social pressure to be in a couple – a pressure which impinged disproportionately on women, especially those in their late thirties. In spite of the pressure on women to get married, the results showed that it is more difficult for them to find a partner. This was also true of older people (35–49). While there were few differences among men of all social classes in terms of their ease in finding a partner, among women, those in the middle and highest social class groups found it significantly more difficult to do so. Given the disparity in men and women's educational and occupational status – with women being more likely to have third level education as well as more likely to hold jobs of higher occupational status – it is not surprising that women felt men were threatened by their career advancement. While men did not endorse this to the extent that women feared, better educated women, particularly those over 35, are finding it more difficult to find a partner. This is undoubtedly one of the contributors to the increasing proportion of single people in the population, as well as the later age at marriage, older age of women at the birth of their first child and the decreasing birth rate overall.

10.5.2.2 *Attitudes to having children*

The study revealed discrepancies between people's ideal, expected and actual number of children. When asked how many children they would "ideally" like to have, the average number was 2.73. However, when asked how many children they expected to have over the course of their lifetime, the average was 2.41 children. People thus expect to have fewer children than they would ideally like to have. The actual number of children that the average woman has when she completes her childbearing (total fertility rate) is currently approximately 2, which is far less than people's ideal or even expected family sizes. However, attitudes to having children have changed considerably over the last 25 years. In the 1970s the ideal number of children that people wanted was four (Fine-Davis, 1976). People no longer think that it is necessary to have a child in order to be fulfilled and attitudes to childlessness are much more accepting than they were before, reflecting a change in attitudes over the last 25 years. Previous attitudes favouring larger families are being replaced with new attitudes favouring smaller families. Almost three-quarters of the sample believe that having fewer children is better since they "are being had by choice" and two-thirds believe that having fewer children is better because "you can give more to each child". However, the results also show that economic factors are having a major influence on people's attitudes to having children and their childbearing intentions. More than three-quarters think that "these days most couples simply cannot afford to have more than two children" and more than two-thirds said that the cost of living was restricting the number of children that they would have.

10.5.2.3 Attitudes to childcare, work–life balance and related policies

The study explored people's attitudes to childcare, work–life balance and related social policies in relation to their attitudes to having children. There was almost unanimous support for the universal provision of childcare and a national programme of childcare facilities for pre-school-aged children. Most supported a policy for free pre-school education available to all children in the same way that primary education is. Given that such facilities do not exist at present and most parents have to pay a significant portion of their income on childcare, there was strong support for tax concessions for childcare costs. The vast majority felt that if people had to spend a lot on childcare they would be less likely to have more children. It is clear that choices regarding family size are being significantly influenced by childcare costs.

Flexible working policies were also seen as relevant to childbearing decisions. Over 60% felt that if people had flexible working conditions, this would make it more likely that they would have more children. In terms of new social policies, there was strong support for fathers to have a right to paid paternity leave. There was also moderate support for maternity leave to be changed into leave for one or the other parent. The results also showed quite high support for "co-parenting". Half of the sample felt that both men and women should ideally work part-time and co-parent. While this was the wish of many, part-time working and job sharing were seen by some as leading to career disadvantages, particularly for men, a finding also obtained in previous Irish and cross-cultural research (Fine-Davis *et al.*, 2004, 2005). Nevertheless, these attitudes signal a readiness for greater sharing of childcare between men and women.

10.5.2.4 *Effects of family status, gender and socio-economic status on well-being*

While much research has documented demographic changes which have been taking place in our society and in societies around us, relatively little research has examined the effects of these changes on people's well-being. The present study compared the well-being of single, cohabiting and married people, while also simultaneously examining the effects of other relevant variables, such as gender, parenthood and socio-economic status. Married people were found to have the highest level of well-being on most measures, including social integration, life satisfaction, positive life experiences, etc. They were followed by cohabiting people. Compared to married and cohabiting people, single people had the lowest level of well-being and were more socially isolated. Single mothers had the lowest life satisfaction and were the loneliest of all groups. Their life satisfaction was less than that of single women with no children and less than that of single fathers. While there is an acceptance of single parenthood and a belief, especially among women, that one parent can bring up a child as well as two parents, it is clear that this comes at a high price in terms of the poorer well-being of this group.

Socio-economic status was also found to be related to well-being. Men in the highest socio-economic group were the most likely to say their life is "close to how they would like it to be", followed by women in this group. The group least likely to feel this way was men of lower socio-economic status, who also manifested lesser psychological well-being on a range of measures. This group had the highest level of unemployment, which undoubtedly contributed to their lesser psychological well-being. As other results found, this group of men was also more likely to feel threatened by women's career advancement, not surprisingly, given their own vulnerable circumstances. This finding echoes those seen in our earlier research in 1975 to the effect that lower socio-economic status and being male were associated with holding more traditional attitudes and also being more likely to perceive women as inferior to men (see Chapters 3 and 4). These characteristics were also associated with conservative views on maternal employment specifically. These effects still were apparent in 1978 and in 2005, but had considerably lessened by 2005 (see Chapter 6).

10.5.3 *Overall policy implications*

The increasing education of women and their greater role in the labour force is leading to postponement of couple formation and childbearing.

In addition the increasing value placed on autonomy, freedom and independence is also contributing to changes in family formation. As a result, young men and women who want to start families, while at the same time fulfilling their own needs for autonomy and development, are facing dilemmas. These issues are particularly facing women with higher education, who are making strides in the labour force. They are postponing family formation because of extended time in education, followed by a focus on their careers. When they are ready to form more permanent relationships – often in their mid thirties – they find that it is difficult to find a partner. This is so because potential male partners do not have the same biological clock exigencies and also have a wider pool of potential partners, since it is more usual for men to marry younger women.

If women do have a partner it is often difficult to make the choice to have a child since childcare is so expensive and flexible working not always available. Women know that they are the ones who will be expected to provide domestic work and childcare and they are the ones who will be expected to work part-time, rather than their partners, and many are not ready to relinquish satisfying full-time jobs at a time when their career development is at an important stage. While many people would like to "co-parent", this is rarely possible since most flexible working arrangements tend to be more available to women than to men (Fine-Davis *et al.*, 2005), in addition to the fact that childcare costs are prohibitive. As a result people are having fewer children than they ideally would like to have. Such findings underscore the need for new social policies to address the dilemmas faced by young people who want to start families, while at the same time fulfilling their own needs for autonomy and development. Provision of necessary supports such as universal childcare and more widespread availability of various modes of flexible working that are compatible with parenthood will be essential if men and women are to be able to perform the dual roles of worker and parent. Unless social policy facilitates the sharing of childrearing by both parents, women will continue to face dilemmas which prevent them from forming families at an optimal time and having the number of children that they ideally wish to have (Esping-Andersen, 2009; Fagnani, 2012).

While some social policies will be beneficial for all groups, different social policies may also need to be targeted to different groups. Those with less education are actually having more children than they would ideally like to have and are less able to afford to raise the children they have. As Lunn *et al.* (2009) have suggested in their analysis of demographic trends in family formation, outreach programmes to assist with family planning may be required for this group. Accessible and affordable childcare is also essential to enable people to obtain the training and education needed to fully participate in the labour force. Solutions to problems such as this will need to be found to break through the cycle of poverty which is endemic to most single mothers (OECD, 2003).

The policy response for well-educated women who are deferring family formation needs to be different and may involve linkages between educational and family policy. For this group, awareness programmes may need to be introduced into educational settings to make young women aware of the need to have children before fertility begins to steeply drop. Beginning to form relationships and hoping to have children in one's mid thirties may be too late. Social policy should also address the need for supports to enable women to remain in the labour force if they so choose and at the same time to have children. This means policies which go beyond maternity leave and parental leave. They need to include high quality childcare which is flexible and affordable, as well as flexible working arrangements for both men and women. These must truly be flexible and include such practices as tele-working and flexible hours, which do not impinge on income, as this has been found to be a critical barrier to male take-up of flexible working (e.g. Drew *et al.*, 2003). Consideration also needs to be given at policy level to the synchronisation of childcare times and parental working times, as much research has shown that parents make many ad hoc childcare arrangements to fit in with their employment and that unsatisfactory childcare arrangements lead to stress in the workplace and lesser well-being (Fine-Davis *et al.*, 2004).

Unless social policy facilitates the sharing of childrearing by *both* parents, women will continue to face dilemmas which prevent them from forming family relationships at an optimal time in terms of their fertility. Family policies, such as maternity leave, primarily acknowledge women's role in childcare. It is time for these policies to broaden to acknowledge the role of father as parent.

There is evidence of significantly poorer well-being and social isolation of single people, particularly single mothers, but also of older single women, as well as working class men. As noted above, single women are under pressure to form relationships, marry and have children, while at the same time they have increased educational qualifications and more opportunities in the workplace. Women are caught between their biological clocks and their wish to continue actively in the labour market. It is apparent that these factors are contributing to delays in couple formation, delays in marriage, postponement of the first birth, a decrease in fertility, an increase in the proportion of single people and an increase in childlessness. These trends are likely to have a long term cost in terms of a decreasing population and diminishing ability to support the ageing population, as seen in other countries (European Commission, 2006; Esping-Andersen, 2009). However, other social costs are also being paid in terms of the greater social isolation and lesser well-being of single people. These issues need to be addressed in the development of social policies which support not only families but also the increasing proportion of single people in the population.

Balbriggan
Library
Ph: 8704401

References

Adorno, T. W., Frenkel-Brunswik, E., Levinson, D. J. and Sanford, R. N. (1950). *The Authoritarian Personality*. New York: Harper.

Adshead, M. (1996). Sea change on the isle of saints and scholars? The 1995 Irish referendum on the introduction of divorce. *Electoral Studies*, 15 (1), 138–142.

All Party Oireachtas Committee on the Constitution. (2000). *Fifth Progress Report: Abortion*. Dublin: The Stationery Office.

Allport, G. W. (1958). *The Nature of Prejudice*. New York: Doubleday.

Bailyn, L. (1964). Notes on the role of choice in the psychology of women. *Daedalus*, 93, 700–710.

Bailyn, L. (1970). Career and family orientations of husbands and wives in relation to marital happiness. *Human Relations*, 23 (2), 97–113.

Banaszak, L. and Plutzer, E. (1993). The social bases of feminism in the European community. *Public Opinion Quarterly*, 57, 29–53.

Barristers Against the Amendment. (December 1982). *Possible Consequences of the Proposed Constitutional Amendment*. Dublin: The Anti-Amendment Campaign.

Barry, U. (2008). Changing economic and social worlds of Irish women. In U. Barry (ed.), *Where Are We Now? New Feminist Perspectives on Women in Contemporary Ireland*. Dublin: Tasc at New Island, pp. 1–29.

Beale, J. (1986). *Women in Ireland: Voices of Change*. Dublin: Gill & Macmillan.

Binchy, D. A. (ed.) (1936). *Studies in Early Irish Law*. Dublin.

Bishop, G. F. and Frankovic, K. A. (1981). Ideological consensus and constraint among party leaders and followers in the 1978 election. *Micropolitics*, 1 (2), 87–111.

Blackwell, J. (1986). *Women in the Labour Force*. Dublin: Employment Equality Agency.

Bourke, A. (1987). *Women's Lives in the Fairy Legends*. Paper presented at Workshop on the Role of Women in the Folklore of Ireland and Scotland. UCD Women's Studies Forum, University College, Dublin, 21 February.

Braun, M. and Scott, J. (2009). Gender-role egalitarianism – is the trend reversal real? *International Journal of Public Opinion Research*, 21 (3), 362–367.

Breen, M. J. (1998). *Press and Polls in Irish Politics: The Influence of Media Content on Public Opinion Regarding Divorce Referenda in Ireland*. Paper presented at the European Federation of Associations and Centres of Irish Studies Inaugural Conference, Université de Lille, France, 11–12 December.

Breslin, A. and Weafer, J. A. (1983). *Survey of Senior Students' Attitudes towards Religion, Morality, Education*. Maynooth: Council for Research and Development, St Patrick's College.

Breslin, A. and Weafer, J. (1984). *Religious Beliefs, Practice and Moral Attitudes: A Comparison of Two Irish Surveys 1974–1984*. Maynooth: Council for Research and Development, St Patrick's College.

Broverman, I. K., Vogel, S. R., Broverman, D. M., Clarkson, F. E. and Rosenkrantz, P. S. (1972). Sex-role stereotypes: A current appraisal. *Journal of Social Issues*, 28 (2), 59–78.

Burley, J. and Regan, F. (2002). Divorce in Ireland: The fear, the floodgates and the reality. *International Journal of Law, Policy and the Family*, 16 (2), 202–222.

Callan, T. and Farrell, B. (1991). *Women's Participation in the Irish Labour Market*. Dublin: National Economic and Social Council.

Callender, R. and Meenan, F. (1994). *Equality in Law between Men and Women in the European Community – Ireland*. Dordrecht/Boston/London: Martinus Nijhoff and Luxembourg: Office for Official Publications of the European Communities.

Campbell, D. T. and Stanley, J. C. (1963). *Experimental and Quasi-experimental Designs for Research*. Chicago: Rand McNally.

Cherniss, C. (1972). Personality and ideology: A personological study of women's liberation. *Psychiatry*, 35 (2), 109–125.

Chubb, B. (1971). *The Government and Politics of Ireland*. Oxford: Oxford University Press, (2nd edn) London and New York: Longman, 1982.

Clines, F. X. (1988). For Irish women, even talk of abortions is long distance. *International Herald Tribune*, 16 June, p. 1.

Cochrane, R. and Stopes-Roe, M. (1981). Women, marriage, employment and mental health. *British Journal of Psychiatry*, 139, 373–381.

Collins, S. (2013a). Over 70% support X-case legislation on abortion. *The Irish Times*, 11 February, p. 1.

Collins, S. (2013b). Big rise in support for legislation on abortion. *The Irish Times*, 11 February, p. 5.

Colombotos, J. (1969). Physicians and Medicare: A before-after study of the effects of legislation on attitudes. *American Sociological Review*, 34 (3), 318–334.

Commission of Inquiry into the Civil Service. (1932–1935). *Volume I., Final*. Dublin: The Stationery Office.

Commission of the European Communities. (1987). Men and women of Europe in 1987. *Supplement No. 26, Women of Europe*. Brussels: Commission of the European Communities.

Commission on the Status of Women. (1972). *Report to Minister for Finance*. Dublin: The Stationery Office.

Converse, P. E. (1964). The nature of belief systems in mass publics. In D. E. Apter (ed.), *Ideology and Discontent*. New York: The Free Press, pp. 206–261.

Cotter, D., Hermsen, J. M. and Vanneman, R. (2011). The end of the gender revolution? Gender role attitudes from 1977 to 2008. *American Journal of Sociology*, 117 (1), 259–289.

Craven, F. E. V. (2006). *An Analysis of the Social, Religious and Gender Role Attitudes of Catholic and Protestant Women in the Republic of Ireland: A Comparative Study*. PhD Dissertation, Centre for Gender and Women's Studies, Trinity College, Dublin.

Craven, F. E. V. (2010). *A Comparison of the Social, Religious, and Gender Role Attitudes of Catholic and Protestant Women in the Republic of Ireland*. Lewiston, Queenston, Lampeter: The Edwin Mellen Press.

Crowley, L. (2011). Irish divorce law in a social policy vacuum – from the unspoken to the unknown. *Journal of Social Welfare and Family Law*, 33 (3), 227–242.

CSO. (1971–97). *Labour Force Surveys.* Dublin: The Stationery Office.

CSO. (1999). *Population and Labour Force Projections: 2001–2031.* Dublin: The Stationery Office.

CSO. (1999–2009). *Quarterly National Household Surveys.* Dublin: The Stationery Office.

CSO. (2007). *Census 2006: Principal Demographic Results.* Dublin: The Stationery Office.

CSO. (2009a). *Quarterly National Household Survey, Quarter 2, 2009.* Dublin: The Stationery Office.

CSO. (2009b). *Measuring Ireland's Progress 2008.* Dublin: The Stationery Office.

CSO. (2013). *Vital Statistics: Second Quarter 2013.* Dublin: The Stationery Office.

CSO. (2014). *Measuring Ireland's Progress 2012.* Dublin: The Stationery Office.

Cullen, P. and Holland, K. (2013) Consultant refused termination over "legal position", she tells Galway inquest. *The Irish Times,* 10 April, p. 1.

Cumming, E., Lazer, C. and Chisholm, L. (1975). Suicide as an index of role strain among employed and not employed married women in British Columbia. *Canadian Review of Sociology and Anthropology,* 12 (4), 462–470.

d'Addio, A. C. and Mira d'Ercole, M. (2005). *Trends and Determinants of Fertility Rates in OECD Countries: The Role of Policies.* OECD Social, Employment and Migration Working Papers: No. 27. Paris: OECD.

Daly, M. (1975). *The Church and the Second Sex.* New York: Harper and Row.

Daly, M. E. (1978). Women, work and trade unionism. In M. MacCurtain and D. Ó Corráin (eds), *Women in Irish Society: The Historical Dimension.* Dublin: Arlen House, pp. 71–81.

Darcy, R. and Laver, M. (1990). Referendum dynamics and the Irish divorce amendment. *The Public Opinion Quarterly,* 54 (1), 1–20.

Davis, E. E. and Fine-Davis, M. (1979). *Continuing Social Survey No. 1: Social Indicators (Health and Housing) and Attitudes to Social Issues in Ireland.* Dublin: Economic and Social Research Institute and Institute of Public Administration.

Davis, E. E., Fine-Davis, M., Breathnach, A. and Moran, R. (1977). A study of the factor structure of attitudinal measures of major social psychological constructs in an Irish sample. *The Economic and Social Review,* 9 (1), 27–50.

Davis, E. E., Grube, J. and Morgan, M. (1984). Attitudes toward poverty and related social issues in Ireland. *Paper No. 117.* Dublin: The Economic and Social Research Institute.

Davis, J. A. and Smith, T. W. (1982). Have we learned anything from the General Social Survey? *Social Indicators Newsletter,* 17 August, 1 et seq.

Deutsch, M. and Collins, M. E. (1958). The effect of public policy in housing projects upon interracial attitudes. In E. E. Maccoby, T. M. Newcomb and E. L. Hartley (eds), *Readings in Social Psychology.* New York: Holt, Rinehart and Winston, pp. 612–636.

Doctors Against the Amendment. (1982). *Some Medical Implications of the Proposed Constitutional Amendment.* Dublin: The Anti-Amendment Campaign.

Drew, E. (1998). Re-conceptualising families. In E. Drew, R. Emerek and E. Mahon (eds), *Women, Work and the Family in Europe.* London and New York: Routledge, pp. 11–26.

Drew, E., Humphreys, P. and Murphy, C. (2003). *Off the Treadmill: Achieving Work Life Balance.* Dublin: National Framework Committee for the Development of Family Friendly Policies.

Editor. (2010). Sex, sin and society. *The Irish Times*, 18 September, p. 17.

Esping-Andersen, G. (2004). Preface. In M. Fine-Davis, J. Fagnani, D. Giovannini, L. Højgaard and H. Clarke, *Fathers and Mothers: Dilemmas of the Work-life Balance – A Comparative Study in Four European Countries.* Dordrecht, Boston and London: Kluwer, pp. v–vii.

Esping-Anderson, G. (2009). *The Incomplete Revolution: Adapting to Women's New Roles.* Cambridge: Polity Press.

Ester, P., Halman, L. and de Moor, R. (1993). *The Individualizing Society: Value Changes in Europe and North America.* Tilburg: Tilburg University Press.

European Commission. (2006). *The Demographic Future of Europe – from Challenge to Opportunity.* Brussels: Commission of the European Communities.

Eurostat. (1981). *Economic and Social Position of Women in the Community.* Luxembourg: Statistical Office of the European Communities.

Eurostat. (2006). *Population Statistics.* Luxembourg: Office for Official Publications of the European Communities.

Eurostat. (2008). *Statistics in Focus.* Luxembourg: Eurostat.

Expert Working Group on Childcare. (1999). *National Childcare Strategy – Report of the Partnership 2000 Expert Working Group on Childcare.* Dublin: The Stationery Office.

Fagnani, J. (2008). *The Future of Integrated Family Policy – the Long-term Prospects: 2025/30.* Scoping Paper, Advisory Unity to the Secretary-General, International Futures Programme. Paris: OECD.

Fagnani, J. (2012). Work-family life balance: Future trends and challenges. In OECD, *The Future of Families to 2030.* Paris: OECD, pp. 119–187.

Fahey, T. (2012). Small bang? The impact of divorce legislation on marital breakdown in Ireland. *International Journal of Law, Policy and the Family*, 26 (2), 242–258.

Fahey, T. and Field, C. A. (2008). *Families in Ireland: An Analysis of Patterns and Trends.* Dublin: The Stationery Office.

Fahey, T. and FitzGerald, J. (1997). *Medium-term Report.* Dublin: Economic and Social Research Institute.

Fahey, T., Hayes, B. C. and Sinnott, R. (2005). *Conflict and Consensus: A Study of Values and Attitudes in the Republic of Ireland and Northern Ireland.* Dublin: Institute of Public Administration.

Faludi, S. (1991). *Backlash: The Undeclared War Against Women.* London: Chatto & Windus.

Family Support Agency. (2005). *Submission to the All Party Oireachtas Committee on the Constitution.* Dublin: Family Support Agency.

Farley, M. A. (1976). Sources of sexual inequality in the history of Christian thought. *Journal of Religion*, 56 (2), 162–176.

Faulkner, J. E. and De Jong, G. F. (1965). Religiosity in 5-D: An empirical analysis. Paper presented at the American Sociological Association Convention, Chicago.

Ferree, M. M. (1976). Working class jobs: Housework and paid work as sources of satisfaction. *Social Problems*, 23 (4), 431–441.

Ferriter, D. (2009). *Occasions of Sin: Sex and Society in Modern Ireland.* Dublin: Profile Books.

Festinger, L. (1957). *A Theory of Cognitive Dissonance.* Evanston, IL: Row Peterson.

Fine-Davis, M. (1976). *Structure, Determinants and Correlates of Attitudes Toward the Role and Status of Women in Ireland, with Particular Reference to Employment Status of*

Married Women. Unpublished Doctoral Dissertation. Department of Psychology, Trinity College, University of Dublin.

Fine-Davis, M. (1977). *Attitudes Toward the Status of Women: Implications for Equal Employment Opportunity.* Report to the Department of Labour. Dublin: Department of Psychology, Trinity College, Dublin.

Fine-Davis, M. (1979a). Personality correlates of attitudes toward the role and status of women in Ireland. *Journal of Personality,* 47 (3), 379–396.

Fine-Davis, M. (1979b). Social-psychological predictors of employment status of married women in Ireland. *Journal of Marriage and the Family,* 47 (1), 145–158.

Fine-Davis, M. (1983a). A society in transition: Structure and determinants of attitudes toward the role and status of women in Ireland. *Psychology of Women Quarterly,* 8 (2), 113–132.

Fine-Davis, M. (1983b). *Women and Work in Ireland: A Social Psychological Perspective.* Dublin: Council for the Status of Women.

Fine-Davis, M. (1983c). Mothers' attitudes toward child care and employment: A nationwide survey. In Working Party on Child Care Facilities for Working Parents, *Report to the Minister for Labour.* Dublin: The Stationery Office, pp. 73–168.

Fine-Davis, M. (1985). Housework versus employment: Quality of working life and psychological well-being among Irish married women. In M. Safir, M. T. Mednick, D. Israeli and J. Bernard (eds), *Women's Worlds: From the New Scholarship.* New York: Praeger, pp. 105–116.

Fine-Davis, M. (1988a). *Changing Gender Role Attitudes in Ireland: 1975–1986* – Vol. I: Attitudes toward the Role and Status of Women, 1975–1986. In *First Report of the Second Joint Oireachtas [Parliamentary] Committee on Women's Rights* (Pl. 5609) Dublin: The Stationery Office, pp. 1–100.

Fine-Davis, M. (1988b). *Changing Gender Role Attitudes in Ireland: 1975–1986* – Vol. II: Issues Related to Equal Employment Opportunity. In *Second Report of the Second Joint Committee on Women's Rights* (Pl. 5673). Dublin: The Stationery Office, pp. 1–66.

Fine-Davis, M. (1988c). *Changing Gender Role Attitudes in Ireland: 1975–1986* – Vol. III: Attitudes Towards Moral Issues in Relation to Voting Behaviour in Recent Referenda. In *Third Report of the Second Joint Committee on Women's Rights* (Pl. 5796). Dublin: The Stationery Office, pp. 1–80.

Fine-Davis, M. (1989). Attitudes toward the role of women as part of a larger belief system. *Political Psychology,* 10 (2), 287–308.

Fine-Davis, M. (2009). *Attitudes to Family Formation in Ireland: Preliminary Findings – The Qualitative Study.* Report to the Family Support Agency. Dublin: Social Attitude & Policy Research Group, Trinity College Dublin.

Fine-Davis, M. (2011). *Attitudes to Family Formation in Ireland: Findings from the Nationwide Study.* Dublin: Social Attitude and Policy Research Group, Trinity College Dublin & Family Support Agency.

Fine-Davis, M. (2014). Gender role attitudes, family formation and well-being in Ireland. In L. Eckermann (ed.), *Gender, Lifespan and Quality of Life: An International Perspective.* Social Indicators Research Series, Vol. 53. New York and Heidelberg: Springer, pp. 203–227.

Fine-Davis, M., Davis, E. E. and Bolger, N. (1981). *The Quality of Working Life in the European Community: Multivariate Analyses of the Irish Data.* Final report to the Statistical Office of the European Community. Dublin: Dept. of Psychology, Trinity College Dublin and The Economic and Social Research Institute.

Fine-Davis, M., Fagnani, J., Giovannini, D., Højgaard, L. and Clarke, H. (2004). *Fathers and Mothers: Dilemmas of the Work-Life Balance – A Comparative Study in Four European Countries.* Dordrecht, Boston and London: Kluwer.

Fine-Davis, M., McCarthy, M., Edge, G. and O'Dwyer, C. (2005). *Work-life Balance and Social Inclusion in Ireland: Results of a Nationwide Survey.* Dublin: National Flexi-Work Partnership (Centre for Gender and Women's Studies, Trinity College Dublin; IBEC; ICTU; Age Action Ireland & Aware).

Flanagan, D. (1975). The more subtle discrimination. *Studies,* Autumn, 231–242.

Fogarty, M., Rapoport, R. and Rapoport, R. N. (1971). *Sex, Career and Family.* London: Allen and Unwin.

Fogarty, M., Ryan, L. and Lee, J. (1984). *Irish Values and Attitudes: The Report of the European Value Systems Study.* Dublin: Dominican Press.

Fowler, M. G. and van de Reit, H. K. (1972). Women, today and yesterday: An examination of the feminist personality. *Journal of Psychology,* 82, 269–276.

Francome, C. (1984). *Abortion Freedom: A Worldwide Movement.* London: Allen and Unwin.

Gaffney, M. (2010). All change – how Ireland turned its back on dogma. *The Irish Times,* 18 September, p. 14.

Galligan, Y. (1998). *Women and Politics in Contemporary Ireland: From the Margins to the Mainstream.* London: Pinter.

Galligan, Y. and Knight, K. (2011). Attitudes towards women in politics: Gender generation and party identification in Ireland. *Parliamentary Affairs,* 64 (4), 585–611.

Garvin, T. (2004). *Preventing the Future: Why Was Ireland Poor for so Long?* Dublin: Gill & Macmillan.

Glock, C. and Stark, R. (1965). *Christian Beliefs and Anti-Semitism.* New York: Harper and Row.

Green Paper on Abortion. (1999). Dublin: The Stationery Office.

Griffin, The Very Reverend Victor, Dean. (1983). *Statement on the Anti-Abortion Referendum.* Dublin: St Patrick's Cathedral, 14 February.

Gump, J. P. (1972). Sex-role attitudes and psychological well-being. *Journal of Social Issues,* 28 (2), 79–92.

Haavio-Mannila, E. (1971). Satisfaction with family, work, leisure and life among men and women. *Human Relations,* 24 (6), 585–601.

Haavio-Mannila, E. (1972). Sex-role attitudes in Finland, 1966–1970. *Journal of Social Issues,* 28 (2), 93–110.

Hall, J. and Jones, D. C. (1950). The social grading of occupations. *British Journal of Sociology,* 1, 31–55.

Haller, M. and Rosenmayr, L. (1971). The pluridimensionality of work commitment. *Human Relations,* 24 (6), 501–518.

Hannon, E. and Sinclair, J. (1999). *The Implications of the Employment Equality Act 1998.* Dublin: European Foundation for the Improvement of Living and Working Conditions. www.eurofound.europa.eu/eiro/1999/09/feature/ie9909144f.htm.

Hayes, B. C., McAllister, I. and Studlar, D. T. (2000). Gender, postmodernism and feminism in comparative perspective. *International Political Science Review,* 21 (4), 425–439.

Hederman, M. (1980). Irish women and Irish law. *The Crane Bag,* 4 (1), 55–59.

Heider, F. (1946). Attitudes and cognitive organisation. *Journal of Psychology,* 21, 107–112.

Hibernia Review/Irish Marketing Surveys Limited. (1974). Contraception poll, *Hibernia*, 12 April, 5.

Hinds, K. and Jarvis, L. (2000). The gender gap. In R. Jowell, J. Curtice, A. Park, K. Thomson, L. Jarvis, C. Bromley and N. Stratford (eds), *British Social Attitudes: Focusing on Diversity (17th Report)*. London: Sage Publications and National Centre for Social Research, pp. 101–117.

Hornsby-Smith, M. P. and Whelan, C. T. (1994). Religious and moral values. In C. T. Whelan (ed.), *Values and Social Change in Ireland*. Dublin: Gill & Macmillan, pp. 7–44.

HSE Crisis Pregnancy Progamme. (2013). *Number of Women Giving Irish Addresses at UK Abortion Clinics Decreases for Eleventh Year in a Row According to UK Department of Health*. Press Release. Dublin: HSE Crisis Pregnancy Programme, 11 July. www.crisispregnancy.ie/news/number-of-women-giving-irish-addresses-at-uk-abortion-clinics-decreases-for-eleventh-year-in-a-row-according-to-uk-department-of-health/.

Hussey, B. (1976). Women and family law. *Hibernia*, 16 January, 14.

Hutchinson, B. (1969). Social status in inter-generational social mobility in Dublin. *Paper No. 48*. Dublin: The Economic and Social Research Institute.

Hyer, M. (1988). U.S. Catholic bishops say sexism is sinful and urge its removal. *International Herald Tribune*, 13 April, p. 3.

Inglehart, R. and Norris, P. (2003). *Rising Tide: Gender Equality and Cultural Change Around the World*. Cambridge: Cambridge University Press.

Inglis, T. (1987). *Moral Monopoly: Catholic Church in Modern Irish Society*. Dublin: Gill & Macmillan.

Inglis, T. (1998). *Moral Monopoly: The Rise and Fall of the Catholic Church in Modern Ireland*. (2nd edn) Dublin: University College Dublin Press.

Ipsos/MRBI(2013). Poll on attitudes to abortion. *The Irish Times*, 11 February.

Irish Times. (1976). Fewer births trend shown, 5 May.

Irish Times. (1988). Pope stresses theme of women, 30 March.

Jelen, T. G., O'Donnell, J. and Wilcox, C. (1993). A contextual analysis of Catholicism and abortion attitudes in Western Europe. *Sociology of Religion*, 54 (4), 375–383.

Joesting, J. (1971). Comparison of women's liberation members with their non-member peers. *Psychological Reports*, 29 (3, pt. 2), 1291–1294.

Kaiser, H. F. (1958). The varimax criterion for analytic rotation in factor analysis. *Psychometrika*, 23, 187–200.

Kennedy, F. (2001). *From Cottage to Crèche: Family Change in Ireland*. Dublin: Institute of Public Administration.

Kingston, J., Whelan, A. and Bacik, I. (1997). *Abortion and the Law*. Dublin: Round Hall Sweet & Maxwell.

Kirkpatrick, C. (1936). The construction of a belief pattern scale for measuring attitudes toward feminism. *Journal of Social Psychology*, 7, 421–437.

Klein, D. P. (1975). Women in the labor force: The middle years. *Monthly Labor Review*, 98 (11), 10–16.

Kohler, H. P., Billari, F. C. and Ortega, J. A. (2002). The emergence of lowest-low fertility in Europe during the 1990s. *Population and Development Review*, 28 (4), December, 641–680.

Labour Women's National Council. (1983). *Stop the Confusion*. Dublin: Labour Women's National Council.

Lansdowne Market Research. (2001). *Lansdowne Market Research Abortion Reform Topline Results*. Dublin: Lansdowne Market Research.

Lee, J. J. (1978). Women and the Church since the Famine. In M. Mac Curtain and D. Ó Corráin (eds), *Women in Irish Society: The Historical Dimension*. Dublin: Arlen House, pp. 37–45.

Levinson, D. and Huffman, P. (1955). Traditional family ideology and its relation to personality. *Journal of Personality*, 23, 251–273.

Levinson, D. J. and Sanford, R. N. (1944). A scale for the measurement of anti-Semitism. *Journal of Psychology*, 17 (2), 339–370.

Lott, B. E. (1973). Who wants the children? Some relationships among attitudes toward children, parents, and the liberation of women. *American Psychologist*, 28 (7), 573–582.

Lunn, P. and Fahey, T. (2011). *Households and Family Structures in Ireland: A Detailed Statistical Analysis of Census 2006*. Dublin: Economic and Social Research Institute.

Lunn, P., Fahey, T. and Hannan, C. (2009). *Family Figures: Family Dynamics and Family Types in Ireland, 1986–2006*. Dublin: Family Support Agency.

Lysaght, P. (1985). The wailing woman. In E. Ni Chuilleanain (ed.), *Irish Women: Image and Achievement*. Dublin: Arlen House, pp. 25–35.

MacCana, P. (1980). Women in Irish mythology. *The Crane Bag*, 4 (1), 7–11.

MacCurtain, M. (1978). Women, the vote and revolution. In M. MacCurtain and D. Ó Corráin (eds), *Women in Irish Society: The Historical Dimension*. Dublin: Arlen House, pp. 46–57.

MacCurtain, M. and Ó Corráin, D. (eds), (1978) *Women in Irish Society: The Historical Dimension*. Dublin: Arlen House.

MacGréil, M. (1974). Church attendance and religious practice of Dublin adults. *Social Studies*, 3 (2), 163–211.

MacGréil, M. (1996). *Prejudice in Ireland Revisited*. Maynooth: Survey and Research Unit, St Patrick's College.

Mason, K. Oppenheim, Czajka, J. L. and Arber, S. (1976). Changes in U.S. women's sex-role attitudes, 1964–1974. *American Sociological Review*, 41 (4), 573–596.

Mason, K. Oppenheim and Lu, Y. (1988). Attitudes toward women's familial roles: Changes in the United States, 1977–1985. *Gender and Society*, 2 (1), 39–57.

McBride, O., Morgan, K. and McGee, H. (2012). *Irish Contraception and Crisis Pregnancy Study 2010 (ICCP-2010): A Survey of the General Population*. Crisis Pregnancy Programme Report No. 24. Dublin: HSE Crisis Pregnancy Programme.

McGinnity, F. and Russell, H. (2007). Work rich, time poor? Time use of women and men in Ireland. *Economic and Social Review*, 38 (3), 323–354.

McShane, I. (2010). Public morality of more concern. *The Irish Times*, 16 September, p. 6.

Millward Brown. (2013). *National Opinion Poll: Late May* (for publication in *Sunday Independent*, 2 June 2013).

Nielson, J. M. and Doyle, P. T. (1975). Sex-role stereotypes of feminists and non-feminists. *Sex-Roles*, 1 (1), 83–95.

Nye, F. I. (1974). Sociocultural context. In L. W. Hoffman and F. I. Nye (eds), *Working Mothers*. San Francisco: Jossey-Bass, pp. 1–31.

O'Carroll, J. P. (1984). *Some Sociological Aspects of the 1983 Abortion Referendum Debate in the Republic of Ireland*. Seminar Paper read at the Economic and Social Research Institute, Dublin, 24 May.

O'Connor, P. (1998). *Emerging Voices: Women in Contemporary Irish Society*. Dublin: Institute of Public Administration.

Ó Corráin, D. (1978). Women in early Irish society. In M. MacCurtain and D. Ó Corráin (eds), *Women in Irish Society: The Historical Dimension*. Dublin: Arlen House, pp. 1–13.

OECD. (2003). *Babies and Bosses – Reconciling Work and Family Life: Vol. 2 Austria, Ireland and Japan*. Paris: Organisation for Economic Co-operation and Development.

Ó hÓgáin, D. (1987). *Famous Women in Irish Folklore*. Paper presented at Workshop on the Role of Women in the Folklore of Ireland and Scotland. UCD Women's Studies Forum, University College, Dublin, 21 February.

O'Halloran, M. (2010). Women cannot get abortion to save lives, says group. *The Irish Times*, 1 March, p. 7.

O'Keefe, B. E. (1972). Attitudes toward women's liberation: Relationships between cooperation, personality and demographic variables. *Dissertation Abstracts International*, 33 (3-B), 1293.

O'Leary, C. (1987). The Irish referendum on divorce. *Electoral Studies*, 6 (1), 69–74.

Osgood, C. E., Suci, G. J. and Tannenbaum, P. M. (1957). *The Measurement of Meaning*. Urbana, IL: University of Illinois Press.

O'Sullivan, S. (2007). Gender and attitudes to women's employment. In B. Hilliard and M. Nic Ghiolla Phadraig (eds), *Changing Ireland in International Comparison*. Dublin: Liffey Press, pp. 135–162.

O'Sullivan, S. (2012). All changed, changed utterly? Gender role attitudes and the feminisation of the Irish labour force. *Women's Studies International Forum*, 35, (4), 223–232.

Ó Tuathaigh, G. (1978). The role of women in Ireland under the new English Order. In M. MacCurtain and D. Ó Corráin (eds), *Women in Irish Society: The Historical Dimension*. Dublin: Arlen House, pp. 26–36.

Pawlicki, R. E. and Almquist, C. (1973). Authoritarianism, locus of control and tolerance of ambiguity as reflected in membership and nonmembership in a women's liberation group. *Psychological Reports*, 32, 1331–1337.

Philbin Bowman, E. (1976). *The Sexual Behaviour and Contraceptive Practice of Single Irish Women*. Unpublished master's thesis, Department of Psychology, Trinity College, University of Dublin.

Philbin Bowman, E. (1977). Sexual and contraceptive attitudes and behaviour of single attenders at a Dublin family planning clinic. *Journal of Biosocial Science*, 9 (4), 429–445.

Pope John Paul II. (1981). Encyclical on Human Work. *Laborem Exercens*. London: Catholic Truth Society.

Powell, B. (1977). The empty nest, employment, and psychiatric symptoms in college-educated women. *Psychology of Women Quarterly*, 2 (1), 35–43.

Prendiville, P. (1988). Divorce in Ireland: An analysis of the Referendum to Amend the Constitution, June 1986. *Women's Studies International Forum*, 11 (4), 355–363.

Punch, A. (2007). *Marriage, Fertility and the Family in Ireland – A Statistical Perspective*. Presidential address from Central Statistics Office to the Statistical and Social Inquiry Society of Ireland, 31 May.

Purcell, B. (1980). 10 years of progress? Some statistics. *The Crane Bag*, 4 (1), 556–559.

Raab, E. and Lipset, S. M. (1959). *Prejudice and Society*. New York: Anti-Defamation League.

Randall, V. (1982). *Women and Politics*. London: Macmillan.

Randall, V. (1987). The politics of abortion: Ireland in comparative perspective. *Working Paper No. 1*. UCD Women's Studies Forum, University College Dublin, pp. 13–22.

Randall, V. (1992). The politics of abortion: Ireland in comparative perspective. *The Canadian Journal of Irish Studies*, 18 (1), 121–128.

Redlich, P. (1978). Women and the family. In M. MacCurtain and D. Ó Corráin (eds), *Women in Irish Society: The Historical Dimension*. Dublin: Arlen House, pp. 82–91.

Report of the Task Force on the Travelling Community. (1995). Dublin: The Stationery Office.

Reuther, R. (1974). *Religion and Sexism*. New York: Simon and Schuster.

Riffault, H. (1983). *European Women and Men in 1983*. Brussels: Commission of the European Communities.

Robinson, M. (1978). Women and the new Irish state. In M. MacCurtain and D. Ó Corráin (Eds), *Women in Irish Society: The Historical Dimension*. Dublin: Arlen House, pp. 58–70.

Robinson, J. P. and Shaver, P. R. (1973). *Measures of Social Psychological Attitudes*. Ann Arbor: Institute for Social Research, University of Michigan.

Ruane, F. P. and Sutherland, J. M. (1999). *Women in the Labour Force*. Dublin: Employment Equality Agency.

Rundle, K., Leigh, C. McGee, H. and Layte, R. (2004). *Irish Contraception and Crisis Pregnancy [ICCP] Study: A Survey of the General Population*. Dublin: Crisis Pregnancy Agency.

Ryckman, R. M., Martens, J. L., Rodda, W. C. and Sherman, M. F. (1972). Locus of control and attitudes toward women's liberation in a college population. *Journal of Social Psychology*, 87, 157–158.

Safilios-Rothschild, C. (1971). Towards the conceptualization and measurement of work commitment. *Human Relations*, 24 (6), 489–493.

Safir, M., Mednick, M., Israeli, D. N. and Bernard, J. (eds) (1985). *Women's Worlds: From the New Scholarship*. New York: Praeger.

Scannell, Y. (2000). The taxation of married women – Murphy v. Attorney General (1982). In E. O'Dell (ed.), *Leading Cases of the Twentieth Century*. Dublin: Round Hall Sweet and Maxwell, pp. 327–352.

Scott, J. (1989). Conflicting beliefs about abortion: Legal approval and moral doubts. *Social Psychology Quarterly*, 52 (4), 319–326.

Scott, J. (1998). Generational changes in attitudes to abortion: A cross-national comparison. *European Sociological Review*, 14 (2), 177–190.

Scott, J. (2006). Family and gender roles: How attitudes are changing. *Arxius*, 15, 143–154.

Scott, J. (2008). Changing gender role attitudes. In J. Scott, S. Dex and H. Joshi (eds), *Women and Employment: Changing Lives and New Challenges*. Cheltenham: Edward Elgar, pp. 156–178.

Second Joint Committee on Women's Rights. (1988). *Third Report of the Second Joint Committee on Women's Rights* (Pl. 5796), I–VII.

Sexton, J. J. (1981). *The Changing Labour Force*. Paper presented at Conference on "The Irish Economy and Society in the Eighties", The Economic and Social Research Institute, Dublin.

Sexton, J. J. and Dillon, M. (1984). Recent changes in Irish fertility. In T. J. Baker, T. Callan, S. Scott and D. Madden. *Quarterly Economic Commentary*. Dublin: The Economic and Social Research Institute, May, pp. 1–38.

Shaver, P. and Freedman, J. (1976). Your pursuit of happiness. *Psychology Today*, 10 (3), 26–33.

Simms, K. (1978). Women in Norman Ireland. In M. MacCurtain and D. Ó Corráin (eds), *Women in Irish Society: The Historical Dimension*. Dublin: Arlen House, pp. 14–25.

Smyth, A. (ed.) (1992). *The Abortion Papers: Ireland*. Dublin: Attic Press.

Spence, J. T. and Helmreich, R. (1972). The Attitudes Toward Women Scale: An objective instrument to measure the attitudes toward the rights and roles of women in contemporary society. *JSAS: Catalogue of Selected Documents in Psychology*, 2, 66–67 (Ms. No. 153).

Stoloff, C. (1973). Who joins women's liberation? *Psychiatry*, 36 (3), 325–340.

Tangri, S. S. (1970). Role-innovation in occupational choice among college women. *Dissertation Abstracts*, 30 (9-A), 4021.

Tatalovich, R. and Daynes, B. (1981). *The Politics of Abortion: A Study of Community Conflict in Public Policymaking*. New York: Praeger.

Thornton, A. and Freedman, D. (1979). Changes in the sex role attitudes of women, 1962–1977: Evidence from a panel study. *American Sociological Review*, 44 (5), 831–842.

Thornton, A. and Young-DeMarco, L. (2001). Four decades of trends in attitudes toward family issues in the United States: The 1960s through the 1990s. *Journal of Marriage and Family*, 63, 1009–1037.

Thornton, A., Alwin, D. F. and Camburn, D. (1983). Causes and consequences of sex-role attitudes and attitude change. *American Sociological Review*, 48, 211–227.

Tomeh, A. K. (1978). Sex-role orientation: An analysis of structural and attitudinal predictors. *Journal of Marriage and the Family*, 40, 341–354.

Treas, J. and Widmer, E. D. (2000). Married women's employment over the life course: Attitudes in cross-national perspective. *Social Forces*, 78 (4), 1409–1436.

Trewhela, P. (1975). How Irish women fell from power. *The Irish Times*, 14 November, p. 12.

Triandis, H. C. (1971). *Attitude and Attitude Change*. New York: Wiley.

van der Wal, E. and Oudijk, C. (1985). *Women on the Move: Developments in Facts and Figures*. Rijswijk: Sociaal en Cultureel Planbureau.

van Egmond, M., Baxter, J., Buchler, S. and Western, M. (2010). A stalled revolution? Gender role attitudes in Australia, 1986–2005. *Journal of Population Research*, 27, 147–168.

Walsh, B. M. (1973). *Women and Employment in Ireland: Results of a National Survey*, Paper No. 69. Dublin: The Economic and Social Research Institute.

Welch, S. (1975). Support among women for the issues of the women's movement. *The Sociological Quarterly*, 16 (2), 216–227.

Whelan, B. J. (1977). *RANSAM: A national random sample design for Ireland*. Seminar paper presented at the Economic and Social Research Institute, Dublin, 3 November.

Whelan, B. J. (1979). RANSAM: A random sample design for Ireland. *Economic and Social Review*, 10 (2), 169–175.

Whelan, C. T. (ed.) (1994). *Values and Social Change in Ireland*. Dublin: Gill & Macmillan.

Whelan, C. T. and Fahey, T. (1994). Marriage and the family. In C. T. Whelan (ed.). *Values and Social Change in Ireland*. Dublin: Gill & Macmillan, pp. 45–81.

Whyte, J. H. (1971). *Church and State in Modern Ireland 1923–1979*. Dublin: Gill & Macmillan.

Wilcox, C. (1991). The causes and consequences of feminist consciousness among Western European women. *Comparative Political Studies*, 23 (4), 519–545.

Williams, J. E. and Best, D. L. (1986). Sex stereotypes and intergroup relations. In S. Worchel and W. G. Austin (eds), *Psychology of Intergroup Relations*. Chicago: Nelson-Hall, pp. 244–259.

Wilson-Davis, K. (1974). Irish attitudes to family planning, *Social Studies*, 3 (3), 261–275.

Wood, H. L. (1985). Women in myths and early depictions. In E. Ni Chuilleanain. (ed.), *Irish Women: Image and Achievement*. Dublin: Arlen House, pp. 13–24.

Working Party on Child Care Facilities for Working Parents. (1983). *Report to the Minister for Labour*. Dublin: The Stationery Office.

Worell, J. and Worell, L. (1977). Support and opposition to the women's liberation movement: Some personality and parental correlates. *Journal of Research in Personality*, 11, 10–20.

Yorburg, B. and Arafat, I. (1975). Current sex-role conceptions and conflict. *Sex Roles*, 1 (2), 135–146.

Index

Page numbers in **bold** refer to tables and those in *italics* refer to figures.